ACEQUIA

Published in cooperation with the William P. Clements Center
for Southwest Studies, Southern Methodist University, and
with the support of the Ethel-Jane Westfeldt Bunting Foundation.

ACEQUIA

Water Sharing, Sanctity, and Place

Sylvia Rodríguez

A School for Advanced Research Resident Scholar Book

Santa Fe, New Mexico

School for Advanced Research Press

Post Office Box 2188

Santa Fe, New Mexico 87504-2188

www.sarpress.sarweb.org

Co-Director and Executive Editor: Catherine Cocks
Copy Editor: Kate Whelan
Design and Production: Cynthia Dyer
Proofreader: Margaret J. Goldstein
Indexer: Catherine Fox
Printer: Cushing-Malloy, Inc.

Library of Congress Cataloging-in-Publication Data:

Rodríguez, Sylvia, 1947-

    Acequia : water-sharing, sanctity, and place / Sylvia Rodríguez.

      p. cm. — (A School of American Research resident scholar book)

    "Published in cooperation with the William P. Clements Center for Southwest Studies,

    Southern Methodist University, and with the support of the Ethel-Jane Westfeldt Bunting Foundation."

    Includes bibliographical references and index.

    ISBN 1-930618-55-7 (pa : alk. paper)

    1. Human ecology—New Mexico—Taos Region. 2. Indigenous peoples—Ecology—New Mexico—Taos
Region. 3. Stream ecology—New Mexico—Taos Region. 4. Water supply—New Mexico—Taos Region.
5. Water resources development—New Mexico—Taos Region. 6. Communication in water resources—New
Mexico—Taos Region. 7. Water—Symbolic aspects—New Mexico—Taos Region. 8. Taos Pueblo (N.M.)—
Environmental conditions. 9. Taos Region (N.M.)—Environmental conditions.
I. William P. Clements Center for Southwest Studies. II. Title.
GF504.N47R63 2006
304.209789'53—dc22

                    2006023875

Portions of chapters 6 and 7 first appeared as "Procession and Sacred Landscape in New Mexico," *New Mexico Historical Review* 77 (Winter 2002): 1-26. Copyright 2002 by the University of New Mexico Board of Regents. All rights reserved.
Ralph Meyers' map appears courtesy of Ouray Meyers.
The entrega reprinted in chapter 6 appears courtesy of Frank Gusdorf.
Front cover photograph © Sylvia Rodríguez. Back cover: *San Ysidro,* by Belarmino Esquibel, 1996. Museum of Spanish Colonial Art, Collections of the Spanish Colonial Arts Society, Inc. Photo by Addison Doty (1996.1).

Contents

Figures

Color Plates

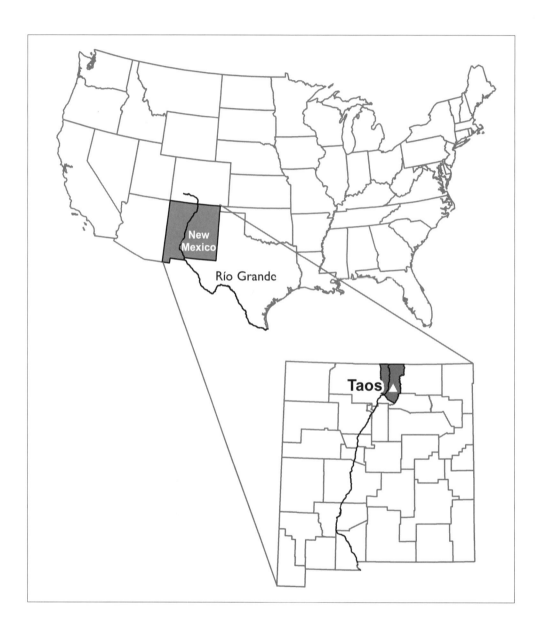

Acknowledgments

Many people have contributed to the making of this book. First and foremost among them are the officers, staff, board of directors, and members of the Taos Valley Acequia Association, the organization that funded the study on which the book is based. Palemón Martínez, president of the TVAA, was a guiding presence, as well as a source of knowledge about the history, ditches, and *repartos* of the Arroyo Seco and upper Río Lucero watersheds. Without his vision, leadership, and instruction, this study would not have been possible. Board members who were of particular help to me include Steve Trujillo and Augustín (Atilano) Montoya. Both gave me interviews, and Steve also showed me the acequias in Upper Ranchitos.

The board as a whole authorized the study. In addition to the aforementioned, this group includes Ernest Coca, Moises Mascareñas, and Alex Ortiz on the Río Chiquito; Arthur Martínez and Ray Mondragon on the Río Fernando; Paula Martínez, Bennie Mondragon, and Joe Mondragon on the Río Grande del Rancho; Elías Espinosa, Chilton Anderson, and Fernando Martínez on the Río Hondo; Leroy Graham on the Río Lucero–Arroyo Seco; and Ronald Jones and Antonio Lavadie on the Río Pueblo.

The always helpful TVAA staff included Priscilla Rael, Carol Ortega, and Diana Trujillo. Fred Waltz, the attorney for the TVAA, played a key role, providing information, advice, and feedback at every stage.

Mario Barela gave generously of his time in arranging for ditch tours and interviews with parciantes; he also gave me a tour of the entire Río Grande del Rancho watershed and accompanied me on the 1996 Good Friday procession in the San Francisco parish. Others who gave me tours of their ditch systems, as well as interviews, include Ernesto Montoya, Gus García, Joe Gomez, and Fermín Torres. I consulted more than once with Ernesto, who also arranged for me to photograph ditch cleaning on the Acequia Madre del Prado, and with Gus, who patiently revisited with me a particularly intricate nexus of acequias to make sure that I grasped their workings and layout. Other ditch officers and parciantes who granted me interviews and acted as my teachers on acequia matters include the late J. J. Montoya; Eliverio García; Bolivar Quintana; Ezequiel Torres; Elizardo Pacheco; Donaciano Torres; Telesfor Eliverio García; the late Tom Tarleton Sr.; Fernando Romo; Rudy Pacheco; Eliseo García; Lee Gonzales; Luís Martínez; Francis Quintana; Roberto Martínez, who mesmerized me with his stories and even made me lunch; Benton Bond; Rafael Vigil; Felix Miera; George Trujillo; the late Leo Baca; and Orlando Ortiz.

Several parciantes and members of the Río Grande del Rancho watershed/St. Francis parish gave me interviews and helped me to understand the San Isidro novena and feast day celebration, as well as other local devotional practices. Corina Santistevan guided me through the novena, and her extensive knowledge of Taos history, its cultural traditions, and the premodern geography of her community was invaluable. Others who shared their wisdom, knowledge, and good grace were Feloníz Trujillo, Gabriel Chávez, the late Polito Valerio, and Candido and Anita Valerio. I am especially grateful to Agnes García, mayordoma of the San Isidro chapel in 1996 and twice since, who generously and patiently answered questions, gave advice, and provided feedback on my chapter 6 about the San Isidro celebration.

Many other Taoseños contributed to this project by sharing their knowledge, memories, stories, and insights; offering advice, feedback, and encouragement; showing me places; accompanying me on trips to investigate particular sites; allowing me to observe their acequia meetings and practices; and generally putting up with my strangely secretive obsession with ditch matters and related local traditions. Naming everyone is impossible, but among them are my cousin Juanita Jaramillo Lavadie, my sister Anita Rodríguez, and dear friends Vicente Martínez and Fabi Romero. Roberto Lavadie kindly read and gave feedback on what I presumed to write about his brother, Eduardo. Joe Jeantete showed me the lower reaches of the Spring ditch, and Ramona Montaño showed me the hidden meanders of the lower Río Fernando and the brand new, red compuerta of the Acequia de San Franciso de Pauda. Felimón Pacheco allowed me to photograph him irrigating his field, and Mayordomo Victor Chávez allowed me to photograph *la saca* (the cleaning) of the Acequia del Finado Francisco Martínez.

Fathers George Salazar and Terry Brennan each gave me interviews that helped to illuminate Catholic processional traditions in Taos. Over the course of a long telephone conversation, Father William McNichols gave me the benefit of his keen insight into the spiritual qualities of native Taoseños. Father Thomas Steele also offered valuable insight into New Mexican religious practices. Sister Catherine Mary shared her perspective on the intensity of local attachment to paraliturgical traditions and awakened me to the heavy personal demands parishioners can make on their clergy.

Conversations and exchanges with numerous scholars over the years added immeasurably to my grasp of irrigation history and practice in the Upper Rio Grande Valley. They include Michael Meyer, Malcolm Ebright, José Rivera, Marc Simmons, Em Hall, and Fran Levine. Several archaeologists—Patty Crown, Michael Adler, Kurt Anschuetz, Linda Cordell, Vern Scarborough, and Ann Ramenofsky—indulged my many questions about prehistoric and early colonial water management in the region and beyond and directed me to important sources. Enrique Lamadrid reawakened my long buried memory about the old custom of asking for water and alerted me to its parallel in the Muslim world.

Three institutions provided material support at crucial stages of this project. The UNM Department of Anthropology maintained the field station at the Harwood Foundation in Taos, which served as the base for all my ethnographic fieldwork. I am deeply grateful to David Weber and the William P. Clements Center for Southwest Studies for giving me an idyllic semester at Southern Methodist University, where I happily enjoyed the company of historians and completed the first draft of the book. Andrea Boardman and Ruth Ann Elmore contributed in countless ways to the productivity and pleasure of my stay there. The Clements Center also provided funding for the maps and other publication costs. I could not have been more fortunate in finding a press and an editor at the School for Advanced Research. There, as a summer fellow, I revised the manuscript. Thanks to James F. Brooks, then press director, and Catherine Cocks, my editor, for believing in this book and for understanding and accommodating the complex circumstances that surrounded its making. Catherine's editorial skill and unerring clarity of judgment were crucial to the final transition from manuscript to book.

In addition to two anonymous reviewers, my esteemed colleagues Marta Weigle and Keith Basso gave careful, constructive readings to early versions of the manuscript. Marta's brilliant editorial insights, merciless yet extraordinarily generous, were delivered with a scandalous humor impossible to resist. Her friendship, support, and knowledge of things New Mexican have nourished my work for many years.

María Dolores Gonzales and Joan Chernock transcribed the tape-recorded interviews. Kurt Menke made the maps, patiently and skillfully reworking them as my understanding of ditch layout evolved. Amy Sánchez began work on the bibliography, and Moanna Wright completed it. Kate Whelan ably copyedited the book manuscript.

Last but not least, I am thankful to Nan MacCurdy, who, having nothing to do with acequias, Taos, or academe, has shown me the way to life and laughter beyond them.

Prologue and Dedication

This book is dedicated to the memory of Eduardo Lavadie and Geoffrey Bryce, two close friends without whom it could not have been written. Each so profoundly influenced the focus and course of my work on the Taos acequia system that the project would be unimaginable without either of them. Yet neither lived to see this book in print. Their tragic and unexpected deaths framed the beginning of my research in June 1995 and the approval of the book manuscript for publication almost nine years later to the day. My involvement in the project is so inseparable from their friendship that I must say something about each of these extraordinary individuals. Their work contributed not only to this endeavor but also, more important, to the future viability of acequia organizations in northern New Mexico.

Both Eduardo and Geoff were dedicated to the cause of protecting and preserving the acequia systems of New Mexico. Each in his own way was a quiet, unsung hero who put his work before self-interest and ignored the opportunity for public visibility or recognition. Both were convinced that this mission required widespread public education about the nature, workings, and significance of New Mexico's traditional irrigation communities. Although each belonged to a ditch and an acequia association, his commitment was always to the larger, collective interest. Eduardo and Geoff saw the big picture—beyond the Taos Valley and beyond the statewide coalition of acequia associations they helped to build. Both saw the acequia associations' struggle to survive as part of a global struggle over who will enjoy rights to a finite quantity of freshwater. Both understood how the right to use local water is tied to the right of traditional, place-based communities to endure and to have a voice in the future sustainability of their ecological habitats. Both realized that water issues are not simply economic—they are also about cultural identity, social welfare, and political self-determination.

Eduardo

Eduardo died on the day before my research was supposed to begin, in 1995. Our last telephone conversation, two days before his death, was charged with his urgent command that I get to Taos as soon as possible to begin the project. The spring semester had ended in May, and Eduardo showed no patience for my excuse that it was hard to disengage from university commitments in order to begin a long-awaited sabbatical leave. He died of a massive heart attack in the early afternoon of June 24, Día de San Juan, the day when the devout are supposed to immerse themselves at daybreak in the divinely purified waters of the rivers, lakes, and acequias. I learned of his passing en route to Taos. Instead of arriving full of excitement and energy, I drove into town in a state of shock, grief, and disbelief. His death was sudden and unexpected. He had gone home after lunch with a mutual friend and suffered the attack in his front yard. Eduardo was only 52 years old.

In the coming days, friends and family gathered to mourn him, trying to piece together some sense of how we would proceed, in our lives and in our work, without him. The loss each of us suffered was immense. In small, genealogically dense communities like Taos, the ties that bind people are inescapably multiple. Eduardo was not only a close friend but also the husband of my cousin Juanita. His death also reverberated throughout the acequia communities in Taos and northern New Mexico. He was a founder and the executive director of the Taos Valley Acequia Association, the organization that had hired me to conduct ethnographic research on water-sharing customs in the Taos Valley.

For weeks, I could not imagine how to carry out the research without his guidance, advice, and feedback. Yet during the period of mourning and its aftermath, my resolve to conduct the study and bring it to fruition deepened. The *cargo* (obligation) of this task, which would have been important and consuming anyway, took on a deeper, heavier significance as our last conversation replayed itself again and again in my mind. His final words to me were "I trust you to do this." Eduardo did not trust easily. The year of fieldwork that followed was permeated with sorrow and elation, perplexity and thrill, privilege and loss—and an emerging sense of awe at the picture that came slowly into focus. Gradually, the project, and especially the book that grew out of it, came to represent my fulfillment of a private *promesa* (sacred vow) to Eduardo.

My friendship with Eduardo began around 1981 when I returned to Taos, where I was born and spent the first 14 years of my life before going off on a scholarship to boarding school in Arizona. After my first academic job many years later, I returned to Taos to begin ethnographic research on interethnic relations and social change since World War II. I had been acquainted with Eduardo and others in his family, but we got to know each other as adults initially because of Juanita. We shared a sense of anguish at what was happening to Taos and those who live there, a sentiment common among Taoseños of all kinds. We talked endlessly about what was happening in northern New Mexico, who did what and why, and whether people could change direction and how. We collaborated with others in various organizing projects, including the 1982 Valdez Condo War, and local efforts to create protective zoning in acequia communities threatened by escalating resort development (see Rodríguez 1987). Eduardo belonged to a generation of organic intellectuals who live, work, and are politically active in northern New Mexico and southern Colorado. Today, their children have children of their own, and, much to our alarm, we are now becoming the elders. Eduardo stood on that cusp when he died.

A turning point for me occurred in 1985 when civil rights lawyer Richard Rosenstock asked me to provide expert testimony in a water rights transfer case in Río Arriba County. I flew in from Los Angeles, where I taught anthropology at UCLA, and stayed at the home of a *parciante* (member) of the Ensenada ditch. The hearing was held in the hallowed Tierra Amarilla courthouse, where Tijerina's famous raid took place in 1967.[1] Eduardo, Juanita, and Geoff drove through the mountains in deep winter to attend the trial and observe my testimony. To our amazement, the acequia association won its case against the transfer for resort development, on the grounds that it threatened the public welfare. Although reversed on appeal because a crucial new public welfare statute was not retroactive, Judge Art Encinias's decision in the Sleeper case became a milestone in New Mexico water law (Rivera 1998:161–162). In the late 1980s Eduardo and others formed the Taos Valley Acequia Association (TVAA), opened an office, and secured nonprofit status.

Eduardo was an outsider all his life and a community activist for much of it. He had committed the unspeakable during the Vietnam War by becoming a conscientious objector, an unforgivable *vergüenza* (disgrace) in a town where people pride themselves on their Purple Hearts. He was a recovering alcoholic who, during the 1970s, founded and directed a detox treatment center in Embudo. Later on, as someone who openly protested resort development, he became virtually unemployable, yet somehow he always managed to generate his own employment as an organizer or administrator. Although members of his extended family have property in Ranchitos, Eduardo himself owned very little when he died. He was a parciante and commissioner on the Sánchez ditch off the Río Pueblo. He had wanted cremation. Juanita bought him a little piece of *terreno* (ground) just outside the fence under a cedar tree, off one corner of the San Cristóbal *camposanto* (cemetery). There his ashes are buried.

Eduardo's funeral mass at the Guadalupe church in town was packed. Father Luís Jaramillo, a personal friend and counselor to many, presided over it. Delivering the eulogy as part of the sermon, Father Luís compared Eduardo to the irascible, intense, and difficult prophet Jeremiah. Priestly consolation usually seems threadbare in the cold face of loss. But somehow Father Luís's words felt uplifting, probably because he was honest and talked about Eduardo with humor, as well as pain. There was little doubt in many minds that stress over the water rights adjudication and the vicissitudes of ongoing negotiation between the TVAA and Taos Pueblo had contributed to Eduardo's untimely death. The sense of urgency and threat of impending, irretrievable loss (of acequia water rights) that permeated his work and the last years of his life had probably killed him. During the mass, a little dog wandered in through an open side door of the church, sat down right in front of the altar, and began barking. Father Luís did not miss a beat, and everyone else pretended to ignore it. Suddenly, my quiet, uncontrollable sobbing became quiet, uncontrollable laughter, switching back and forth in agonizing sequence as I struggled desperately to control my emotions. Eduardo would have loved it!

Geoff

It bears testimony to Eduardo's good judgment that he recruited Geoff to work in the TVAA office, sometime around 1993–94. He had befriended Geoff more than a decade earlier when this newly arrived stranger had worked hard but almost invisibly to assist grassroots community acequia resistance to water rights transfers from agricultural use to resort development. He met Geoff through me. Gradually, perhaps even grudgingly, Eduardo came to like and even trust this laconic, intensely private individual who came to Taos to work as an independent community organizer.

I first met Geoff in 1977 when I got a temporary teaching job at Carleton College in Northfield, Minnesota. He was married to my Carleton colleague María Lugones. Commuting between Madison, Wisconson, and Northfield, Geoff was struggling over his dissertation in political philosophy. The three of us became fast friends, ultimately sharing a house next to campus that served as headquarters when the Carleton service staff went on strike. When I left Carleton for Taos to begin a year of anthropological fieldwork, María and Geoff came with me. María and I continued to pursue academic careers, but Geoff abandoned his dissertation and stayed in Taos, supporting himself at various odd jobs until Eduardo hired him at the TVAA.

It took me a while to get used to Geoff's long silences and biting sarcasm. At first, he scared me. He rarely spoke and openly avoided most social interaction. Very slowly, I came to understand his humor and appreciate his lucidity and depth. Geoff grew up middle-class in rural Pennsylvania and was the only academic I ever knew who had been in the marines. The one member of his family he identified with was his Welsh grandfather, a coal miner and Methodist preacher who died of black lung. I gradually saw what mattered to him. Together with María, we dreamed of starting a school to promote grassroots popular education and political organizing in northern New Mexico, modeled after the Highlander School in Tennessee. In the hundreds of hours we spent conversing, I talked incessantly about the social and economic conditions of northern New Mexico and the history and character of its people and land. Somehow, I knew that Geoff would find his place there, and indeed he did.

As it turned out, I left the school project after a few years because, under María's direction, it had lost touch with local people and needs. The three of us had bought a parcel of irrigated land in the community of Valdez outside Taos. Geoff took up residence there around 1982 and never left. Valdez became his home, his community, and, in some sense, his family. The attachment was mutual. Connie Espinosa, an old friend and the postmaster of Valdez, told me after Geoff's death, "We were his family here." He ended up being commissioner on the San Antonio ditch off the Río Hondo.

During the approximately five years Eduardo and Geoff worked together at the TVAA, they became a formidable, if unusual, team. What now seems remarkable about the early TVAA years is how the organizers managed to bring together both conservative and progressive elements among the local ditch and water rights advocates. Two men who had been on opposite sides during the Valdez Condo War, Eduardo and Palemón Martínez, ended up running the TVAA together.[2] Despite any initial reservations, Eduardo and then Geoff worked for many years side by side with Palemón, the dedicated, taciturn, widely respected president of the TVAA.

In the aftershock of Eduardo's death, Geoff stepped in to manage the office, write grants, advocate and organize, and shepherd various consultants' research projects through seemingly endless stages. He was so effective that, before long, the board made him executive director. Under his low-key, self-effacing management, the office flourished and became a respected source of information and advocacy within the statewide acequia community. Always behind the scenes, Geoff never told people what to do but quietly advised them, when appropriate. He worked incredibly hard, with unbroken concentration and meticulous attention to detail. Better than anyone I know, Geoff mastered details of water law and regional and local water politics. He brought to this work a brilliant and disciplined mind, deep political understanding, razor-sharp humor, and sheer strength of character.

It was largely through Geoff that I communicated with the TVAA's 18-person board of directors. He organized the dozens of meetings he and I had over the years with Palemón and Fred Waltz, the TVAA lawyer, as well as my meetings with other board members and with scholars doing research for the case. Fred, Geoff, and I met periodically at every major stage of the project, from the first days of planning the fieldwork through the final days of preparing the book for press. Because of the confidential nature of the work, Geoff was the only person with whom I could freely discuss the project, and he found the material as exciting and provocative as I did. An intellectually curious man, Geoff perfectly understood the ironic ambiguity of my position while never losing sight of what was needed for the case. Ours was a conversation in progress.

One week after we had all three gone over the book manuscript together and the day before Geoff and I were to meet again so that he could update me on the case, Geoff was killed in a car accident. It happened on the beautiful, sunny-stormy

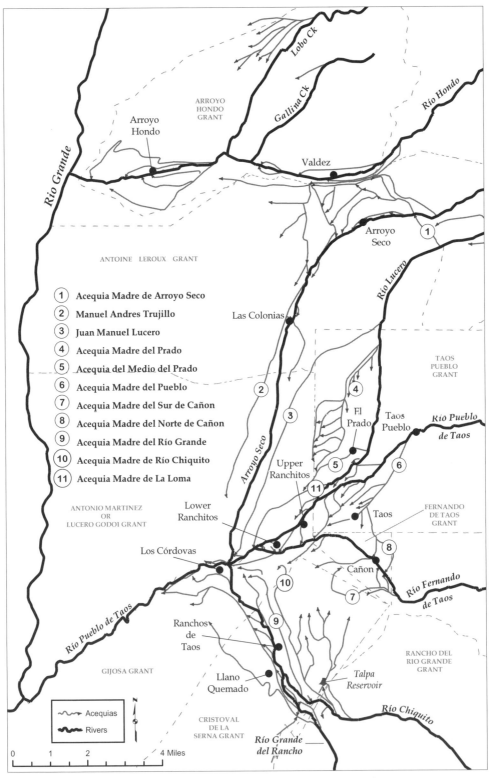

Figure P.1 Taos Valley acequias. Drawn by Kurt A. Menke. © Sylvia Rodríguez.

afternoon of June 15, 2004, at the crossroads north of Taos known as the Blinking Light. His pickup was T-boned by a well-drilling rig in a crash involving neither alcohol nor skid marks. One of Taos's occasional power failures had occurred shortly before, and it is possible that the traffic light was not working. No one seems to know exactly what happened. Geoff was DOA at Holy Cross Hospital, where the staff would not let his frantic Valdez neighbors see him (the news traveled quickly) because they were "not family."

Once again, the TVAA and the larger New Mexico acequia community were in terrible shock over a loss impossible to absorb. A few days later, at least 200 people from around northern New Mexico showed up at the Taos County Agricultural Center to pay their respects at a secular service organized by the TVAA, the people from Valdez, and Geoff's widow, María, who flew in from New York with an entourage of friends. The spontaneous testimony so many bore to his work and character was overwhelming, but words gave me no consolation this time. He was buried on his land in Valdez, where he wanted "to live, die, and be buried," he had told me only a year before. Perhaps because he was so steady and calm and dependable, Geoff was the sort of person one expected to be there always. I realize now, I just assumed that he was in for the long haul and would live to be a wise, spry old man. His death has undone me.

One winter day in early 1994, Eduardo and Geoff drove down to Albuquerque to ask me to do two things: serve as an expert witness for the Abeyta case (Taos water rights adjudication) and write a book about the case. My report for the TVAA and this book represent my fulfillment of their first request. The second request was driven by their conviction that unless the full story of the case was told, putting a human face to the perspective of the acequia associations, national public sentiment would inevitably go against Mexican American small farmers whose irrigation water is needed elsewhere for urban "progress" and "the greater good."[3] They promised full cooperation and access to TVAA records, knowing that the project would be long and difficult. Partly because of the second request, I feel compelled to write about these two valiant men, now that they have gone and left me holding the bag. Surely this is "anthropology that breaks your heart" (Behar 1996). Whether or how the story of the case is told and by whom depend on its outcome. We can be certain that the consequences will outlast us all.

Preface

This book is about ditches. It is also about the people who use and maintain them in the urbanizing communities of the Taos Valley in northern New Mexico. The Taos Valley contains the largest and most elaborate acequia (community irrigation ditch) system in New Mexico. Traditional ditch irrigation and water sharing involve a moral economy or system of principles and values that supports and guides cooperative, interdependent economic practice. In these pages, I describe two areas of acequia-related activity: the traditional *reparto de aguas* (division of waters) and the religious rituals that sanctify agriculture and place. The moral economy of acequia practice and belief integrates these seemingly distinct realms. What people do and say about their ditches and how they divide and use the water reveal the tenets of this moral economy, as do the religious and moral beliefs permeating the day-to-day lives of parciantes (ditch association members). Here, I explore the relationship between water sharing, belief, and attachment to place. But there is more to this story than how parciantes share a vital and limited resource and how religious belief and practice reinforce the moral economy of water.

In 1995 I began anthropological fieldwork for this study at the request of the Taos Valley Acequia Association (TVAA); throughout my study, I worked in close cooperation with its executive board. The TVAA is a federation of 74 community acequias in the Taos Valley. It was established in 1986 to coordinate a response to the intensifying pressure of resource competition in the late 20th century—particularly the Taos water rights adjudication, a lawsuit known as Abeyta. I designed the research project in collaboration with the president, both executive directors, and the attorney for the TVAA, with input from a consulting historian.

Our primary goal was to document the living practice of water-sharing customs among Taos Pueblo and neighboring acequia associations on two tributaries of the Rio Grande: the Río Pueblo and the Río Lucero. We also wanted to investigate the cultural and religious significance of water in Hispano acequia communities—a previously unexplored topic that the TVAA officials considered crucial to an understanding of parciantes' core values. Finally, they requested that I assess the potential impact of water loss on the acequia associations. My role was to write a report and to testify as an expert witness in the Abeyta case.

The support of the TVAA opened doors that otherwise would have been walls to me. I was fascinated by the topic and grateful for the opportunity to do ethnography under the least invasive circumstances possible—when people invite you to examine what they consider important. One commissioner, Mario Barela, graciously arranged for tours, interviews, and opportunities to photograph irrigation and ditch cleaning.[1] The men who escorted me along the ditches and gave me more than 50 in-depth interviews were at least 40 years of age, recommended by their peers, and selected for their intimate knowledge of and long involvement with the acequias. Many of them I had known since childhood. Almost all were commissioners (ditch officers) or *mayordomos* (ditch bosses). Parciantes from the Río Pueblo, Río Lucero, and Río Grande del Rancho watersheds gave me tours of their respective ditch systems while I asked questions and photographed. Each explained the layout and workings of his ditches, including the repartos. During separate interviews, parciantes spelled out how they divide the water on their rivers and on specific ditches.

Fieldwork became a progressive revelation about the magnitude, complexity, and ingenuity of the Taos Valley acequia system. Even though I grew up in the town of Taos and spent my childhood exploring its neighborhoods and ditches, I soon realized that I had barely glimpsed what was really there. Gradually, I discovered how the many smaller components, each with its own features and history of disputes and compromises, form part of a larger entity. Another world slowly emerged, one tour at a time, out of a once seemingly familiar landscape: hidden, cultivated places nestled behind more prominent ones, all interconnected by ditches that carry water to nearly every square meter of arable land in the Taos basin. Punctuating these many miles of hand-dug canals are *compuertas* (headgates) that divert and regulate flow, making water-sharing agreements "concrete."

My ditch guides were like psychopomps leading me through the watery underworld, showing me where to walk and what to look for while they recounted the perils, strengths, and pitfalls of each place. The guides possessed a wealth of local knowledge accumulated over a lifetime of using, working on, and talking about their ditches. Perhaps a linguist and skilled videographer could have done justice to the vast amounts of information transmitted by my interlocutors on each of these unforgettable tours. But as it was, juggling a notebook and camera while trying to navigate ditch banks and record major features, I was constantly overwhelmed. Later, working with field notes, photographs, and maps, I would try to reconstruct the basic content of each tour.

I also began to appreciate the blend of pragmatism, ownership, and pride the parciantes conveyed when showing me their ditches. Individual personality aside, every parciante clearly took deep pleasure in walking along the acequias out among the fields in the open air. I learned that ditch knowledge is extremely local. Any given parciante knows every detail, including assets and liabilities, of his own ditches and neighborhood, but the fields, ditches, and water-sharing customs in the next valley might be quite unfamiliar to him. It dawned on me that perhaps no one, either today or in the past, has ever kept the entire basinwide system "in his head" with the same degree of intimate familiarity mastered in his own locale. This point was brought home one afternoon when Gus García showed me the middle Río Lucero watershed. Standing in a low, fertile field where acequias from the Río Lucero and the Río Pueblo intertwine, we were marveling at this engineering achievement when he asked rhetorically, "I wonder if there was a master plan."

His question stuck in my mind and nagged. The idea of a master plan is intriguing, but surely the answer to Gus's question must be no. For one thing, the acequias were dug a section at a time over the course of several generations by different parties, all scrambling for an agricultural foothold. The system was never planned or laid out as a whole but gradually evolved into an entity comprising many carefully husbanded and ardently defended local parts, each with its own acequia association and set of problems. Indeed, the very notion of the system as a unitary whole is a modern construct, a defensive, imagined community that corresponds to all the acequias along the seven rivers whose sum of diversions defines the Taos basin. The Taos acequia system emerged as a self-conscious, organized entity with the establishment of the Taos Valley Acequia Association. The acequia associations' engagement of me to document contemporary water-sharing customs and practices was likewise part of their defensive strategy. Thus, my ethnography will further reify the system. The TVAA Taos Valley acequias map (figure P.1) graphically portrays this entity.

In addition to ditch tours and interviews, I took part in religious activities of the local Catholic parishes, focusing on rituals related to themes of agriculture and water. I had grown up *coyote*, Catholic, and middle-class—on an acequia, but unaware of its inclusive webwork, and in a parish, but without appreciating the intensity and depth of people's religious devotion.[2] Ritual telegraphs its message through the body. The psychophysical impact of ritual participation on an adult who long ago left the church amounted to a reindoctrination in values I learned as a child and spent my youth rebelling against. My visceral response to the familiar power of ritual prayer evoked an inner conflict between an impulse to convert and the refusal of reason. Without participating, however, I would never have felt the bonding power of a novena (a nine-day prayer ceremony) or grasped the moral economy that its teaching engenders.

The moral import of religious teachings came clear as I joined in the novena, the rites of passage, and the unending cycle of feast days. The ethos of this moral economy seems most compellingly modeled by *ancianos*—elders in their seventies, eighties, and nineties who embody the "old way" ideal of proper comportment. This is an elusive yet unmistakable quality subsumed by the term *respeto* (respect). To show respect is to elicit respect. Respeto prescribes relations between generations, genders, and, ideally, neighbors.

One elderly couple, Anita and Candido Valerio, so evoked my respeto that before leaving their home I asked them to give me their blessing. We had talked about the ditches and the celebration of San Isidro in Los Córdovas. There were old ties between Anita's family and mine, and she had reminisced about how parents in two generations had hoped, without success, to effect marriages between their children. Even as a secret unbeliever, I dropped spontaneously to my knees to receive their blessing.

The link between ditch business and parish ritual emerged when I saw that these involve the same families and when I reflected on the values that parciantes and parishioners voice in both settings. By walking the ditches and joining the processions, I came to see where folk Catholic holy sites are located in physical relationship to bodies and sources of water. The pathways of irrigation and the pathways of procession overlap and intertwine. Repeated acts of irrigation, like repeated processions, inscribe the landscape with meaning and also inscribe the human body of the one who participates in them. The irrigated landscape becomes the sacred landscape through procession and prayer. Cooperative action and words spoken in specific places produce local subjects and instruct them how to live. In this moral economy, the principles of equity and need governing the repartos also manifest in the normative value of respeto.

The Abeyta case, which occasioned this study and shaped its trajectory, was filed in 1969, and the portion dealing with the water rights claims of Taos Pueblo has still not gone to trial. The purpose of the Taos and other New Mexico water rights adjudications is to determine the nature and extent of all water right claims on the Upper Rio Grande and its tributaries, as well as those of other river systems, including groundwater, in the state. Adjudication applies the doctrine of prior appropriation to oppose senior-against-junior water claims and to rank them according to seniority. The parties in Abeyta include Taos Pueblo, the TVAA, the town of Taos, and several federal and state agencies, as well as other entities.[3] All have been preparing for years. The stakes are so high and the issues so complex that the parties still are not ready to step into the courtroom, which looms on the horizon like a slow giant.

From the beginning until almost this moment of writing, my research project has been shrouded in secrecy because of the rule of confidentiality while the TVAA coordinates the acequias' preparation for the case. Discovery still continues. This means that I have been unable to speak publicly about my involvement or write about my findings, much less publish them. Not until well after I submitted my report to the TVAA did the board finally give me permission to publish writings based on the research. I had always wanted to write and publish articles and a book, but it was clear that permission was required and my manuscripts would remain subject to review by the executive director, the attorney, and the president—a little like working for a tribal council.

As the years went by and I became steeped in the study and in privileged conversations about the case, certain parallels between the TVAA and Taos Pueblo struck me. Despite the obvious differences and legally imposed adversarial relationship, these two parties share some common ground. They have been the two authoritative, local, strategizing agents in this litigation, representing the two traditional "stakeholder" communities living side by side, sharing and competing for water since the 17th century. As designated corporate agents in this matter, both have been made up almost exclusively of culturally conservative men more than 40 years of age and involved in agriculture. Both have worked to ensure the survival of a traditional, land-based community by protecting their respective water rights. Both represent long-standing communities of identity and place. But if I have enjoyed full and privileged access to acequia knowledge and culture, I have had none whatsoever to the Pueblo side of things, not only because of the case but also because of the Pueblo norm of secrecy.[4] Therefore, I have been subject to a double rule of secrecy that has rendered me invisible and mute.

The awkwardness of my position was brought home to me one July during the town of Taos's summer fiesta. This is about the only occasion when one is likely to see a large number of native Taoseños on the plaza (Rodríguez 1997, 1998). I happened to be standing in front of an information booth operated by the TVAA when I spotted Josephine and Frank Marcus, old friends from Taos Pueblo, walking along the street. Josephine's parents and mine, now deceased, were good friends many years ago. Her parents would come to our house to eat, drink, dance, and sing, and we would go to theirs and do the same. I remember picnics at their summer camp near Arroyo Seco and even watching Josephine's father, Eliseo, irrigate a small cornfield up there. If only I had paid more attention when I was a child. Eliseo and my father, who spoke a little Tiwa, knew each other all their lives. Eliseo visited my father when he was ill and sang at the gravesite for my father's funeral. Eliseo told me that his pickup truck, parked with its brake on, had moved about ten feet the night my father died, which we took to be a sign of my father's *despedida* (farewell).

We greeted one another warmly and reminisced, lamenting that our parents were gone and now our scattered, busy families hardly knew each other. Suddenly, Frank, who sat on the tribal council and had served on the governor's staff more than once, spotted the TVAA sign. Jumping in mock surprise, he muttered something about "the other side" in the pueblo's fight to keep its water. I sympathized and said what a pity that old neighbors who had always shared now opposed one another, when their interests were really so similar. I felt a stab of guilt. Here I was, working secretly for the "other side," a fact that no doubt would come out one day. I wanted desperately to hear his side of the story but knew I dare not ask.

Since 1990 the major players have been struggling to reach a negotiated settlement rather than go to court. In reality, they have been engaging simultaneously in two contrary efforts: to prepare for a bloody courtroom battle and also to avoid it. This negotiation has gone through many vicissitudes. It was at a low point when Eduardo suffered his fatal heart attack; it seemed to be verging on resolution when Geoff was killed nine years later. As I write these words in 2005, a negotiated settlement is said to be imminent, although anything can happen until an agreement is signed. I am told that representatives from the pueblo, the TVAA, the town of Taos, and the El Prado Water and Sanitation District have held daylong negotiation sessions up to several times a week for the past two years. This level of intensity has taken a heavy toll on those involved, but the goal is worthy. One can only hope that a fair and mutually acceptable settlement will be reached, because a court decision is less likely to be accommodating or to be appealed.

If the case never goes to court, I will never have to testify. After so many years, such an outcome might seem anticlimactic, but this would be a great relief—not only for me but also, probably, for all the dedicated souls who have given their lives to the ongoing struggle over Taos Valley water. Either way, I must bear witness, speaking from a position both inside and outside the action, inside yet outside the communities of interest. I can make no claim to objectivity or detachment. Taos is my hometown, and these are my friends and family. I care deeply about the issues. Yet ethnography is inherently a divided project: between inside understanding and outside analysis. Eduardo and Geoff had to have known that I would bring this split to the story about acequias and identity in northern New Mexico.

o n e
Introduction

The story told in these pages is born out of the struggle of acequia systems to survive in a world where water scarcity and competition are no longer local issues but part of a global crisis. Small farmers and ranchers in New Mexico are fully immersed in the urban wage economy, and few subsist exclusively or primarily by agriculture. Yet in communities in Taos, Río Arriba, Mora, and other northern counties, people still clean their ditches and irrigate, and ditch associations increasingly mobilize and litigate to defend their water rights against competing claims and demands. The regional pressures that face them include population growth, urbanization, and industrial or resort development, all of which require ever greater amounts of water—water that most city dwellers comfortably assume will be transferred for their needs and out of agricultural use.

Water scarcity and the legal status and ownership of water and water rights are major world issues in the 21st century. The acequia associations of New Mexico, like other local water-use and water-sharing communities around the world, are caught in a dilemma: the legal transition of water as a substance to which all humans have a right, to water as a commodity available to the highest bidders. This worldwide crisis magnifies their significance as an example of a workable, even elegant solution to the age-old problem of dividing water where it is scarce.

Every society, whether hunting-foraging, agricultural, pastoral, or industrial,

...ust have a system for capturing, storing, and distributing water. This requires some form of technology and associated practices, rules, and meanings. The larger and more complex the society, the larger and more complex the waterworks. Archaeologists have long recognized canal irrigation as a cornerstone of human civilization in both the Old World and New World. Karl Wittfogel's hypothesis (1957) that massive irrigation works require the centralized authoritarian power of a state sparked an ongoing debate over the relationship between hydraulics and social structure. Although many cases challenge his formulation, scholars agree that power and water control are intimately related. The question is, how will their relation vary and under what conditions? Even more important, how should they correlate in a fair and just society?

In New Mexico, the Arabic derivation *acequia* refers to both a canal structure and a social institution whereby river water is diverted and distributed via gravity flow among a community of irrigators or water right user-owners called *parciantes*. Historically, acequias made possible the Spanish colonial settlement of the semiarid Upper Rio Grande Valley of New Mexico, starting in the late 16th century. Acequias appropriated and transformed whatever irrigation structures and practices were operating among Pueblos in the Upper Rio Grande Valley at the time of European contact.

During the colonial and Mexican periods and into the American era, acequias proliferated. For roughly 350 years, they formed a core component of the technological infrastructure of New Mexico's agropastoral economy. Their local, interlocking networks of canals transformed and shaped the entire riparian ecology of the region. The body of irrigation law brought from Spain and adapted through customary practice to frontier conditions became incorporated into territorial and finally New Mexico state water law.

Today's acequia associations are political subdivisions of the state. Local associations of parciantes elect a *mayordomo* and commissioners to oversee the annual operations of the acequias and to maintain, use, improve, and defend them. At the start of the 21st century, approximately one thousand acequia associations still existed in New Mexico. The humble earthen ditches crisscrossing the fields and arable valleys along the Rio Grande and its tributaries are arguably the oldest living, non-indigenous public works system in North America.

Acequias occupy a paradoxical position along the hypothetical water-control continuum between extremes of centralized control at one pole and autonomy or consensus at the other. Historically, acequias partake of both extremes. At the outset, they were a colonial or colonizing institution. In concert with roads, architecture, mines, and the agriculture they supported, acequias transformed the indigenous landscape radically and forever. Subordinated workers dug the first colonial ditches. Yet despite invasive beginnings, acequias became integral to the New Mexican environment.

In our own era, acequia associations continue to promote a fluctuating balance between cooperation and competition, as well as seasonal, face-to-face interaction among parciantes on a ditch. They are a democratic institution in that parciantes elect their mayordomo and commissioners, with usually one vote per parciante. Ownership of water rights is normally inherited but can transfer with the land. Nowadays, a water right is also a prime commodity bought and sold separately from the land to which it was once implicitly attached, and it can be transferred to urban uses. The market in detachable water rights escalates with each passing year. Use rights to a ditch depend on exercise through irrigation, compliance with rules, and proportional contribution to maintenance of the system. Each ditch operates according to its own variant of a common set of principles. Some are written as law; some are observed, spoken, but not written; and others are simply unspoken practice.

Origin

The principles that organized Spanish irrigation crossed the Atlantic with the colonists to take root in the New World in three contexts: private systems that were built and maintained by wealthy landowners, public community systems that met the domestic and agricultural needs of incorporated communities, and private community systems that served "non-incorporated agricultural clusters" (Meyer 2000:79). The latter, *acequias de común*, predominate in New Mexico. Today's one thousand New Mexican acequia associations, or local irrigation communities, arose out of diverse beginnings such as private individual grants, community grants, or de facto settlements along a stream.[1] These "rural agricultural clusters" survived through an organizational strategy for ditch construction and maintenance, water sharing, and irrigation management (Meyer 2000:79–93). The scarcity of water demanded some means of allocating the vital substance. Lacking formal governmental structures, the colonists resorted to a form of "democratic collectivism motivated by self-interest" (Meyer 2000:88). Some kind of water-sharing plan accordingly became the key ingredient in every local setting (Meyer 2000:89).[2]

From the late colonial through Mexican periods, ditch organization and water-sharing practice coalesced into broad uniformity on the Rio Grande and its tributaries, notwithstanding variation in local custom. Acequia associations sprang up along the "mother ditches," *acequias madres*, according to regulations that originated in Spain and were published in 1680 in a compilation of laws for the colonies, known by specialists as the *Recopilación*. Community ditch associations in the Upper Rio Grande Valley and Río Arriba worked out their specific water-sharing customs in an unending dialectic between the word of law and day-to-day practical accommodation. Water law and acequia practices remained in place under Mexican rule and were preserved by the Kearny Code enacted upon Americanization in 1846 (Clark 1987; Wozniak 1997; Rivera 1998).

In 1895 the New Mexico legislature defined community acequias as corporate bodies with powers to sue and be sued; each association was required to elect three commissioners to assist a mayordomo in regulating ditch operation and maintenance (Clark 1987:30). The status of acequias was clarified in a series of court decisions following statehood in 1912 (Apodaca and Zokan 1999). In 1945 the state legislature tightened the administrative requirements for mayordomos and acequia commissioners (Clark 1987:350) and 20 years later declared acequias to be political subdivisions of the state of New Mexico (Wozniak 1997:131; Rivera 1998:148–149).[3]

Custom

Repartimientos de agua (or more colloquially, *repartos*) are basic to how community acequia systems operate. They follow the pattern for Spanish colonial customary law, in which "customs vary from place to place, are locally accepted and obeyed, and for officials to enforce them, the custom must be clear, contain reasonable and immemorial practices not contradictory to each other, and lastly they must be continuous and remain undisputed" (Tyler 1995:152–153; Rivera 1998:168). Custom originally arose out of conflict, secreted like a pearl around the grain of perpetual dispute. Rather than crystallize into a static measure, custom persists as the ongoing, elastic process of negotiation or conciliation itself, of meeting year after year to divide the water according to an agreement forged in crisis long ago.[4]

Scholars recognize two basic models of water allocation found in irrigation systems around the world: Syrian and Yemenite (Scarborough 2003:97–99). In the former, water is allocated in proportion to the amount of land under irrigation. In the latter, water is allocated on a fixed, time-release basis. Historian Thomas Glick links these two models to different conditions and suggests that an irrigation system may shift sequentially from a Syrian to a Yemenite model when demand exceeds availability (Glick 1970:1972). Anthropologists Robert and Eva Hunt (1976) report the Yemenite model in the private sector and the Syrian on *ejido* (common) land in rural Mexico and tell how, in one case, the Syrian gave way to the Yemenite method during a protracted drought.

Interestingly, repartos implemented on a single stream in the Upper Rio Grande Valley often combine both models. Both operate on the Río Pueblo and the Río Lucero, involving slightly different combinations of proportional and rotational methods. Both apply among the acequias themselves in that each parciante receives an amount proportional to his or her cultivated acreage but all parciantes are subject to fixed time releases when demand exceeds supply. The Yemenite system holds between Taos Pueblo and the downstream acequia madre on the Río Lucero except in times of abundance; the Syrian prevails between Taos Pueblo and the acequia madre on the Río Pueblo. Responding to contingencies of weather and supply, the mayordomo calculates need and enunciates a measured equity when he must rotate the water among large and small irrigators.

Most significant is that in extreme scarcity the mayordomo must allocate every drop according to need and give priority to animals. Seniority does not confer, and has never conferred, exclusive right on either stream. Instead, sharing arrangements on these and other rivers include *sobrante* (surplus) water that others petition to use and the *auxilio* (special dispensation) made during crises. Although not articulated as such, the principle at work here resembles—and may well derive from—both the Islamic Right of Thirst, which dictates that all living creatures have a right to water, and the Islamic Right of Irrigation, which gives all users the right to irrigate their crops.[5]

Autonomy and Globalization

Each acequia association, as well as the stream as a whole, constitutes a self-regulating entity that anthropologists call an autonomous irrigation community. Small-scale autonomous irrigation communities in Latin America, the Philippines, Bali, and elsewhere generally operate according to six principles: "autonomy, uniformity, contiguity, proportionality, regularity, and transparency, which results from the others and allows for accountability within the system" (Trawick 2001a:366–377; see Coward 1980b).[6] Such systems are autonomous only insofar as they control their own flow of water. Local irrigation communities are always embedded within larger state, national, and global systems, in which they occupy marginal and subordinated positions. Each is locked in struggle with larger systems, as well as internal interests, over the ownership and control of the water it depends on. The battles intensify as the privatization of water accelerates.

A set of procedures or lawsuits known as water rights adjudications, brought by the New Mexico State Engineer, has forced all acequia systems to defend in court the water rights claimed by individual parciantes. Each adjudication suit is a separate case. The purpose of each case—which assumes a different name in each watershed according to the names of the defendants, listed in alphabetical order, such as Aamodt for Pojoaque and Abeyta for Taos—is to determine the nature and extent of all water right claims on the Upper Rio Grande and its tributaries, as well as those of other river systems (including groundwater) located in the state.[7]

These cases are driven by the imperative to quantify and rationalize every drop of water in these finite, fully allocated river systems. Because of the US doctrine of prior appropriation, this litigation places all water right claimants in adversarial relation to one another and threatens to rank them according to priority of right based on priority in time. Acequia associations contend that Spanish and Mexican law, which is based on a system of equitable apportionment, applies. Parciantes believe that water should be shared according to need and equity rather than owned exclusively, based on a principle of prior appropriation. In 1991 and again in 1993, the US district court recognized the importance of customs in the apportionment among acequias, a point critical to my focus on customs of water sharing (Rivera 1998:166, n. 55).

Acequia associations contend that the doctrine of prior appropriation is inimical to their very basis of operation, a flexible principle of equity and the common good. Prior appropriation privileges seniority of water rights exclusively during times of abundance and scarcity alike. It imposes an all-or-nothing, zero-sum formula on what has been a fluid process of negotiation that, in principle at least, spreads the last drops among the thirsty. Ditch coalitions contend that their customary repartos—which, despite their diversity, share a common ethic—should receive full legal recognition.

Acequia Practice

Acequia practice encompasses the annual spring cleaning of the ditch and other work of repair, maintenance, and improvement; changing the headgate and dividing the water; and attending meetings of the parciantes. Irrigating the fields, orchards, and gardens is the basic secular activity, and far from the simplest. Stanley Crawford's (1988) memoir, *Mayordomo*, about his year of service as mayordomo on a ditch in Dixon, in southern Taos County, offers the most detailed account of everyday acequia activities. His narrative begins and ends with cleaning the ditch but also covers the daily tasks—repair, crisis management, planning, improvement, dues collection, record keeping, meeting, and negotiation—that make up the seasonal operation of an acequia.

Curiously, Crawford never describes the actual process of irrigation. Perhaps, like riding a horse or driving a car, it is taken for granted and laborious to explain. Irrigation involves bodily skill learned through observation in the context of practice. Practitioners do not describe it in the abstract or narrate it outside its execution. Irrigation is kinesthetic, visual, spatial, technical, and interactive, but not especially verbal.

Anyone who has watched the minimalist gestures of a parciante irrigating a field will allow that at first glance it does not look like much. Yet anyone who has tried to control the gravity-driven flow of water over an irregular gradient of variably porous, plowed ground so that it will soak in slowly, deeply, and evenly will tell you how difficult this job is. Success requires experience, patience, knowledge, and control. One must be familiar with the terrain and responsive to the contingencies of weather and water flow. One must not lose the water or let it get away. Given the undeniable power of flowing water, little apparent exertion can become a mark of skill rather than lassitude. Each act of irrigation is particular to a piece of land (plate 9). My own first attempt years ago at what looked like a simple project ended in ruined, washed-out rows and tears of frustration and shock. I failed to anticipate the force of the water as it rushed off the mountain and over my neatly planted rows of seeds. Seventy-eight-year-old Corina Santistevan of Cordillera put it this way:

> But there was, there is, a real craft about how to irrigate a field. It isn't done,
> it can't be done, by just anybody. I have been paying for people to do it for
> me, and they don't know how to irrigate. They either flood one spot, or they
> never get the water to another, and they don't have that sense of how the water
> runs. [April 1996]

La saca, or *la limpia de la acequia* (the annual spring cleaning of the ditch), requires each parciante to contribute labor toward physical maintenance of the system. Each parciante goes, sends a *peón* (surrogate), or pays for hired labor, according to how much acreage he or she irrigates. Contribution to ditch maintenance is proportional. On the morning of the designated day, each worker arrives with a shovel and spends the day clearing away underbrush and digging dirt and debris out of the ditch (plates 6 and 7). The mayordomo marks and calls out the sections and supervises the labor. This is the *tarea* (task) to which generations of parciantes have committed their sons from the age of puberty. Today, most parciantes hire or pay for peones rather than go, or they send their sons. Each spring, a few young boys can still be found performing this rite of passage on their acequia madre. Some ditches take more than one day to clean. Along with irrigation, la limpia enables parciantes to become familiar with their ditches and keep their use rights. It is a day of common labor by the members— or their peones—of an acequia community. It affirms and socializes members into a cooperative, subsistence institution. "Ditch cleanings are all very much the same," Crawford (1988:224) writes, "and in this they often feel more like ritual than work." The warm glow of mutualism notwithstanding, Crawford still perceived an underlying tension in acequia work:

> The collective power of a ditch crew of twenty or thirty men can often be felt as threatening or dangerous, but what holds it in restraint are the conventions and traditions that have evolved out of hundreds of years of maintaining acequias—a complex social fabric binds a ditch crew together far more than the character of a mayordomo or the commissioners, recalling it to a sense of common purpose and preventing the inevitable disputes from flaring into political divisiveness or even physical violence. [Crawford 1988:23–24]

Meetings are the major venue for the cooperative, organizational, and managerial aspects of acequia practice. Each acequia must hold an annual meeting to elect the mayordomo and commissioners and to deal with other routine ditch business. Parciantes also hold meetings to deal with crisis situations and the rationing of water during drought. New Mexico state statute requires mayordomos and commissioners to meet each spring to decide how the water will be divided on their common stream under pending conditions. A parciante meets with the mayordomo at a given time and headgate to transfer the water from one ditch to another. Crawford evokes the everyday seesaw of structure and agency played out among individuals and families through time along a ditch. The medium of meetings is public language, employed as an instrument of organization, control, and power.

The mayordomo plays a key role in the New Mexican community acequia complex. The mayordomo and commissioners manage all ditch business. They supervise la saca, preside over meetings, resolve minor disputes between parciantes, and organize repair jobs. The mayordomo assigns the water and manages the reparto de agua according to custom. Each tributary and acequia madre has its own, distilled out of generations of struggle and negotiation or conciliation among parciantes or between parciantes and pueblo irrigators over their respective shares of river water. Each reparto synthesizes principles of law with the pragmatics of compromise. Some customs, such as the ones governing the division of water on the Río Pueblo and the Río Lucero, enjoy the force and formality of a legal decree or agreement. Others persist in memory and practice but go unwritten and jurally unrecognized.

Today's parciantes describe mayordomos of a generation or two ago as powerful, authoritarian figures regarded with a mixture of respect, trust, and fear. Gus García put it succinctly: "They were like dictators, and what the mayordomo said was the law and you did it" (personal communication with the author, July 1995). A good mayordomo must know and uphold the customary repartos on his ditches, as well as on the river as a whole. He must be fair and evenhanded, possess intimate knowledge of local topography and hydraulics, and be able to deliver the water despite adversity or conflict. He must command respect. The authoritarian nature of the position is counterbalanced by the fact that parciantes in good standing on a ditch elect the mayordomo and the commissioners. The mayordomo is both a leader and an equal among peers.

Mayordomos are still respected, and the position carries status along with responsibility. They exert less power, however, and are less feared than in the old days when nearly everyone farmed for a living. State statute has spread the mayordomo's former power among the commissioners. A person's boss can potentially impact household economy the way the mayordomo of the acequia once did. Today people rarely seek the role of mayordomo and often accept it reluctantly, under subtle, irresistible pressure. The acequia association pays the mayordomo a modest stipend that hardly covers the hours, miles, worry, and labor involved. The variety of mayordomos is as diverse as the ditches themselves. Some are adept and fair; others are inept or self-serving. Acequias and their mayordomos have always had to adapt to local conditions shaped by larger forces. These days, officers are as preoccupied with defending their acequia rights in court as with dividing the water or maintaining their ditch.

The acequia is predominantly a male domain. The full significance of this cannot be explored here. Women have been known to irrigate, to dig and clean ditches, and even to serve as commissioner or mayordomo. But such cases remain exceptional. Women who actively participate on a ditch usually do so because there is no man around to fulfill the role. Depending on who she is in both personal and familial terms, according to the temper of the community and other circumstances, a woman parciante may be barely tolerated, may be treated with respect, or may be silently erased. The rare woman who assumes the role of mayordomo, probably a late-20th-century innovation, will invariably admit to difficulty, if not hostility, encountered while trying to maneuver inside this deeply patriarchal domain.[8]

My own experience in conducting this study seems like an exception that proves the rule. Individual men graciously escorted me through each watershed, granting every access, answering every question, patiently but firmly instructing me about their ditches. But I was working for them rather than trying to run a ditch. The patriarchal face of acequia culture is pervasive and undeniable. Patriarchy structures the honor code and gender norms, not to mention a division of labor that domesticates women and relegates most public and outdoor space to men. Even though women have chopped wood, hauled water, tended livestock, and irrigated, perhaps only in ritual were they allowed to move out of doors into the open air, to pray and walk in procession. Only men showed me the ditches. But when it came to religious ritual, my guides and advisers were mostly women.

The Pueblo Enigma

The water rights adjudications promote opposition between local acequia associations and their longtime neighbors, the Rio Grande Pueblos. These two populations are historically the oldest and economically the poorest owners of New Mexico's scarce and precious rights to river water. Both peoples entered the United States under the Treaty of Guadalupe Hidalgo but now have very different legal statuses vis-à-vis federal and state governments. The theme of Pueblo-Hispano relations weaves inextricably throughout the pages of this study. On the one hand, water rights adjudications serve to highlight the history of oscillating cooperation and competition that has characterized four centuries of Pueblo and acequia-based Hispano coexistence. On the other hand, the Abeyta case and similar cases can harden the perennial fluidity of these relations into rigid and fatal opposition. Research for the adjudications by scholars, including me, has generated a wealth of new knowledge about the history of irrigation and water disputes in New Mexico. Yet the adversarial climate of litigation, with its emphasis on asserting a superior claim, can discourage open inquiry into acequia-pueblo interpenetration. The question of what is shared and what is not when it comes to acequia and pueblo irrigation practices remains largely unanswered because no one seems to have asked it.

Although most scholars accept that Pueblo Indian agriculture incorporated acequias, no researcher has compared how ditch water is allocated at the pueblos with how neighboring acequia associations do it. In Hispano communities, ditch maintenance and water allocation are always vested in the hands of a mayordomo elected from among the parciantes on an acequia madre, or main ditch. Usually, two elected commissioners assist him. Pueblo ditch management may rest with the governor or a mayordomo, but little is documented about how Pueblos divide their water internally.[9] In a rare study of the irrigation technology at a Northern Tiwa pueblo, anthropologist Richard Ford (1977:147) reports: "No authority in Picurís allots water; no calendar is followed." He says nothing about how water is shared during times of scarcity.

My research confirms customary water-sharing practices between Taos Pueblo and the acequia associations on both the Río Pueblo and the Río Lucero, but it also indicates that parciantes do not know how their pueblo neighbors divide the water among themselves or precisely how they manage their ditches. This raises questions. Is it possible that they knew in the past, when people were more engaged in the cooperative endeavor of farming? Do some pueblos follow the mayordomo system and employ repartos, and others do not? Does this vary according to relative placement within a watershed? How is water managed internally at Taos Pueblo during times of shortage? How does canal irrigation relate to the Pueblo moral economy of water? Are Pueblo and Hispano moral economies alike? How do they differ, and why?

The Plan of the Book

In chapter 2, I provide the historical context for this two-part ethnography about contemporary acequia practice and belief. Part One, titled "Reparto," contains two chapters in which I describe, drawing on the words of the parciantes themselves, how they divide the water on the Río Pueblo (chapter 3) and the Río Lucero (chapter 4). In Part Two, titled "Respeto," I briefly discuss the concept of moral economy (chapter 5) and then describe the novena (chapter 6) and procession (chapter 7) performed each May in Los Córdovas in honor of San Isidro, the patron saint of farming. Drawing on the words of parishioners, the texts of prayers, and participant observation, I examine the religious and moral meanings and values these rituals embody. In chapter 8, the parciantes explain what they think would happen if they lost their water rights through adjudication.

t w o
Irrigation in Taos

Water is always a metaphor of social, economic and political relationships—a barometer of the extent to which identity, power and resources are shared.

—*Veronica Strang,* The Meaning of Water

Irrigation and other forms of water management have a long history in the Taos Valley. Indigenous peoples throughout the region had shaped the landscape to serve their agricultural needs for hundreds of years by the time the earliest Spanish colonists arrived in the Upper Rio Grande Valley. These newcomers introduced a system of live irrigation that gradually transformed Pueblo agriculture. No one knows precisely how or even when this process of transformation took place, but there is little doubt that it did. Historians remain equivocal on this matter because they usually want to have it both ways without bothering much about what this implies. James Vlasich (2005), for example, adheres to the prevailing view that the Spanish introduced the mayor-domo system of ditch management; he also holds that the aboriginal Pueblos were accomplished canal irrigators who produced substantial stores of corn. Yet he notes that the crude laterals dug by Pueblo laborers in the colonial era were less sophisticated than their Iberian models (Vlasich 2005:28). Like other historians, Vlasich glides over the questions of precisely what sort of indigenous canal and related water-management systems operated before contact and precisely how and when the acequias came to be dug, maintained, and extended around the individual pueblos.

Given almost universal scholarly agreement—and debate—that the construction and control of hydraulic systems correlate somehow with the exercise of power, this particular juncture of Indo-Hispano interaction ought to be of special interest to historians and anthropologists. Yet, perhaps because virtually no direct archaeological or archival evidence that can illuminate this process of transplantation and adaptation seems to exist, scholars have failed to problematize its theoretical import. Like others, Vlasich takes for granted that, apart from the initial shock of contact and the introduction of new cultigens, Pueblo agricultural practice remained little changed by colonization through the 18th century. Can this be true? Can we ever know the answer?

In the following pages, I survey the prehistory and history of irrigation in the Upper Rio Grande region and then in the Taos basin, with an eye to how indigenous and *vecino* (Spanish settler, literally "neighbor") irrigation would have intersected in different locations at different points in time. The questions of precisely where, when, and how stream diversion developed in the Taos Valley are not yet answerable, but we need to explore the issue to understand the history of Pueblo-Hispano/Mexican interpenetration and separateness in the Upper Rio Grande Valley.

The Rio Grande Irrigation Hypothesis

Anthropologists once took for granted that the Rio Grande Pueblos had depended primarily on live canal irrigation long before European contact. Indeed, some of the early Spanish chronicles describe it for pueblos well south of Taos.[1] Furthermore, Karl Wittfogel's hydraulic hypothesis appeared to explain the organizational and religious differences observed between the Eastern or Rio Grande Pueblos dependent on irrigation and the Western Pueblos, such as Zuni and Hopi, who predominately dry-farmed (Wittfogel and Goldfrank 1943; Wittfogel 1957; Eggan 1966:138–139; Dozier 1970: 131–133). Wittfogel proposed that the creation and maintenance of a canal system required a centralized, authoritarian organizational structure. Among the Pueblos, anthropologists reasoned, canal irrigation must have led to a more centralized decision-making structure than mere clans could provide and to less reliance on magical techniques of weather control (Dozier 1970:131–133). In Edward Dozier's words, "intensive irrigation practices utilizing water from permanently flowing streams have brought about the centralized orientation of the Eastern or Rio Grande Pueblos" (131).

But the Rio Grande Pueblo irrigation hypothesis has since been refuted on both ethnographic and archaeological grounds. Using modern Picurís Pueblo as a case example, Richard Ford (1977) showed that centralized authority is neither present nor necessary to carry out community irrigation and ditch maintenance. While many accept the prehispanic practice of live stream irrigation by the Rio Grande Pueblos, not all archaeologists agree. Linda Cordell, for example, contends that "the [Rio Grande Pueblo] sites occupied during historic times are not consistently located along sources of permanent water, which could have been used for irrigation, nor is there evidence that ditch irrigation was practiced prior to historic times" (Cordell 1979:146). Similarly, Gwinn Vivian writes, "There is no solid evidence that the Rio Grande river ditch systems were functioning prehistorically" (Vivian 1974:104).

Whether or not they practiced live stream irrigation, the aggregating and relocating Pueblos of the Coalition (AD 1200–1300) through Classical (AD 1300–1540) periods used a variety of other techniques to harvest, capture, and conserve water across a range of environmental microniches. Archaeologists have identified varied and flexible "agricultural tool kits" whereby ancient cultivators "adapted their technologies to interact with highly localized climatological, physiographic, sedimentological, and hydrological conditions" (Anschuetz 2001:66). Dry or runoff ancestral-pueblo farming structures widely documented south of the Taos District include gravel-mulched plots, rock-bordered grids and cobble step terraces, stone-lined ditches, and reservoirs (Vivian 1974; Anschuetz 2001:59–66). Ditches, canals, and laterals for diverting runoff, as well as floodwater, were part of the Anasazi repertoire, but their remnants do not necessarily attest to extensive stream diversion (Clark 1987:7). Archaeologist Kurt Anschuetz gives a more nuanced view:

> While the Pueblos' use of irrigation is beyond refute, I do question whether indigenous northern Rio Grande farmers deployed river and spring water irrigation technologies on a sufficiently large scale from year-to-year to form the principle foundation of their subsistence economies. Rather, river and spring irrigation practices were technological components of a much broader system of water management engineering. [Anschuetz 2001:66]

"Acequiazation"

The uncertain picture of Pre-Columbian stream-diversion irrigation in the Upper Rio Grande Valley is partly due to the sweeping impact of "acequiazation" on Pueblo agriculture. Ditch irrigation would have been but one of several water-management techniques before Spanish conquest, but colonization inaugurated Pueblo dependence on it. A major drought at the end of the 16th century probably encouraged this shift (Simmons 1972:137). An Old World desert society collided—and ultimately fused with—a New World desert society. Both had rules, practices, beliefs, and attitudes related to water management and sharing. Some that persist today are traceable to a specific source, but others are not.

The process I call acequiazation was central to how colonization changed Pueblo farming practice and subsistence economy. Acequiazation gradually superseded aboriginal farming techniques as it appropriated natural and previously exploited lines of drainage into local acequia systems. Acequiazation involved the syncretism of Old and New World ingredients. Originally an invasive strategy of exploitation, it became a process of mutual exchange whereby local indigenous knowledge of the hydrological and microclimatological environments joined with an imposed regime of ditch construction, regulation, utilization, and maintenance. At best, we can reconstruct this generations-long process hypothetically.

After colonizers located water sources and identified potential field sites, the next step for them was the digging of ditches. Soon after arrival in 1598, the first settlers, "with the aid of the San Juan people, began construction on acequias in order to have them ready for the following spring" (Simmons 1972:138). A few years later, relocating the capital to Santa Fe, citizens, "probably with the aid of Mexican Indian servants and conscripted Pueblo laborers, dug two acequias madres (main ditches) to water fields on either side of the small river that passed through their villa" (Simmons 1972:138–139).

The material face of acequiazation involved the construction and proliferation of ditches and fields where few or none had been. Spanish law prohibited settlers from encroaching on land, including ditches, under active use by Indians. Unoccupied land and ditches were another matter, and colonial farmers may well have redug and modified ditches that already existed (DuMars et al. 1984:138–139, appendix C). This process obliterated any clear archaeological evidence of possible aboriginal precursors.

New crops requiring ditch irrigation, such as wheat, vegetables, and fruit trees, joined the Pueblo suite of corn, beans, squash, melons, cotton, and tobacco (Ford 1987:77–78). Indian men dug ditches to irrigate fields of wheat and other cultigens for Spanish consumption. Animal husbandry displaced hunting as a regular source of meat; grazing transformed the landscape. Historian Robert MacCameron summarizes the net impact on Tewa ecology as "a strange admixture of environmental degradation and a 'beneficial and more secure subsistence base' [Ford 1987:86]" (MacCameron 1997:92; also see Doolittle 2000).

Both the Spaniards and the Tlaxcaltecan Indians who accompanied them into New Mexico came from societies with well-developed codes and techniques for canal (including stream-diversion) irrigation. Mexican anthropologist Tómas Martínez Saldaña (1998) argues that Tlaxcaltecans developed hybrid farming methods drawn from both Iberian and Mesoamerican sources, established syncretic practices in central Mexico, and took these north to Colotlán and beyond. He proposes that the Tlaxcaltecan diaspora exerted profound influence on the historic development of agricultural techniques, including irrigation, on the northern Mexican and New Mexican frontiers.

The Tlaxcaltecans had allied with the Spaniards against the Aztecs during the conquest of Mexico. Afterward, they enjoyed privileged status as *caballeros* and *hidalgos* (gentlemen and noblemen), were given land to work, and were permitted to ride horses and carry firearms (Jones 1979:22). They served as agents of colonization, functioning as "teachers and exemplary farmers to Indian neophytes," and as laborers, auxiliary soldiers, and personal servants (Simmons 1964:102.) Although not deployed according to formal plans as in Coahuilia, Tlaxcaltecans did accompany Oñate to New Mexico. They settled near their fields in the barrio of Analco on the south bank of the Santa Fe River (Simmons 1964; Jones 1979:131). During the 1680 Pueblo Revolt, they fled, but some may have returned with the Reconquest (Simmons 1964; Jones 1979:23). Saldaña's theory may be impossible to test, but it raises provocative questions.[2]

Still, scholars generally agree that the observed practices of ditch cleaning and maintenance, which Pueblos share with their parciante neighbors, are of Iberian origin. In any case, the fit seems to have involved the one's inclination to build on the other's predisposition:

> Apparently many of the community irrigation customs of the Pueblos were entirely compatible with Spanish institutions and were allowed to continue. This was in conformity with laws set forth in the *Recopilación*, which provided that ancient customs of the Indians should be retained and respected so far as practicable. Nevertheless, it is apparent that Spanish practices, such as organization of labor under a mayordomo and techniques of dam and acequia construction, were gradually adopted by the Pueblos. They continued to retain, however, ancient ceremonial practices surrounding irrigation, such as the planting of prayer sticks in the ditches and ritual dances following the cleaning of the acequias in spring. [Simmons 1972:144–145]

Acequiazation imposed a new regime on Pueblo irrigation. It required workers to dig the ditches that linked the Pueblos with their vecinos, acequia neighbors who used the same rivers. In pueblos such as Taos, the function of mayordomo, or ditch boss, was ultimately subsumed under the exogenous, secular governor's office. Given the importance of water in Pueblo religion, acequia management somehow coordinated with traditional ceremonial practice to serve community purpose. Anthropologist Elsie Clews Parsons reports:

> Of all the communal undertakings, work on the irrigation ditches is the most important. Throughout the farming season work on the ditch is called for, literally, by town officers, and there is the annual spring cleaning. The procedure at San Juan is fairly typical. Toward the close of February, the chiefs meet at the Governor's house, to "talk about the day for cleaning the ditch." Late in the afternoon before the appointed day, the crier goes about town calling out the order. Food is supplied the workers on the first day by women of the south-side houses; on the second day by women on the north side. The women are counted, and if anyone delays, the Fiscal goes after her.[3] [Parsons 1974:110–111]

Anthropologist Alfonso Ortiz hypothesizes that the introduction of wheat and the Spanish system of irrigation canals caused a shift in the Tewa ceremonial calendar. Once, the winter and summer chiefs enjoyed evenly divided reigns each year. But wheat must be planted earlier than native crops, and the ditches that irrigate it, shared by San Juan Pueblo and its Hispano neighbors, must be cleaned and repaired by early March. In Ortiz's view, the adaptation to the new crop accounts for an asymmetrical shortening of the winter chief's ceremonial rule in a dual organizational system or moiety that would otherwise be symmetrical (Ortiz 1968:115–117, 174–179 nn. 21, 22, 23, 24). Other Pueblos would have integrated the Iberian system into their lives in different ways, depending on local conditions. Pre-Columbian Tewa and Northern

Tiwa peoples relied more heavily on hunting for their subsistence than did Pueblos farther south, but their economy was nevertheless transformed by Spanish agriculture and animal husbandry (Ortiz 1968:176 n. 23).[4]

The postconquest drop in Indian population was succeeded during the coming centuries by a slow tide of *mestizaje* (miscegenation). Initially, newcomers did not come in sufficient numbers to replace Pueblo losses. "Paradoxically," one historian notes, "this reduction in Pueblo population meant that there were more human beings in the upper Rio Grande valley at the beginning of the Spanish period in 1598 than at its close in 1821" (MacCameron 1997:83).

Vecino Settlement

Spanish colonial history in New Mexico is generally divided in two parts. The earlier period dates from the first settlement colony established by Juan de Oñate in 1598 to the great Pueblo Revolt of 1680, when an unprecedented coalition of Pueblo forces managed to drive the Spaniards out of New Mexico for 12 years. The second part is the Reconquest, led by Diego de Vargas starting in 1692, which succeeded in reasserting the colonists' foothold. It was during the century after 1692 that vecino settlement spread, at first tenuously and slowly, finally gaining momentum by 1800. Mexico, of which New Mexico was part, won its independence from Spain in 1821. Twenty-five years later, New Mexico became part of the United States as a result of the Mexican American War, along with the rest of what is now the US Southwest.

Using longitudinal census data, geographer Richard Nostrand maps Hispano expansion as beginning in the 1700s and culminating at the end of the 19th century. The initial core area centered on the Rio Grande pueblos and gradually spread outward to define a homeland that ultimately encompassed much of the state and extended into southern Colorado:

> Hispanos capitalized on the Pueblo decline. They infiltrated Pueblo villages...and encroached on Pueblo lands to establish their own communities, for which they pre-empted Pueblo village names—Taos, Pojoaque, Tesuque, San Ildefonso, Galisteo, and, in the early nineteenth century, Pecos. Such encroachment forced Spanish officials to recognize each Pueblo group as having a minimum four-square-league land base. The ever-growing Hispano population meanwhile filled in, as it were, between the Pueblos, and beginning in the 1790s, in a modest way, Hispanos began to expand beyond the outermost Indian villages. Thus, by the end of the Spanish era, no longer did the geography of Hispanos merely reflect that of the Pueblo Indians, and their numerical superiority ensured that their Homeland was also their Stronghold. [Nostrand 1992:55–57]

Vecinos during the 17th and 18th centuries preferred to disperse into *ranchitos* scattered across the countryside rather than follow governmental regulations to form nucleated settlements. They did this for better access to their fields and water sources such as streams, springs, and acequias. Ultimately, officials managed to enforce the law, "collecting scattered families and obliging them to dwell in compact units" so that they could better defend themselves against nomadic Indian attacks (Simmons 1969:18).

The Taos Basin

If little is known about the first acequias and farms in the *villas* (towns) of Santa Fe or Santa Cruz, we know even less about where and how colonization began in Taos. As one historian observes, "Hispano land and water use near Taos during the seventeenth century is almost completely undocumented" (Baxter 1990:4). To introduce the question of acequiazation with specific reference to Taos, therefore, I must backtrack in time and begin with the prehistory of this particular setting.

The Taos basin offers a remarkable set of opportunities for human settlement. This fertile, awesomely beautiful valley has been a magnet for human migration and settlement since mobile hunters first discovered it roughly nine thousand years ago. Over the past millennium, the valley has sustained at least three successive patterns of human habitation and growth: Pueblo Indian; the Spanish colonial, acequia-based multicommunity; and the potent, expanding overlay of modern American urban development. Each society has exploited the environment in a different way and transformed the landscape accordingly. Each has used significantly more water than its predecessors.

The first humans to enter the Taos Valley were Paleoindian hunters, whose archaeological traces consist of sporadic distributions of fluted spear points. Archaic remains, dating from 6000 BC to AD 750, consist of concentrations of chipped stone, waste debris with ground stone, but no ceramics. They attest to hunter-collectors living in camps on ridgetops, "usually in foothill areas with good visibility and easy access to permanent springs and other water sources" (Woosley 1986:146). The earliest evidence of ancestral pueblo occupation in the Upper Rio Grande Valley dates from what archaeologists call the Developmental period, between about 750 and 1200. Remains include dispersed pithouse sites and mineral-pigmented ceramics, which appear in the Taos district around AD 1000.

By 1150, there were aboveground structures with circular kivas. During the Coalition phase, between 1200 and 1400, settlements aggregated into larger pueblo units that contained multiple room blocks and kivas. Ceramics associated with these sites were decorated with organic ceramic pigments. By 1250, population in the Taos district had coalesced into just two or three pueblos. They included Pot Creek Pueblo, established in the upper Río Grande del Rancho watershed where the Rito de la Olla joins the Río Grande del Rancho, and Old Picuris Pueblo, located outside the Taos basin in a separate watershed several miles to the southwest. Pot Creek was abandoned around 1320, evidently followed by the construction of Cornfield Taos at the foot of

Taos Mountain and the rebuilding of Picuris, father south, by 1350. Scholars assume the greater antiquity of Pot Creek and Old Picuris because the Taos Indians consider them ancestral and because these pueblos are excavated, whereas, with one tiny exception, Taos is not.[5] Archaeologists date the Classic period from 1400 to 1610, when Spanish settlement took hold. Between 1450 and 1500, Cornfield Taos was replaced by present-day Taos Pueblo, located about a quarter of a mile to the southwest on the upper banks of the Río Pueblo at the base of Taos Mountain (Bodine 1979:258).

The establishment of Taos Pueblo on both banks of the upper Río Pueblo would seem conducive to the development of diversion canals to irrigate fields on the north and south sides of the village. In any case, the river divides the pueblo into north and south sides, or moieties. Perhaps the move from Cornfield, located upstream on the north side of the river, to the present site on both banks signaled greater investment in stream diversion. Indeed, today an extended network of ditches exists around the core of the village, but when or how it came into existence is not precisely known.

A handful of archaeologists debate whether people practiced canal irrigation in the Taos district before 1600. Some hold that a period of drought with reduced stream flows forced ancestral pueblo farmers to aggregate upstream along alluvial fans where they could divert water to irrigate (Boyer 1995; Moore 1995a, 1995b). Ann Woosley argues for site coalescence in the lower Río Grande del Rancho watershed by 1100, when "in addition to the appearance of larger sites, the diversity and extent of agricultural features with dry and irrigated farming are clearly represented" (Woosley 1986:148). Greiser and Greiser (1995) claim, on the basis of a cursory survey, widespread stream-diversion irrigation in the 12th and 13th centuries along the upper and middle Río Lucero watershed, as well as in what is now lower Des Montes above the Río Hondo watershed.

Most archaeologists seem skeptical of the Greisers' claim (for example, Adler1993). Crown and colleagues even raise doubt about the canal Moore identified at Pot Creek (Crown, Orcutt, and Kohler 1996:201 n. 3). They note that "no known habitation sites dating between AD 1250 and 1350 occur in close proximity to the rich agricultural land farmed today along the Río Pueblo de Taos and the lower reaches of the Río Grande del Rancho (from Talpa to the confluence of the Rio Grande)" (201 n. 4). More recently, however, Fowles has confirmed Moore's canal, identified additional segments, and even documented a second canal just north of Pot Creek. He suggests that these structures were experimental (Fowles 2004:446–451).[6] Interestingly, no prehistoric canals are reported for Old Picurís, and according to Brown, the modern Picurís themselves say that they acquired canal irrigation from the Spaniards. Their word for "ditch foreman," *akissawin*, presumably derives from acequia (Brown 1999: 28,30). Ford, however, alludes to a folk belief in the ancient origin of irrigation canals that remains unverified (1977:143).

Moreover, skeptics doubt that the conditions thought to drive aggregation ever existed in Pre-Columbian Taos. These boil down to population pressure against environmental carrying capacity: "There is no evidence," write Crown and colleagues, "that population had reached carrying capacity by AD 1250, or that resource depletion encouraged aggregation" (Crown, Orcutt, and Kohler 1996:192). They report that "population levels remained low in all time periods," and until the 15th century, when trade with Plains Indians probably increased, only low levels of exchange existed between Taos district populations and surrounding populations (192). Perhaps in the Taos hinterland, "aggregation was an indirect competitive response to increasing population levels and the establishment of aggregated pueblos *outside* of the Taos district to the south" (192, emphasis added). Perhaps, they suggest, aggregation into concentrated pueblos was part of a regional "domino effect" (201).

In the end, two basic possibilities emerge: either the Taos were already irrigating off the Río Pueblo and possibly the Río Lucero when Europeans arrived, or they soon began under colonial rule. Familiarity with live irrigation, perhaps advanced experimentally at Pot Creek, would have eased acceptance of Iberian methods and perhaps predisposed the people of Taos Pueblo to a structure of ditch oversight. In either case, the introduction of Old World cultigens, animal husbandry, and agricultural technology pushed Taos Pueblo into reliance on a network of acequias to grow crops.

Physiography

The Taos basin is defined geologically by the Sangre de Cristo Mountains, the Rio Grande, and the northern Chihuahuan Desert. The mountains run north-south, curling around the eastern perimeter of the valley, roughly parallel to the river. The Rio Grande cuts through the length of Taos County much as it bisects the state. West of the river, the high desert stretches for hundreds of miles into Arizona. On the east, seven tributaries drain out of the mountains into the Rio Grande across the fertile plain of Taos Valley. Each of these perennial streams originates in a spring or lake high in the mountains, descends an alpine canyon, flows through a valley, and drops down an arroyo.

North to south, these rivers are the Río Hondo, Arroyo Seco, Río Lucero, Río Pueblo, Río Fernando, Río Chiquito, and Río Grande del Rancho. The Río Chiquito has an upper branch (not counted among the seven) known as Rito de la Olla or Pot Creek. The largest and most central of these rivers is the Río Pueblo, of which all the others except the Río Hondo are tributaries. The Río Hondo joins the Rio Grande north of the Río Lucero. Lush meadows cover the delta where the other tributaries come together, at the hydrological "vortex" of the valley. The Río Pueblo drains into the Rio Grande Gorge a few miles below that, above Pilar.

According to the US Geological Survey, the average annual flow of the Río Pueblo is 20,850 acre-feet a year. This river drops almost five thousand feet in the roughly twenty-one-mile journey from its alpine source to confluence with the Rio Grande. It is followed in volume by the Río Hondo (20,000 acre-feet), Río Lucero (16,080), Río Grande del Rancho (14,270), Río Chiquito (5,850), and Río Fernando (4,780) (L. Wilson 1978:V-13, table 14). All these streams are 15 to 25 miles long. The

Arroyo Seco, which lies between the Río Hondo and Río Lucero, is considered too meager to gauge. Today, these watersheds are irrigated and densely inhabited. Each has its own ecology and history. After the first colonial footholds were established, these places were settled in rapid, overlapping succession, according to a logic of practical advantage with respect to access to water and mutual proximity.

Colonial Taos

Permanent European presence in the Taos Valley began with the imposition of the Catholic mission of San Gerónimo at Taos Pueblo. No more than 80 colonists seem to have occupied the valley up to the Pueblo Revolt in 1680. Plotted from a kiva at Taos Pueblo, the revolt destroyed the San Gerónimo Mission, killed most settlers in the area, and drove away the others. Few, if any, returned. The San Gerónimo Chapel was reinstated under Reconquest leader Don Diego de Vargas in 1696 and remained the parish seat until 1826.

The 18th century was one of slow but enormous change in the Taos Valley. Vecinos settled downstream from the pueblo and spread into the neighboring watersheds. A few land grants were made to individuals during the first half of the century, but the settler foothold remained fragile. Waves of Comanche warriors swooped in on horseback to wage battle and seize captives. These depredations finally forced settlers to retreat inside the fortified walls of Taos Pueblo, where they joined forces with their Indian neighbors for mutual protection. They lived inside the pueblo off and on for years, finally returning to their ranchitos permanently after relations with the Comanches improved (Simmons 1969:15). In 1776 Fray Francisco Atanasio Domínguez visited the Taos Valley and described it as "very pleasant, for in addition to its wide view, it is watered by four fair-sized rivers"(Adams and Chavez 1956:111). Baxter summarizes the friar's report:

> Taos Indians cultivated broad fields of wheat and corn irrigated from the ríos Lucero and Pueblo, raising bumper crops that made the region New Mexico's breadbasket when shortages threatened elsewhere. At the pueblo, Fray Francisco admired the large pond, surrounded by cottonwoods and plum trees, that diverted water from the river to benefit the resident friars' vegetable garden. To the south, along the Trampas, Spanish vecinos also made good use of water resources to produce bountiful harvests of everything except chile and frijoles. At Los Estiércoles, the swamp grew a big hay crop annually with enough grazing left over to sustain local cattle and the enormous horse herds that accompanied visiting Comanches. [Baxter 1990:15]

The acequiazation of Pueblo agriculture proceeded at full throttle during this period, when vecinos and Pueblo Indians cooperated for mutual defense and subsistence labor. Over time, Taos Indians hunted and foraged less but farmed more, expanding and consolidating a network of ditches that watered tribally allocated family plots.

They grazed horses and burros in their communal pasture northeast of Los Estiércoles. Not until 1790 did the non-Indian, or Spanish and *casta* (various categories of miscegenation), population outnumber Indians. Then, between 1794 and 1811, the non-Indian population doubled. In the same period, vecinos began to concentrate into *placitas* (little plazas) or more nucleated settlements. This phase of Hispanic "aggregation" is signaled by the issuing of the Don Fernando de Taos land grant, which made official the de facto settlement already in place.

Multicommunity

The pre-American Taos Valley settlements constitute a multicommunity or constellation of villages around a central town, all situated at strategic intervals along and between the seven rivers at critical points of diversion along the ditches originally dug to sustain food production. All the villages that make up the Taos multicommunity exist in some kind of upstream-downstream relationship to one another. Each is situated in an upper, middle, or lower watershed zone. A village's location dictates its relationship to the neighbors with whom it must share irrigation water. Every village enjoys certain assets and suffers certain liabilities with respect to its acequias and water sources. Its history and character are further shaped by the topography and microclimate of its fields, orchards, pastures, and mountain access.

During the last 25 years of the colonial era, vecino population growth in the Taos Valley increased competition among the colonists and their Pueblo neighbors. The 1796 census listed a total of six smaller placitas in the Taos Valley besides Taos Pueblo, each named for a patron saint: San Francisco, Santa Gertrudis, Nuestra Señora de Guadalupe, La Purísima Concepción, San Francisco de Paula, and Nuestra Señora de Dolores. All but Santa Gertrudis exist today. They cluster along the banks of the Río Pueblo, Río Lucero, Río Fernando, and Río Grande del Rancho.

Soon more settlements sprang up in these watersheds, as well as on the Arroyo Seco, Río Hondo, and San Cristóbal streams to the north. By the early Mexican period, the number of placitas or communities scattered around the valley had more than doubled. These settlements coalesced into bounded, self-identified entities as populations reached the carrying capacities of their respective watersheds (Snow 1979). As each community delineated its resource base, it crystallized into a placita located within a larger constellation. The exact sequence of settlement in the Taos Valley is not known.

Don Fernando de Taos is the town of Taos, also known as the placita of Nuestra Señora de Guadalupe. It was formally established by a land grant dated just before the 1796 census. The town sits downstream from Taos Pueblo on the Río Pueblo and downstream on the Río Fernando from Cañon, or la placita de Nuestra Señora de Dolores. Cañon, a few miles below Taos Canyon, also sits on the Don Fernando grant. The following year, in 1797, people in town petitioned for and received rights to surplus waters, sobrantes, on both the Río Pueblo and the Río Lucero. La Purísima, or Upper Ranchitos, took root downstream where the Río Lucero meets the Río Pueblo.

Lower Ranchitos, or the old placita de San Francisco de Paula (alternatively, Pauda), sprang up even farther downstream, just east of where the Río Fernando runs into the Río Pueblo.

Historians believe that the two Ranchitos communities contain some of the oldest ditches in the valley (Jenkins 1978; Meyer 2000). The placita de San Francisco de Asís, or las Trampas and later Ranchos, sprang up to the south in the middle Río Grande del Rancho watershed. The placita de Santa Gertrudis remains a mystery.[7]

By the early 19th century, both the upper Río Lucero, near the mouth of the Arroyo Seco, and the Rio Hondo watershed a few miles to the north and west were populated by overflow from the town. San Cristóbal was established some twenty miles to the north in its own separate watershed, miles beyond Arroyo Hondo. Thus nearly a dozen more communities came into being, including Talpa, Llano Quemado, Cordillera, and Los Córdovas (unless it had been Santa Gertrudis) in the Río Grande del Rancho watershed and Valdez (originally San Antonio), Arroyo Hondo, Des Montes, and Cañoncito in the Río Hondo watershed. Des Montes and Arroyo Seco, as well as Las Colonias to their southwest, also draw on the Río Lucero. Las Colonias even receives an infusion from the Río Hondo via the Rebalse ditch and the Mariposa lateral of the Des Montes ditch.[8]

Half or more of the 17 or 18 agriculturally based communities founded before 1846 in the Taos Valley draw on more than one river. They include two upper-watershed villages (Talpa and Arroyo Seco), four middle-watershed communities (Taos, El Prado, Ranchos, and Des Montes), and five lower-watershed communities (Upper and Lower Ranchitos, Cordillera, Los Córdovas, and Las Colonias). There are zones along and between the four central streams that contain *ciénegas*, lush wetlands with high water tables fed by springs and sustained by underground waters related to the rivers.

Taos Valley Acequias

To get water to their fields, individuals working in different microbasins dug the Taos Valley acequias madres and their laterals a little at a time over the course of several generations. Before the Pueblo Revolt, coerced Indians probably did most of the digging. Later, both Indians and Mexicanos performed ditch labor as peones (for pay), parciantes, tribal irrigators, or conscripts (unpaid). Some of the earliest ditches may have followed natural lines of drainage known to indigenous farmers. Some ditches served communities, some the pueblo, some the church. Many parciantes claimed a patchwork of resources that included sobrantes and water from more than one river. Transforming the landscape, the acequias extended riparian zones along drainages, across fields, through orchards, and along roads and windbreaks. Acequias created and defined new boundaries: between green land and dry, between properties, between communities. They proliferated around the Pueblo village and spread into the Río Lucero watershed, where they mingled and competed with acequias belonging to other communities.

Vecino settlement on and near the pueblo did not occur without conflict, because the growing population increased demand on irrigation water. Litigation over land or water started in 1730 and continues into the 21st century (Jenkins 1966:93).[9] Pueblo and Mexicano farmers on the Río Pueblo and Río Lucero shared and fought over the water, worked together, traded, went to church, enjoyed *compradrazgo* (ritual coparenthood), cohabited, yet remained separate. Each irrigation community maintained its own customs governing water control and allocation. Apart from the acequias madres diverting directly off the Río Pueblo and the Río Lucero, the pueblo ditches remained separate from other community acequias. The pueblo governor oversaw ditch repair and water allocation, and a ritual chief presided over associated prayer (Parsons 1939:1117–1118). Indians who were Catholics petitioned the saints and, accompanied by vecinos, processed them through their fields for blessings. This shared practice reveals the interpenetration of Indian and Mexicano communities. Indeed, the pervasive fact of water sharing involved every local system in a larger project of river-wide cooperation.

When Brigadier General Stephen W. Kearny arrived in Santa Fe in 1846 to claim New Mexico for the United States, the Taos Valley acequias were a mature system running full force. According to court records for the Abeyta case, all acequias in Taos were established before 1848 (Fred Waltz, personal communication with the author, June 8, 2004). As historian Frank Wozniak has argued, "given the limitations of locally available technology, the irrigation resources of the upper Rio Grande had already been developed to virtually their fullest extent by 1846" (Wozniak 1997:79). Yet the Territorial period (1850–1912), until New Mexico became a state, may well have been the high point of agricultural intensification and productivity for both Pueblo and Mexicano farmers in Taos. American conquest proletarianized Mexicanos, contained Indians, and promoted resource exploitation by newcomer capitalists on a massive scale. It engendered a new era of labor exchange and economic interdependency between Indians and Mexicanos that today's *ancianos* (elders) remember from their childhoods.

Taos in 1896

In the summer of 1896, Merton Miller, an anthropology graduate student from the University of Chicago, spent three months at Taos Pueblo conducting fieldwork for his doctoral dissertation. Little is known about Miller's subsequent career, but his dissertation, completed in 1898 as "A Preliminary Study of the Pueblo of Taos New Mexico," offers a rare if fleeting glimpse of irrigation and agricultural practice a century ago. I quote from Miller's study in some detail because it provides a kind of baseline from which to move into the modern period of my own fieldwork among the pueblo's acequia neighbors. His work also underscores how much anthropology itself has changed since he and his more prominent successors presumed to conduct ethnographic research at Taos Pueblo.

Miller reports that in 1890 the population of Taos Pueblo was 401. Citing Bandelier and noting the nearby ruins (presumably Cornfield Taos) where the Taos said their ancestors had lived, he suggests that the multistoried adobe complexes on the upper banks of the Río Pueblo, still seen today, were not the original structures the Spaniards saw in 1540 (Miller 1898:10). Turning his focus to subsistence, Miller notes that "perhaps no crop, excepting maize, the staple Indian product, could be raised without irrigation" (5). He corroborates the assessment published in the *US Eleventh Census Report* of 1890 that "it would be difficult to find in the west, where farming is dependent upon irrigation, a more desirable tract of land than that owned by these Indians. The water, carried in subwaterways, or acequias, commands a large portion of the reservation" (6).

Miller reported that the pueblo owned a grant of 27.5 square miles, half of which had been encroached upon by Mexican settlers originally allowed on Indian land for mutual defense against nomadic raiders. The pueblo grant encompassed both common and individually owned lands:

> The uncultivated land is today, as the whole area undoubtedly was at one time, owned in common by the pueblo. The pasture lands in the foothills, and the mesa lands north and west of the village, still lie open for the use of anyone in the pueblo. The only valuable piece of land which is not owned individually, and which is near the village, is a common pasture of twenty or more acres. It is so poorly fenced that everyone who has horses, cattle, or burros, must take his turn watching the stock to prevent their wandering out into the fields of grain. [Miller 1898:16]

Miller quotes from the eleventh census (1890) in describing individually owned lands:

> At Taos, as everywhere else, some men are more prosperous than others; so the amounts of land owned vary greatly. The sections of land are small, but one man often owns several pieces, separated from one another by one or two miles. "The fields behind the town towards the mountain are divided by scrub willow, wild plum, and blackberry bushes, and seldom contain more than three or four acres" [1890 census report]. A fence is not often seen. There is a fence the greater part of the distance around the common pasture, and there are, besides, a few pastures belonging to certain families which are fenced. Sometimes a rude, temporary fence is built along a roadway when growing crops are in the fields near by. The boundaries between the plots of ground are usually irrigation ditches, along which grow plum bushes and willows. These are often very dense, and furnish a satisfactory and effectively marked line. [Miller 1898:16–17]

He is uncertain about individual land ownership, adding: "While I cannot speak positively about it, I believe the Taos Indian may do what he pleases with his land, till it, lease it, let it lie fallow, or sell it, so long as he does not sell it outside the tribe" (Miller 1898:16).

Miller then describes the pueblo ditch system:

> About two miles above the village the first irrigation ditches branch off from the creek. Three or four main ditches tap the stream on each side, and these ramify into small channels until the whole of the cultivated land is reached. There are other ditches to bring water from Lucero Creek, which comes down from the mountains a short distance north of Pueblo Creek. One of the larger ditches was made by the Indians years ago, under the direction of the priests, to carry water to a mill about three miles away. It is still used, but now only for irrigation. [Miller 1898:17]

The pueblo governor was responsible for seeing that the ditches were kept in repair, and "as they are of use to all and belong to no one in particular, work on them is done by all in common" (Miller 1898:37). The governor also assigned "times to the men for their use in irrigating" (38). Miller adds: "As the Mexicans have the use of the water of the creek three days in the week, they may often be seen at the governor's house talking with him about some misunderstanding which has arisen" (32).

Miller also discusses crop production:

> The principal crops of Taos are corn and wheat. Occasionally a field of oats is seen, or a few beans and peas and melons. Considerable quantities of squashes are also raised. Much of the wheat and corn is sold at the stores three miles from the pueblo or traded for meat, sugar, coffee, syrup, soap, cloth, or whatever else the Indian wants or can buy. What game he can get, deer, turkeys, grouse, rabbits, and doves, supplements his other supplies, though much less than it once did, when game was plenty and methods of cultivation much more crude than now.
>
> In summer the work of the men is, of course, mainly farming. But the Indian farmer is not a very hard worker. At certain times, in harvest time for example, or when he is irrigating, he has to work hard and steadily, but ordinarily he works a part of the day and sits on the housetop or goes to town for the rest of the day. When spring comes and the planting time is at hand, the land has first to be irrigated. Two or three days later it is ready for the plow. By the hour I have watched the planting of corn. Indian ponies, less often oxen, are used. Behind the one following the plow comes an old man or a boy dropping the kernels of corn which the next turning of the furrow will cover. After the field is planted, the oxen are hitched to a long pole by rawhide traces fastened to the yoke and to each end of the pole. The Indian steps on the pole and, holding on by the tails of the oxen, rides around the field to level it off. When the corn is a few inches above the ground, the field is trenched for irrigating. If the water is scarce, as it is in July, one has to engage the use of it several days beforehand and has to use it whenever it is assigned to him,

whether it be day or night. I have several times known an Indian to work in the field irrigating all night after having worked all day, and sometimes even two nights in succession. [Miller 1898:21–22]

He reports that the laborious harvesting of wheat was done with a small sickle and that goats threshed the wheat by treading on it inside a small bounded area, adding that "as the Taos Indians do not keep sheep and goats, a Mexican is hired to come with a flock and drive them around til the [threshing] plot is hard almost as baked clay" (Miller 1898:22).

Other relevant observations from Miller's account include his impression that Indian attendance at Catholic mass seemed small; one man told him that they disliked the priest and wished that he would leave. Nevertheless, Miller reports that "one may see at Taos an image of the Virgin Mary carried about the fields in the summer to secure good crops. It is shaded by a rude awning, and accompanied by a few Mexican and Indian women, and some young men with rifles, which they occasionally fire off into the air" (Miller 1898:40).

Miller was told that the Taos people had originally emerged from a lake and lived in the north before coming to their present place. In the north they had had many neighbors, including the Picuris, who then lived just south of them. He recorded the following tale about Taos, Picuris, and farming: "One day a Picuris man was planting some white corn. He had some grains in his hand and was showing them to a Taos man, when the latter hit his hand from below and scattered the corn. From that time the two peoples were enemies, and the Picuris moved away to the south" (Miller 1898:43).

When Miller visited Taos Pueblo more than a century ago, he was easily able to observe and inquire about farming practices but got nowhere when he asked about religion or language. Like all outsiders who dare to pry at Taos Pueblo, Miller encountered the hard shell of secrecy for which this and other pueblos are so famous. Today, he probably would not even be allowed to observe irrigation.

Merton Miller belonged to an era when anthropologists walked brazenly into indigenous villages, armed with notebooks and cameras, determined to ferret out truth in the name of science. His more famous successors in the field at Taos, Matilda Cox Stevenson and Elsie Clews Parsons, were less successful in gaining access to the pueblo. Neither was allowed to stay on pueblo land, and the family that had lodged Miller and later talked to Parsons suffered social reprisal (Zumwalt 1992:252). While doing fieldwork in 1906, Stevenson called her off-reservation accommodation Camp Defiance (240). Thirty years later, Parsons would get into trouble at Taos for publishing kiva names in an obscure monograph (Parsons 1970). Firmly entrenched in anthropologists' traditional fixation on Indians, these early ethnographers made no effort to investigate irrigation practice or ritual behavior among the valley's neighboring Mexicanos. Neither did they question their moral right to pursue scientific inquiry regardless of native resistance.

The Taos that Miller visited in 1896 was on the verge of touristic discovery by the painters and founding art colonists Ernest Blumenschein and Bert Phillips, whose broken wagon wheel in 1898 would furnish the plotline for the Taos art colony origin myth. Englishman Arthur Manby had already arrived and embarked on his relentless, ill-fated scheme to acquire and develop the Antonio Martínez land grant. The grassy green at the center of Taos plaza was primly enclosed with a white picket fence. Soon the Commercial Club would be staging festivities and entertainment in town to draw business during the pueblo's saint day celebration of San Gerónimo on September 30. My paternal grandfather, Justino Olguín Rodríguez, had perhaps already arrived from Parral, Chihuahua, to take up his career as a professional monte dealer in Taos, marry into the Trujillo clan on La Loma, and operate a meat market on the plaza. Most important, both an 1893 decree dividing the Río Lucero three ways and, as Miller notes, the 1893 agreement of water sharing on the Río Pueblo were in effect.

By chance, another investigator, W. W. Follett, visited Taos in the summer of 1896. Follett was commissioned by the US Corps of Engineers to conduct a study of "the use of water for irrigation on the Rio Grande del Norte" (Follett 1898:47). His mission was to prepare a report "for the purpose of investigating the claim of the Mexican Government that the people of the United States have taken from the inhabitants of Mexico water which was theirs by ancient right of appropriation," as well as to determine whether there was sufficient water "to successfully serve a reservoir at El Paso" (Follett 1898:47). The report was to help inform government policy concerning settlement with Mexico over reduced flow in the Rio Grande at El Paso.[10]

Follett was in Taos for a few days to count the streams, ditches, irrigated acres, and quantity of water used for irrigation in the Taos Valley. Perhaps he crossed paths with Miller. The "Taos Mesa" section of his report consists of one page of text and one distribution table—thin description compared with Miller's, but informative nonetheless.

Follett reports that in the Taos Valley "the area of arable land is fully 40,000 acres, but the water supply is only sufficient for about half this land, and it has been fully utilised for over forty years" (Follett 1898:79). He provides a candid picture of elusive and mutable ditches on the Ríos Lucero and Pueblo:

> On Lucero and Pueblo creeks the water is all distributed by numerous small
> ditches whose positions are changing each year. It was difficult for me to form
> even an approximate estimate of the acreage in the limited time at my disposal
> as well as to get the exact number of ditches. I believe, however, that the
> aggregate given on the sheet is fairly accurate. [Follett 1898:80]

By his own admission, Follett probably undercounted the entire collectivity of ditches that existed across several watersheds in the Taos basin at the end of the 19th century. What he glimpsed in terms of sheer usage would have been even more overwhelming than what I witnessed 100 years later. He counted only 61 ditches, serving 18,050 irrigated acres off seven creeks. The number of ditches he lists for each stream seems impossibly meager in light of the present system: 1 for the Río Hondo, 2 for

Arroyo Seco, 6 for the Lucero, 20 for the Río Pueblo, 22 for the Taos (Fernando), 9 for the Río Grande del Rancho, and 2 for the Río Chiquito. According to Follett's estimate, 1,440 acres of the total irrigated acreage in the Taos Valley were on pueblo land: 360 acres watered from the Río Lucero and 1,080 from the Río Pueblo.

Even though Follett may have missed a good number of acequias, he was able to comprehend that the local farming population had come to terms with the inherent limitations and possibilities of its environment: "On this mesa the people have learned to be careful in the use of water, so that the average amount used, even in years of plenty, is about 2.5 acre-feet per acre" (Follett 1898:80).

The 1989 Hydrographic Survey Map of Taos Pueblo confirms anthropologist Merton Miller's 1898 description of a network of ditches that border many small, irregularly shaped, individual plots of irrigated land located around and below the village. These plots stand in striking contrast to the typical rectangular strips or long-lots farmed by the Hispano neighbors. Whereas Hispano acequias are typically named for families or individuals, Pueblo ditches often bear more vivid names. Some translate as Cicada Nose, Elk Horn, Pottery, Pull Leaf, and North Trash Pile. Pueblo irrigation practices have changed through time. What today's parciantes perceive to be an absence of a system or method for allocating water among their Pueblo neighbors may, in fact, not be the case. Practice may differ between the oldest ditches around the village core and those installed by the federal government in the 20th century on both rivers.[11] Today, the ditches survive not as a dead relic of bygone subsistence practice but as the living means by which individual irrigators maintain their farmland and manage to circulate river water through the arable soils of the Taos basin.

Modern Taos

The setting in which living parciantes tend, use, defend, and talk about their ditches is modern, urban, and rapidly changing. With a population of 4,700 in 2000 (54.3 percent Hispanic), municipal Taos has paved streets, sidewalks, traffic lights, fire hydrants, and a somewhat irregular grid of city blocks. In 2003 this famed tourist town and immediate environs contained more than 40 motels, 50 bed-and-breakfasts, 80 restaurants, 80 to 100 art galleries, 51 real estate businesses, 60 retail shops, one public school and eight private schools, one hospital, one movie theater, and 25 denominations with churches (Taos Chamber of Commerce figures for 2002; phone book listings for 2003). Downtown Taos offers a motley mix of old and new adobe, cement block, frame, and mobile home residential structures, as well as a growing number of condominiums and multiresidential subdivisions. Many older houses have fenced yards with lawns and trees. There are also empty lots with weeds, decaying sheds, or melting adobe ruins. Occasional properties still have small orchards and vegetable gardens.

The town plaza of Taos sits on a rise just north of the Las Cruces drainage, a wide arroyo between the Río Pueblo and Río Fernando watersheds. The original town core radiates outward from the plaza, evidenced by a concentration of adobe structures and big cottonwood trees. A few remnants betray the town's rural agrarian past, including traces of its once vital ditch system. The town ditch system declined during the last three decades of the 20th century. As gentrification accelerated, new owners of old properties failed to use and maintain their ditches; the city voraciously appropriated their forfeited water rights and, in some cases, may have unlawfully paved over ditches. One can still discern the fading traces of old acequias within a block of the plaza, but some neighborhood ditches last used in the 1960s are now filled in or overgrown and barely visible. Nevertheless, acequias still operate around the eastern, northern, and western edges of the old center.

The burgeoning city of Taos has been eager to annex adjacent areas lying within its extraterritorial zone, but El Prado, Cañon, Ranchitos, and Ranchos continue to fend off its aggressive spread. Each of the neighboring communities, defined by a chapel, a *camposanto* (cemetery), and acequias, persists in maintaining its autonomous identity. Taos's satellite communities retain a more rural character than the town, with fewer paved roads and plenty of mobile homes interspersed among old and new houses, cultivated fields, pastures, orchards, corrals, and livestock. Their acequia systems remain intact and active. Vecinos generally resist imposition of the town's zoning code; newcomers and native returnees have organized to enact protective zoning in order to preserve rural and "traditional" qualities. The farther one goes from the heart of town, the more rural the landscape becomes. Still, the advance of gentrification is unceasing, and its ubiquitous progression has become apparent in "downtown" Ranchos and Arroyo Seco. The old placita of San Antonio (or La Loma) has been swallowed by the town of Taos, but its longtime families maintain their chapel and celebrate their saint's day with a mass and procession.

Like Santa Fe and other tourist towns in the Rocky Mountains, Taos has undergone major demographic change since 1970, mostly the result of amenity migration, the infusion of former tourists (including retirees) who move to a place for its lifestyle amenities rather than for employment. While generations of natives migrate out of the region for employment and education, urban outsiders have moved in ever since the advent of tourism and the art colony in the early 20th century. Often dependent on income external to Taos, amenity migrants have become the principal developers and promoters of tourism.

The rate of amenity migration accelerated in the 1980s. A study published in 2000 indicated that 13,000 in-migrants moved to Taos County between 1990 and 1999 and that 11,000 locals moved out, resulting in a net migratory gain of 2,000. Whereas out-migrants tend to be young, Hispanic, and comparatively poor, most in-migrants are older, wealthier, more educated, and Anglo (BBER 2000b:1–2). According to the 1970 US census, 86.3 percent of the Taos County population (17,516) was Hispanic, 6.9 percent was White Anglo, and 6.8 percent American Indian. In 2000, 57.9 percent of the total population (29,979) was Hispanic, 42.1 percent Anglo, and 6.6 percent American Indian. Between 1990 and 2000, the county population increased by nearly one-third; the Hispanic population grew by 15 percent, and the non-Hispanic population increased by 55.5 percent, mainly because of in-migration. In sum, whereas the American Indian proportion has remained stable during the past 30 years, the Anglo (or non-Hispanic white) proportion has increased sixfold, and the Hispanic proportion has decreased by a third. Thus, like Santa Fe, Taos exhibits a demographic trend that reverses state and national patterns: decrease in the Hispanic/Latino population and increase in the Anglo or non-Hispanic white population.

Gentrification, the gradual replacement of a poorer population by a wealthier one, is also marked by the transformation and expansion of the built environment and dramatic escalation in real estate prices and development. Before 1960 an acre of irrigated land in the Taos Valley might sell for $100, and a modest adobe house for perhaps $2,000. Today, land with water rights is unlikely to sell for less than $60,000 an acre, and the average cost of a home within about a twenty-mile radius of the town is $207,300 (Taos County Chamber of Commerce 2002). Amenity migrants occupy a high proportion of the rental housing in Taos and account for most of the new home construction, including the renovation and expansion of older adobe structures. In 1990, 34 percent of all vacant housing units in the county were reserved for seasonal and recreational use (BBER 2000b:6).

As in other tourist towns, the cost of living in Taos is comparatively high. In 2000 the average per capita income in Taos County was $16,103, and roughly 58 percent of the population older than 16 was employed. Thirty-one percent of the workforce was engaged in management, professional, and related occupations; 22 percent in service positions; almost 25 percent in sales and office occupations; 12.8 percent in construction, extraction, or maintenance; 7 percent in transportation and production; and only 1.2 percent in full-time farming, fishing, or forestry. Sixteen percent of families lived below the poverty level. During recent decades, substantial expansion of the middle class has occurred across all three major ethnic groups; the number of wealthy households increased astronomically between 1989 and 1999. Households with an annual income of between $100,00 and $149,000 increased by 238.9 percent (from 95 to 322), and those with an income of $150,000 or more increased by 454 percent, going from 59 to 327 (BBER 2000a).

Faced with a growing tide of amenity migration and gentrification, coupled with the prospect of water loss through adjudication, native Nuevomexicanos perceive their hold on their land and water base to be increasingly threatened. Land grant and acequia associations have banded together to defend and lobby for their collective interests. In Taos, parciantes belong to the category of "nonmovers," in contrast to in-migrants, out-migrants, and intracounty movers, as defined by the Bureau of Business and Economic Research study of migration in Taos at the end of the 20th century (BBER 2000b:22). According to this study, a little more than half the total population in 1980 and 1990 comprised nonmovers (23). This group includes the oldest age groups and the highest proportion of married couples and Hispanic and native New

Mexican households. They showed overall lower educational attainment, as well as the lowest percentage of households living below the poverty line (perhaps because larger families pool their per capita incomes).[12]

Today, at the start of the 21st century, acequia organization, practice, and discourse persist as a core of subsistence/productive and reproductive or sociocultural patterns established during colonial times that have continuously adapted to changing conditions during successive political and economic eras. Despite precipitous decline during the 20th century, Taoseños still practice agriculture, mostly growing alfalfa and grazing a few cattle and horses. Approximately seventy-five hundred parciantes who are directly or indirectly engaged in the complex of ownership and practices, beliefs, interactions, rights, and obligations that constitute acequia culture live in four thousand rural and semirural, landholding Hispano families in the Taos Valley. Excluding pueblo ditches (and acequia laterals), 74 identified main-stream diversions and roughly two hundred miles of main canals exist in the Taos Valley. They are organized into 56 separate acequia associations, each with its own commissioners and mayordomo (Geoff Bryce, TVAA, personal communication with the author, June 27, 2003).

All non-Indian lands irrigated by the Río Lucero and Río Pueblo are subject to legal agreements between Taos Pueblo and community acequias operated by parciantes who live in Don Fernando (City of Taos), El Prado, Cañon, Las Colonias, and Arroyo Seco. The origins of these agreements or customs are rooted in a mutual history of conflict and conciliation. The repartos on the Río Pueblo and the Río Lucero embody this history.

The modern players in the ongoing drama of reparto, or el repartimiento de agua, understand their present condition as rooted in history, memory of which is passed on orally and through practice from one generation of irrigators to the next.

part one

REPARTO

t h r e e
Dividing the Río Pueblo

Agua que no has de beber, déjale correr [Let run the water you don't drink].

Dicho (saying)

Parciantes on the Río Pueblo know very well that Taos Pueblo commands the upper banks of the river and enjoys more water than it can use. When water is abundant, as it is during spring runoff, Pueblo irrigators divert as they please and still leave plenty in the river for farmers downstream. The reigning agreement, or reparto (customary division of water), between Taos Pueblo and its downstream neighbors ordains that, in times of limited flow, the pueblo enjoys full use of the water for four days a week and then the acequia madre has it for about three days. Acequias downstream from the acequia madre, in El Prado, Ranchitos, and Los Córdovas, divert Río Pueblo water augmented by the Río Lucero, the Río Fernando, and even the Río Grande del Rancho. Thus separate outtakes and ditch systems divert water in the upper, middle, and lower zones of the Río Pueblo watershed.

In this chapter, I draw several lessons from how Taos Pueblo and downstream communities divide the Río Pueblo. First, the singular mix of proportional and rotational methods of water allocation employed on this river derives from a combination of geographic and historical circumstances. The history of relations between neighboring communities is written in how they divide the water on the rivers they share. Even more important is the fact of division itself, as well as the ethic it expresses: water *must* be shared. This is not to claim that irrigators always share it fairly or that no one would ever take it all, which anyone familiar with day-to-day reality knows to be untrue. Therefore, I emphasize the reparto both as practice and as ideal.

The Río Pueblo originates in Blue Lake, located high above Taos Pueblo between Taos and Wheeler peaks. Blue Lake sits like a little round sapphire, surrounded by forest at the head of Glorieta Canyon, about 2,000 feet below Wheeler Peak, the highest mountain in New Mexico at just over 13,000 feet.[1] The river curls around the eastern base of Taos Mountain and descends through miles of aspen and evergreen forest. Once outside the canyon, it cuts through the heart of Taos Pueblo, dividing the village into north and south sides, or moieties known as the Winter People and the Summer People.[2] From there, the river crosses the alluvial plain to rendezvous with the Rio Grande a few miles north of Pilar, some eighteen miles southwest of the famous and much photographed Indian village.

According to the Bureau of Reclamation, the Río Pueblo drains a 66-square-mile area in the Sangre de Cristo mountain range (Baxter 1990:70, n. 2). The Río Pueblo system (including five tributaries) waters about 9,000 of the total 12,500 non-Indian acres under irrigation in the Taos Valley. Taos Pueblo irrigates somewhere between 800 and 1,700 acres, according to different sources.[3]

Pueblo irrigators divert Río Pueblo water at numerous points above and below the bisected central plaza. Two main ditches, the Cicada Nose and the Elk Horn, branch north and south from a large double headgate that sits above the village. At least another ten ditches sprout downstream to irrigate lands lying both north and south of the river and above and below the Indian village.[4] Little seems to be known about how water is allocated inside the pueblo, other than its being the governor's domain.

Intercommunity water sharing on the Río Pueblo begins at the *compuerta* (headgate) for the Acequia Madre del Río Pueblo, located on tribal land less than a mile downstream from Taos Pueblo plaza. Another compuerta on the acequia madre sits about two miles below that, at a juncture just south of the Sierra Vista Cemetery between pueblo land and the town of Taos. This second headgate divides the mother ditch into two branches that run to the east and west sides of town. According to the Taos Valley Acequia Association, approximately five hundred parciantes presently irrigate about 576 acres along more than 12 miles of the acequia madre. This number excludes the Spring ditch south of the plaza, which serves another 30 parciantes irrigating 22.7 acres.[5] All the other laterals are subsumed under the acequia madre.

Starting at the acequia madre and ending at the ditches along the lower reaches of the river, I draw on parciantes' own words to describe the ditches and customs along the Río Pueblo (see figure 3.1).

Acequia Madre del Río Pueblo

When showing me the Acequia Madre del Río Pueblo, Joe Gomez, a former commissioner and then the "ditch records keeper/office manager," estimated that the entire network contains twenty-five miles of ditches. I have known Joe since I was a child, when he managed the meat counter at the local supermarket. Stooped over with a bad back but jovial as ever, he drove me over the bumpy, dirt back roads between Taos and

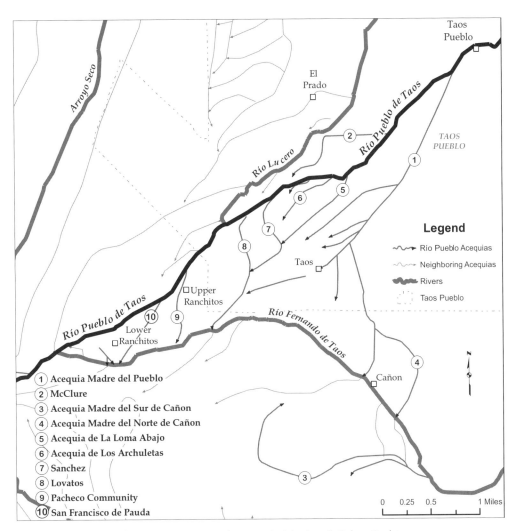

Figure 3.1. Río Pueblo acequias. Drawn by Kurt A. Menke. © Sylvia Rodríguez.

Legend

〰️ Río Pueblo Acequias

〰️ Neighboring Acequias

▬ Rivers

⬜ Taos Pueblo

① Acequia Madre del Pueblo
② McClure
③ Acequia Madre del Sur de Cañon
④ Acequia Madre del Norte de Cañon
⑤ Acequia de La Loma Abajo
⑥ Acequia de Los Archuletas
⑦ Sanchez
⑧ Lovatos
⑨ Pacheco Community
⑩ San Francisco de Pauda

Cañon and walked me along overgrown ditch banks in the Las Cruces neighborhood, near the old wooden flume below the (Las Cruces) *morada* (Penitente chapter house) and the Mabel Dodge Luhan estate bordering Taos Pueblo land. Joe described the acequia madre system as a mother ditch with three branches:

> And its three branches. We have the Loma Arriba town ditch {a lateral}. It irrigates the north part of the town and west of the highway to Colorado. And we have the southwest main ditch, which irrigates on the southwest side near the old Holy Cross Hospital. Our southeast main ditch irrigates the area east of the highway, all the way to where the ditch meets the South Cañon ditch and the place where the North Cañon ditch [both off the Río Fernando] drains across the Fernandez River into the southeast main ditch. The northeast main ditch flows from south of the upper Las Cruces flume all the way to the Raton

highway. The north[ern half] of the main ditch irrigates north of the Las
Cruces flume all the way to the headgate at the Río Pueblo. [July 1995]

In addition to the town, the Don Fernando de Taos land grant seems to have contained another settlement along the middle banks of the Río Fernando, referred to in
the 1796 census as "la placita de Nuestra Señora de Dolores" (Ebright 1985; Baxter
1990; Meyer 2000:136). Known also as Cañon, the old placita de Dolores diverts
water upstream (on the Río Fernando) from Don Fernando de Taos into a system whose
two acequia madres, del Norte del Cañon and del Sur del Cañon, feed into the Acequia
Madre del Río Pueblo.

The Río Fernando originates many miles to the east of Taos plaza in the mountains below Palo Flechado Pass and flows westward through Taos Canyon into the Taos
basin. With an estimated flow of 4,780 acre-feet a year, it is the smallest Río Pueblo
tributary (Wilson 1978:V-13, table 14). Its acequia madre headgate sits near the
mouth of Taos Canyon east of Cañon. Not far below, the mother ditch branches into
the Acequia Madre del Sur del Cañon and the Acequia Madre del Norte del Cañon,
which irrigate fields north and south of Highway 64 East. The Río Fernando flows
through Cañon parallel to the highway and wends its way quietly past the south edge
of Don Fernando de Taos and into the pastures of Ranchitos, where beavers dam it and
springs replenish it. It reaches the Río Pueblo near the old, now vanished placita of
San Francisco de Pauda (Paula), served by the ditch of the same name.

Historians (Ebright 1985:5; Baxter 1990:17–19, 70) report that within a year of
receiving the Don Fernando grant in 1796, settlers petitioned for and were awarded
sobrante rights from both the Río Pueblo and the Río Lucero. Don Fernando settlers
therefore diverted water from all three rivers; those in Cañon used the Ríos Fernando
and Pueblo, and Los Estiércoles or El Prado (located north of Don Fernando) diverted
water from the Río Lucero.

By the 1870s, disputes over water sharing with the pueblo had become a persistent problem. The farmers in Don Fernando had managed to secure a permanent share
of the Río Pueblo instead of mere sobrantes. Still, they complained of insufficient
water when, during times of low flow and drought, pueblo irrigators diverted the
water upstream. A final allocation, dividing the river equally between the pueblo and
downstream irrigators, was made by probate judge Antonio Joseph in 1878 and was
reaffirmed by the Territorial Court in 1893. In that year, drought-provoked conflict
on the Ríos Pueblo and Lucero resulted in formal legal agreements over water division
on each river. In early August, a spontaneous meeting between pueblo and downstream acequia representatives on the Río Pueblo occurred in the county courthouse.
They drew up an agreement that was signed by 20 men from the pueblo and the town
of Taos, including the pueblo governor, Domingo Bernal, and Juan Santistevan, a
prominent property owner in town, as well as the secretary of the pueblo, the secretary
of the town, and one Anglo, Smith Simpson (Baxter 1990:74; Ebright 2005:28,
n. 106). According to Baxter:

The deliberations resulted in an agreement that allocated water from the Rio Pueblo when shortages occurred according to a time schedule. From twilight Friday until dawn Monday, residents of Fernando de Taos received the river's entire flow. Next, irrigators on the Acequia Madre, including those near the cemetery, had exclusive use of the water all day Monday. At other times, the stream belonged to the Indians, giving them complete control about four days a week. [Baxter 1990:74]

Affirmed again in a 1910 court case, the terms of this contract remain in practice today. Every Río Pueblo parciante I consulted—including the mayordomo, a commissioner, the records keeper, and two who remembered pre–World War II days—explained the division, with some variation as to who gets the water on Monday. Eighty-four-year-old Leo Baca from Cañon summarized the overall pueblo-acequia situation ("The Indians always had the upper hand") on the Río Pueblo:

They would only let us have the water on Friday night, let us use it Saturday, Sunday. And by Monday morning, they'd take it away. So we could irrigate only those three days, and they had it the rest of the week. And I suppose that was all the way from the beginning until I wasn't there anymore. I suppose it's still the same. [July 1995]

Now deceased, Leo was a retired schoolteacher and gas station owner whose father sharecropped about seventy-five acres off the Acequia Madre del Río Pueblo before World War II. He was a distant in-law I had known since childhood. Leo recalled that parciantes were not allowed to go up past the headgate until after 6:00 p.m. on Friday. They would proceed all the way to the diversion gate, more than a mile above the pueblo, and turn all the water back toward the acequia madre. Upon closing this upper headgate, Leo explained, more water would stay in the river to supply Hispano irrigators along the acequia madre.

Commissioner Orlando Ortíz described the same customary practice:

That agreement calls for the Indians to share the waters of the Río Pueblo starting at sundown on Friday—the way the agreement stated, I believe sundown on Friday until dawn the following Monday. In other words, the non-Indians have it, according to that agreement, on weekends. So that has worked very well, as far as I know and as far as I've heard from old timers. [July 1995]

Mayordomo George Trujillo likewise told how it is done:

On Friday, I turn the water on at 6. That's when I walk the ditch and I turn their headgates off. I turn the water off all those irrigators in the pueblo, and I get it for myself. Not for myself, but for my irrigators. [July 1995]

Asked to explain how the acequias and pueblo managed to share the water, Joe Gomez responded:

It was done by custom. Custom. People talking to people. People needing water. People sacrificing a little excess water, or even some of the one they needed, so that their neighbors that had none got some at least.... Everybody got some. It's been very unselfish, with a few exceptions. There are people who are selfish, but, in general, the division of the water, both among the acequias and with the pueblo, has generally been a very community-spirited sort of thing. We've never, we've had no trouble on this acequia with the Indian pueblo or the people therefrom. [July 1995]

Orlando Ortíz, a retired high school principal whose wife was my seventh-grade teacher, also described the annual ritual whereby they enact the water-sharing agreement between the acequia madre and the pueblo:

Well, usually the mayordomo meets with the Taos Pueblo governor or his representative in the spring, and arrangements are made to continue [the] sharing agreement. It's kind of a formality, but George [the mayordomo] has been doing it because he feels it establishes a good, harmonious working relationship with people from the pueblo. And so there have been times when the commissioners have gone with him to meet with the governor. This year, we didn't have that meeting, but as I remember, last year we did. The three commissioners went and the mayordomo and Joe Gomez, and we met with the governor and some of the other officials there to talk about the continued use of the diversion gate up there, and so forth. [July 1995]

As noted in chapter 2, anthropologist Merton Miller observed a meeting that signified this agreement a century ago. Long-standing custom governs the use of the ditches as well. Parciantes say that the start of every season always goes much the same way. Joe explained that the pueblo cleans its (upper) part of the ditch and "then they say, 'Get your ditches ready. We've cleaned our part.'" As Mayordomo George Trujillo put it, "It's always been done every year. It's a repeat." Elaborating on pueblo-acequia cooperation, he continued:

They clean up to the boundary of the pueblo. And then, from there on down I clean it. And Ventura Mirabal [of Taos Pueblo] is always very helpful. He's been sick now, but he's been very helpful, you know. He helps me with turning on the water.... If something happens, he gives me a call, tells me if the water is slow or somebody turns it off, or whatever. So I get participation from a few of them. Jeronimo Sandoval is another one that calls me if the water is running somewhere where they don't need it. [July 1995]

Ditch officers stress that the agreement whereby either the Río Pueblo or the acequia madre gets the water is enforced only under conditions of scarcity. In times of plenty, for example, during spring runoff, water flows abundantly in both the river and the acequia madre all week. Parciantes must still ask the mayordomo for the water, but they are not necessarily limited to the weekend. As George explained, when there is enough water, "the system that we have is that everybody calls for their water and first come, first served. That's the way we do it" (July 1995). Parciantes insist that water is never allocated on the basis of priority of ownership in time. People share alike when there is plenty and suffer alike when there is drought. In scarcity, water is allocated on the basis of dire need.

A former county commissioner who owns a bar in Cañon, George described how he manages, as mayordomo, to maintain a balance among parciantes on the acequia madre during each season:

> When the water is slow, it's different, you know. If I have enough for two days, I have to divide it among my irrigators.... Well, I usually just get small irrigators, like lawns and little gardens. My big irrigators are alfalfas, and all that. They don't need water when it's slow. They don't need it until the second cut. About that time, the rains come, and then the water comes down the river again. So I have enough after August for them, you know. But for my small gardens, I divide it into so many hours each, so they can all get some. [July 1995]

Orlando Ortíz spelled out the systematically cooperative nature of all irrigation activity. He described how he and his neighbors had irrigated off the Acequia Madre del Río Pueblo during the preceding week:

> Well, like in our case here, my neighbor Ruben Vigil and I usually share the water when we decide to irrigate. And he called the mayordomo three weeks ago and got the water, after we had cleaned the ditch. And so a certain amount was turned down from the main headgate, which is near the Mabel Dodge Luhan property, turned down into our ditch, which flows behind the Barela property here, and so Joe did it at that time because George was out of town. And he turned so much down at the headgate, and then we get it over here at this headgate and turn it down to our ditch. And then after Ruben finished irrigating, he turned it down to my ditch. Then I got it.
>
> When we're through, we notify the person in charge, and either they ask us to go and close the headgate or they'll go. But this time the man, let's see, somebody else besides Joe—I forget who they say George left in charge—he went out there because there's a padlock on it. He closed the gate and then padlocked it. So that's how it's done, you know, so there isn't water flowing in that ditch all the time. Just when people ask for it, then they'll turn it down. [July 1995]

Ditches in Town

When I talked to him in the summer of 1995, 93-year-old Thomas Tarleton Sr., now deceased, still owned water rights to 1.5 acres near the top of Upper Loma Lateral just north of the town post office. His family lived on this property for 22 years, between 1930 and 1952. They irrigated a large garden and an orchard and kept some cows. The system he described from those days corroborates other accounts of how the water was, and still is, distributed on the Acequia Madre del Río Pueblo:

> All I did was use the water and had a water right for half an acre, and my mother had a water right for an acre, and we just used that and paid our water rights. But I do know that when there was plenty of water, the mayordomo would come and give us all the water we wanted and the water would go on past us to the Loma. [July 1995]

During times of plenty, the mayordomo gave them all the water they needed. When it was scarce, he divided the water among parciantes according to need:

> Generally, you know, the small people that had fruit trees and gardens and places like that, they got water for their little gardens and things over farmers with alfalfa, yes. He [the mayordomo] would make a distinction that if they wanted water, like, Saturday and Sunday, he would give it to them. [July 1995]

Tom also recalled how in 1921 the plaza was irrigated by a covered ditch:

> I came back to Taos from the army in 1921, and it was in the fall, and at that time they had a program on. Something had happened to the irrigation ditch that ran down to the Taos plaza. They irrigated the plaza, and then this ditch ran on down to Alex Gusdorf's place and ran off the hill down there. Now what they were doing was, they were putting this kind of a…making a box out of two-by-tens or two-by-twelves, and they were putting this right down from…it ran from up near Philip's Studio right down Pueblo Street and made the curve into the plaza, and then water would come out at the plaza, and it had to be underground.
>
> Of course, all it was was a little dirt road down there, so they just dug the dirt road up and put this box in there and covered it up so they had a flume down there. And how long that lasted I don't know, but that was in 1921. But when that went out, they didn't have any irrigation water in the plaza anymore. But it must have lasted several years. And then, on each corner of the plaza, there was, like, a barrel, and they would fill these barrels, and they would have the water, too, for flowers around. And then the ditch ran down there and then ran out the southwest corner down out to Alex Gusdorf's place and then out there. [July 1995]

Tom's account indicates that even though the ditch system in town has changed physically through time, the basic reparto has remained the same.

Today, a padlocked, red steel-mesh headgate sits just outside the Lineberry estate fence, across from the Sierra Vista Cemetery between the Taos Pueblo land and the north end of town. Here, the acequia madre branches into the Upper Loma Lateral that feeds west-side neighborhoods all the way to Placitas and La Loma. This ditch crosses North Pueblo Road, where it splits into the lateral Tom described, running south toward the plaza, with the main branch continuing across a motel ground into neighborhoods north and west of the plaza area. Water from this ditch still serves La Loma, an old placita and barrio west of town whose *vegas* (meadows) toward Ranchitos are fed by other ditches, from the Río Pueblo and Río Lucero.

Many of the downtown laterals (off the acequia madre), which ran down the main road toward the plaza, as well as around it into the Loma and Spring ditch drainages below, have fallen into disuse. During the last decades of the 20th century, the town's development obscured many of the ditches. Their fading, overgrown traces are still discernible along roads and fences throughout the town core. Some might debate whether disuse is a cause or a consequence of ditch impairment by town streets. In any case, more than three decades have passed since people regularly irrigated the Placitas neighborhood established north of the plaza during the interwar period when the modern town incorporated.

Originally dug to irrigate farmland, the Placitas laterals still ran through residential properties during the 1950s but started to succumb by 1970. They were the ones on which I grew up, as the offspring of the first—and probably last—generation of Taoseños to irrigate middle-class yards instead of vegetable gardens, fields, or orchards. It has been much longer since acequias watered the plaza itself, during the 1920s.

Although Don Fernando became an *ayuntamiento* (municipal government) soon after the 1796 land grant, it was not laid out according to a central plan. Instead, it coalesced out of a scattering of individual ranchitos. No early maps of the town of Don Fernando or of its acequias are known to exist, and we have few records documenting them. No one has attempted the kind of study archaeologist David Snow (1988) did of the Santa Fe acequia system.[6] Absence of a plan meant that the ditches in and around Don Fernando grew up as individual or private community systems. Michael Meyer suggests that these "patterns of water management and distribution were in place long before corporate status was extended to the town of Taos" (Meyer 2000: 138).[7] My fragmentary sketch of the attenuating system in the center of town draws on my memory of growing up a few blocks north of the town plaza in the 1950s; contemporary observation (late 1900s and early 2000s); an interview with Tom Tarleton, Sr.; and examination of a copy of a map (drawn in 1944 by Ralph Meyers) of the plaza and environs as they were between 1845 and 1875.[8]

Meyers's map, copies of which can be found at the Taos Historical and Millicent Rogers museums in Taos, shows several features of the town's premodern water system (see figure 3.2). It depicts only two "old ditches," both of which would have diverged from the acequia madre, but not their points of diversion. The northern ditch crosses the main road to Taos Pueblo more or less in the present Kit Carson Park area and then turns westward along present Bent Street in front of the old Charles Bent home. It proceeds westward toward La Loma.[9] The other "old ditch" flows from a point behind the Kit Carson home toward the plaza along the road from Cañon now known as Kit Carson Street. It cuts southeast and then southwest, skirting the plaza to run down present-day Ledoux Street, past the old Smith Simpson home, now the Harwood Foundation, toward Ranchitos Road. It is labeled "old ditch for garden and domestic use."

The map shows two wells, one in the center of the plaza and one on the main road north of the plaza but south of the Charles Bent house. The first, labeled "old well for cattle and horses," sits inside the enclosed and gated plaza. The other, the map labels the "first well dug here." A series of springs along a "200 yards" area, labeled "springs water supply for Fernandez" and "Taos Springs Water Supply," appears on the map south of the plaza.

These springs are located in the middle zone of the Las Cruces drainage, which begins in the foothills east of town and runs west toward Ranchitos. This low wetland curves around the south side of the little hill where Taos plaza sits. The Couse pasture lies just above the springs that are the source for the Spring ditch. Meyers's map indicates that they were an important early water source for the town. These springs also fed the old pond on the west side of the main highway, below the site of the La Tuatah Motel between the 1940s and the 1970s. The old pond was paved over in the 1970s to make a parking lot for Taos's first Kentucky Fried Chicken restaurant. B. G. Randall operated a flour mill here in the early part of the 20th century. The drainage descends into a wetland that supplied a fish hatchery for many years. Little by little, this inter-riverine wetland has been drained and covered with landfill and abandoned overgrowth. Yet the springs still survive and supply water for the ditches west of town and in Ranchitos.

Today only a few traces hint at the hydrological importance this area has always had for the town of Taos: the street sign for Ojitos (Little Springs), a dirt road running west below Ledoux Street, and an unobtrusive well house behind a fence hidden by tree branches, near Randall's old mill site. Wedged between two art galleries just north of McDonald's, this tiny parcel contains the Town of Taos Well #5, established around 1970, one of eight municipal wells. Across the highway, a fence encloses the triangle of land where the La Tuatah Motel once stood. A sign proclaims Taos Pueblo ownership of the now empty plot. This property includes a small rectangular extension south across Ojitos Lane, sandwiched between the parking lot over the old pond and an overgrown field, both privately owned. Hidden under landfill, the lower drainage descends into tangles of marshy underbrush, old trees, and dim thickets where drunks go to party and pass out.

In addition to the Loma Arriba branch of the acequia madre, another west-side lateral runs down to the old La Posta site (later, the old Holy Cross Hospital). On the east side of town, the acequia madre runs through a flume near the Las Cruces (or Kit Carson) morada behind the Luhan estate, then south all the way across the Raton highway and the Río Fernando. North of Highway 64 East, it receives an infusion from the Acequia Madre del Norte de Cañon, and south of the highway it receives water from

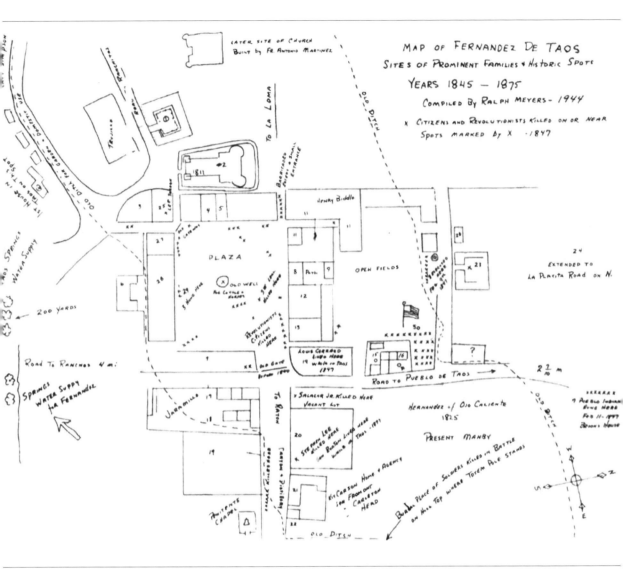

Figure 3.2. Ralph Meyers's map of Don Fernando de Taos.

the end of the Acequia Madre del Sur de Cañon, both Río Fernando ditches. In Cañon and the east side of Taos, then, the waters of both the Río Pueblo and the Río Fernando cross over and meet. Similarly, on the western, Placitas–La Loma–Ranchitos side of town, the Río Pueblo intermingles with the Río Lucero. All three rivers flow together in Lower Ranchitos. South of Ranchitos at Los Córdovas, the Río Grande del Rancho joins the Río Pueblo. There, just below where these four rivers and the end of the Arroyo Seco drainage come together, the people of Los Córdovas built their chapel to San Isidro, the patron saint of farmers.

Lower Río Pueblo Acequias

Like parciantes upstream, irrigators on the lower Río Pueblo depend, when the river is low, on an agreement with the pueblo. At peak times, everyone knows that this river contains more water than can be held back. The amount of water in the river below the acequia madre is sometimes small, but rarely does it go dry. Parciantes downstream say that when water is abundant, the mayordomo allocates it on a first-come, first-served basis, much as in the upper watershed. Priorities based on date of claim are not observed. When water is scarce, the mayordomo allocates it according to need, on a daily or an hourly basis. Felix Miera, who has served as mayordomo, commissioner, and treasurer of the Sánchez ditch, explained that the pueblo normally lets unused water flow on down to the Ranchitos acequias. They, in turn, do the same: "If it's not being used, we just let it go back into the river, and the people below can use it."

Felix knows that, when needed, the pueblo will always help out the Sánchez ditch. He explained:

> When the water gets kind of low, we try to go up into the area [the pueblo] and talk to the people. We've talked to the governor in past years, asking him to somehow let some of that water come down. And he was very good about it. We went there about two, three years ago. That would be about 1992 or '93, I guess, somewhere around that. And we didn't have much water in the river, so we went out there and we asked the governor, we wrote letters, and then we talked.
>
> A commission was appointed to go over there to talk to the governor, and, you know, he was very good about it. He asked that they let some water down, and we had some more water to irrigate. [July 1995]

My homeroom teacher in the eighth grade and now retired, Felix (or Mr. Miera, as I knew him) has served as mayordomo for 17 years. Reviewing the land-use history in his own family, he paid homage to the ideal that enabled parciantes to survive when water was often scarce:

> Well, I would say we go back to the idea of sharing and sharing alike, which has been very good for our people because…it's been the custom traditionally that if there is enough water for everybody to use, go ahead and use all you need. But if there isn't too much water, then use what you need, just the amount that you would need yet not being hoggish with it. Turn it down. Let other people use it. In other words, try to share the water with the people below you or above you, or whatever. That, I think, is a tradition that's been around for quite a while.
>
> My grandmother used to do that with the Acequia de los Molinos. She claimed that was her ditch but, well, the courts didn't agree with it. But my grandfather used to be quite a rancher up in El Prado, in between the two

rivers, and he used to irrigate quite a bit. And the same thing used to be true with Mr. McClure. He lived below, and he and my grandfather would share that water very well. They never had any problem as to who was going to get what.

We had some land up in El Prado also. Her dad [his wife's] used to have quite a bit of land over there, and they never had much problem trying to get enough water. He was irrigating through the Acequia Madre del Prado. We acquired some of that land, which we sold later, regrettably, but we never had any trouble getting enough water to irrigate over there.

But I would say that it's been customary for people to not be selfish, you know, to think about your neighbor, think about the other people, which has been a common thing among Spanish-speaking people anyway. It's always been that way. There are a few selfish people, but 99 percent of the people are very good at that. They say, "Well, I don't need it. You go ahead," which is a good custom. If people were to follow that now, I think we would have a much better world to live in. But, unfortunately, things are changing. They've changed drastically. [July 1995]

Many irrigators in Ranchitos draw on two rivers, in every combination: Río Fernando–Río Lucero, Río Fernando–Río Pueblo, Río Pueblo–Río Lucero. A few use all three. Here, the disadvantage of being at the end of the line is offset by access to a multitude of groundwater and surface water sources: three rivers flowing together with a fourth, in lowlands with a high water table. As the rivers come together at the vortex of the Taos basin, their surface water and groundwater mutually infiltrate and percolate together through the surrounding marsh and pasture.

The *ojitos* along the rivers are what make the basin so fertile and ensure survival during drought. Seventy-five-year-old Roberto Martínez remembered a bad drought in 1934, when farmers at the pueblo used up the Río Pueblo and those in Lower Ranchitos had to rely on water from the Acequia Madre de La Loma off the Río Lucero:

> Pero en la Acequia de La Loma hubo agua, hubo poquito agua de los ojitos del Río Lucero almost all the year around. The only acequia que hubo agua fue en el Río Lucero en la Acequia de La Loma, porque en el Río Pueblo no había nada. Porque los Indios sembraban mucho, regaban mucho entonces. [But in the Acequia de La Loma there was water, there was a little water from the springs along the Río Lucero almost all the year around. The only acequia that had water was on the Río Lucero in the Acequia de La Loma, because the Río Pueblo had none. Because the Indians planted a lot and therefore irrigated a lot.] [July 1995]

Rafael Vigil, a 79-year-old parciante from Lower Ranchitos who uses ditches off the Río Lucero (La Loma) and the Río Fernando (Los Alamitos), recalled how he survived the same conditions:

In my lifetime, and I can only remember two times, twice, that the water was very limited but still we had plenty. Everybody did, used what they needed, and still they had some going down the river. I remember one time this Fernando Creek was completely dry above the Cañon area, you know, the head of the canyon. I remember that one year—it must have been in 1933 or '35, or something like that—the Fernando River got completely dry. I mean the fish and all dried in there, and yet I had plenty of water down here.

Q: From the Río Pueblo, or…?

RV: No, no. Just from the springs coming along the Fernando, below the people of Cañon.

Q: Whereabout is that?

RV: Oh, I would say about maybe half a mile below the town [of Taos]. But there's a lot of springs along both sides. And this is where I was getting the water, my sister was getting the water, McCarthy was getting the water. And the river was completely dry up there. [July 1995]

Rafael confirmed that the allocation of water to parciantes always rests in the hands of the mayordomo, who operates "just based on his experience of the acreage and the time you consume, you know":

Generally, the mayordomo figures out, like, if you have one acre, he'll give you one day, the right one day, twenty-four hours, whatever you want to call it. And if you have, let's say, like, we have more than one acre, well, the mayordomo usually appropriates that according to the time it takes, you know, by experience. The mayordomo usually knows how long it will take to irrigate my share, so he will give me the water, three nights, let's say, three days and three nights, one day and one night, and depending also on weather conditions. [July 1995]

The history and present practice of water sharing on the Río Pueblo de Taos yield several observations. Repartos seem fixed yet elastic; a high degree of consensus persists among parciantes as to how they should operate. The enduring presence of Taos Pueblo on the upper banks of the river confers undisputed first take of the waters, but not their exclusive use. As long as there is plenty of water, everyone may use it, albeit always according to a customary order enforced by the mayordomo. The mayordomo follows custom, but he operates in a flexible manner, taking into account both contingencies and more constant factors. Had it not been for scarcity and a history of conflict, the customs would not exist. Their ongoing practice attests to a legacy of conflict and accommodation. On the Río Lucero, where the history of settlement and intercommunity dispute followed a different trajectory, similar elements combined to create another set of customs.

f o u r
Dividing the Río Lucero

Next to blood relationships, which rule the valley, come water relationships. The arteries of ditches and bloodlines cut across each other in patterns of astounding complexity. Some families own properties on two or three of the valley's nine ditches. You can argue that the character of a man or woman can be as much formed by genetic and cultural material as by the location of their garden or chile patch along the length of a ditch, toward the beginning where the water is plentiful or at the tail where it will always be fitful and scarce. "He's that way because he lives at the bottom of the ditch and never gets any water" is an accepted explanation for even the most aberrant behavior in this valley. The man who lives at the bottom of a ditch is forever expectant, forever disappointed.

—*Stanley Crawford,* Mayordomo

Like the Río Pueblo, a reparto agreement governs the Río Lucero, and each acequia system in its upper, middle, and lower zones has its own internal customs of allocation as well. But compared with the Río Pueblo or any of the other neighboring streams, the Río Lucero has an especially complex and contentious history of disputes over water, many of which sprang initially from disputes over land. Interestingly, division of the Río Lucero into rough thirds became legally formalized in 1893, the same dry year that the rotating allocation on the Río Pueblo assumed legal status. It seems that the early to mid-1890s were as dry as the mid- to late 1990s, when the custom of sharing was again put to the test.[1]

The Río Lucero originates near Bear Lake, located high on the side of a mountain whose opposite face drains into Blue Lake, several miles east of the village of Arroyo Seco. Bear Lake and Lucero Canyon sit on Tract C, which Taos Pueblo acquired in the late 1970s. Lucero Canyon also lies inside the prerevolt Diego Lucero de Godoy land grant, reassigned in 1716 to Antonio Martínez.[2] Beyond the canyon, the river stretches south for miles along the western skirt of the Sangre de Cristo Mountains, above and away from the farmlands it irrigates in Arroyo Seco, Des Montes, and Las Colonias. Several headgates along the Río Lucero divert the water to ditches that irrigate fields belonging to Arroyo Seco, Taos Pueblo, and El Prado. Lands in Des Montes, Las Colonias, and Ranchitos also receive water from the Río Lucero (see figure 4.1).

As on the Río Pueblo, the prehistory of irrigation in the upper Río Lucero watershed remains unclear. Taos Pueblo claims to have diverted water in the upper watershed "from time immemorial," yet pueblo residents have not occupied its banks year-round within historical memory. Aboriginal dry farming in the upper Río Lucero watershed seems very likely, but the question of prehispanic canal diversion on the Río Lucero stands open. Jeancon (1929), Greiser and Greiser (1995), and Doolittle (2000:384–385) identify 12th- and 13th-century riparian canals in the upper and middle watersheds, but most archaeologists remain skeptical (Adler 1993; Crown, Orcutt, and Kohler 1996).

Pueblo ditches used historically in the upper Lucero watershed may or may not have their origins in the colonial period. In any case, non-Indian acequias diverted Río Lucero water in the middle and lower watersheds more or less concurrently with early Spanish settlement along the middle Río Pueblo. In the 1740s, Hispanic settlers built a *torreón* (defensive tower), now in ruin, above Arroyo Seco.[3] Settlers established Arroyo Seco in the early 1800s and dug acequias to irrigate north or west of the river. House construction south of the Arroyo Seco seems to have begun in the late 19th century.

An important historical difference between the Río Pueblo and Río Lucero is that, notwithstanding Taos Pueblo's ancestral claim to both watersheds, the former is inhabited upstream and the latter is not. The lack of permanent, year-round native residency meant that the west or north side of the upper Río Lucero watershed seemed comparatively vacant and open to vecino access and potential occupation. An 1815 land dispute over Hispano encroachment on the Pueblo league along the Río Pueblo and Río Lucero seems to have encouraged Hispano settlers to move northward, into the Río Hondo and Arroyo Seco–upper Río Lucero watersheds and beyond (see chapter 3, n. 9). The settlement of Arroyo Seco placed new demand on the upper Río Lucero and led to conflict with Taos Pueblo and downstream irrigators in El Prado.

The Arroyo Seco placita sits on the upper north bank of the Arroyo Seco stream, roughly two miles west of the Río Lucero. The meager flow of this well-named creek was never enough to meet the settlers' needs, so they diverted Río Lucero water via the Acequia Madre del Río Lucero de Arroyo Seco. At first, this canal supplied fields northwest of the Lucero only on the north side of the Arroyo Seco stream. In the late 1800s, Spanish settlement spread to the south side. A chain of litigation started in 1823 with a lawsuit by Taos Pueblo and parciantes in Don Fernando over Arroyo Seco's de facto diversion of water. Ultimately, the Taos ayuntamiento allotted Arroyo Seco one *surco* "from the Río Lucero when the water is abundant and in times of scarcity it shall be given to them proportionately" (Ebright 2001:23–24).[4]

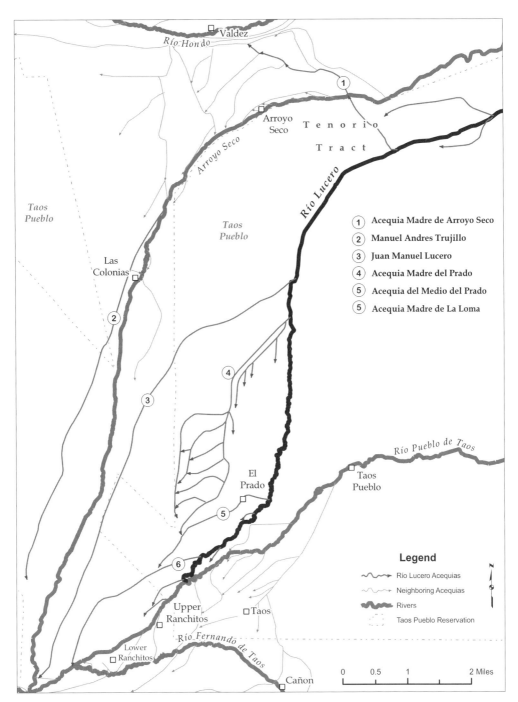

Figure 4.1. Río Lucero acequias. Drawn by Kurt A. Menke. © Sylvia Rodríguez.

Dispute over Seco's share continued to erupt and subside every few years, exacer-
bated by periodic drought. An account from 1838 relates how only a last-minute
cloudburst averted violence between armed Pueblo and El Prado irrigators and the
Arroyo Seco residents.[5] Decades of conflict finally culminated in Judge Edward Seeds's

milestone decree of 1893. More than a century later, the basic threefold division he declared remains engraved in the minds of parciantes all along the river:

> The people of Arroyo Seco, arriba, are entitled to and shall forever have thirty percent of the total water of the Río Lucero, at all seasons of the year; that the people of the Pueblo of Taos, shall forever have thirty-five percent of such total water; that the people of El Prado shall forever have and are entitled to thirty-five percent of such total water of the Río Lucero. And that in the case there shall be any surplus of such waters after supplying the settlement of El Prado and the Pueblo of Taos, the same shall belong to the people of the Arroyo Seco abajo. [*Martínez v. Martínez* final decree by Judge Edward Seeds]

Today, all the land east of the highway that lies between the Río Pueblo and the Arroyo Seco Creek belongs to Taos Pueblo. This vast, mountainous area contains numerous alpine canyons off both the Río Lucero and the Río Pueblo, as well as the ridges between them and the Blue Lake wilderness. Almost the entire length of the Río Lucero lies on pueblo property. Before the 1930s, Hispano settlers enjoyed access to the lake, the canyon, and the upper banks of the river. This area includes the Tenorio Tract between the Arroyo Seco and the Río Lucero, part of which was inhabited and farmed by people from Arroyo Seco until they were ejected by the federal government in 1934.[6]

Las Acequias de Arroyo Seco

The Río Lucero feeds six ditches in the immediate Arroyo Seco area, starting with the Acequia Madre del Río Lucero de Arroyo Seco (AMRLAS). All these acequias were active and in use when I toured them in 1996. The acequia madre is the main channel from which five laterals branch off to fields in the north, west, and south: the Torreón, Alamitos, Espinazo, Martínez, and Brazitos.[7] Along with seven more ditches, they divert water directly off the Arroyo Seco stream to water the placita area and fields north to the Valdez ridge. These seven are the Temporales, El Rito, Juan Márquez, Elizardo Pacheco, Toribio Martínez, La Plaza, and Eraclio Martínez laterals.[8] Lower Arroyo Seco, also known as Upper Las Colonias, draws its water from the Lower Arroyo Seco and the Upper and Lower Manuel Andres Trujillo ditches, which receive an infusion from the Río Hondo via the Rebalse (or Revalse) ditch. Such multiple-ditch service from different rivers underscores the intricate and precarious nature of irrigation in Arroyo Seco.

Today, parciantes in Arroyo Seco irrigate acreage only on the north side of the Arroyo Seco stream. Those 60 years of age or older recall when their relatives and neighbors lived and farmed on the Tenorio Tract, extending south and east from the Arroyo Seco all the way to the Río Lucero. A few melting adobe ruins serve as visual reminders of bygone occupation and irrigation of these lands, which non-Indians were forced to vacate in 1934 after the Pueblo Lands Board recognized Miguel Tenorio's

1818 sale of the tract to Taos Pueblo. The impact of this ejection remains indelibly imprinted on the community memory of Arroyo Seco. The village forfeited both the land and the water used to irrigate it. The residents of Arroyo Seco perceive this loss, which reduced their previous near-third quota of the Río Lucero by 11.7 percent, as a constant deprivation that stings most acutely in dry years. The one-time cash settlements Tenorio Tract ejectees received from the federal government mean far less in group memory than the loss of place, and nothing in comparison to the perennial water deficit.

In addition to numerous casual conversations with parciantes on the Lucero, I interviewed seven present or past commissioners of AMRLAS and an 80-year-old parciante who knew the system well. All of them had been irrigating since they were boys between ages 10 and 12. Collectively, these men represent roughly 111 years of commission experience, and their individual landholdings add up to almost a third (203.5 acres) of the acreage under irrigation from the acequia madre. Most of them use lateral ditches fed by the Río Lucero, as well as the Arroyo Seco, including those that are named for individuals and feed the older, more densely populated village core along the stream. Consensus holds among parciantes as to how the water is divided and distributed within the Arroyo Seco area and also among the pueblo, Arroyo Seco, and El Prado. Although every irrigator offers a unique perspective born of his personal and familial location and experience on the ditch, the overall picture to emerge from these accounts reveals several common, unifying themes.

Foremost is the understanding that Arroyo Seco is supposed to receive nearly a third of the water from the Río Lucero, with Taos Pueblo and El Prado getting slightly larger proportions. Some say the difference is made up by water from the Arroyo Seco stream. Agreement about the three-way allotment, moreover, seems universal even among Río Lucero parciantes who live downstream. It has prevailed through their lifetimes and within the living oral historical memory whence it flows.[9] As 74-year-old Elizardo Pacheco from Arroyo Seco put it, "O ese siempre ha esta'o ya hace mucho. Siempre ha esta'o" [It has always been this way since a long time ago. Always been].

Parciantes on the Acequia Madre del Río Lucero de Arroyo Seco system invariably mention that after the Tenorio Tract ejectments the 30 percent allotment was reduced by 11 percent. They consider this unilateral action by the US government erroneous and unjust because the Tenorio Tract was originally irrigated by contingent, surplus waters granted from AMRLAS. People living north of the river and south on the Tenorio Tract shared the same allotment of water because, as commissioner Palemón Martínez put it, they were "more or less the same people." Palemón used the term *auxilio* to refer to the Tenorio rights. Others called them sobrantes.

Commissioner Fernando Romo from Las Colonias applied the term *sobrante* to Río Lucero water used by irrigators in Upper Las Colonias (sometimes known as Lower Arroyo Seco) and Arroyo Secito (Lower Las Colonias). Fernando, whose younger sister I went to school with, used the variant *arcilio* to describe special dispensations of water made for livestock and gardens in times of scarcity. In any case, all agree with Elizardo's statement: "Este terreno que agarrron [los Indios]…no había agua entonces. Pa'ese terreno, si sembraba pa' aquel la'o, era de temporal" [This land they (the Indians) got…didn't have water then. On this land, if you planted it, was de temporal]. When asked what that meant, Elizardo replied:

> You don't irrigate. You plant like corn or beans or something like that, and you never irrigate. Just hope for the good Lord to give you rain. Ese es temporal…antes no tenían pero hora sí reclamen ellos que sí tienen, sí. [That's temporal…before they didn't have (water rights), but now they claim that, yes, they do.] [May 1996]

The view of Arroyo Seco residents, then, is that Indians who displaced settlers on the Tenorio Tract gained extra water rights because of an official misinterpretation of the nature of those rights. Elizardo implies that pueblo farmers acquired water rights to lands they had previously only dry-farmed. According to Palemón, a flawed computation that inflated the number of irrigated acres inside the Tenorio Tract magnified the consequences of this error. He claims that the United Pueblo Agency diversion structure installed on the river in 1939 was based on a figure of some 800 acres of irrigated land. He insists that only 150 acres, approximately, were watered by auxilio in 1915, an amount that grew to approximately 400 acres by the 1930s.

In 1939 the reduction of Arroyo Seco's allotment from 30 to 18 percent was literally set in concrete with the construction of a new diversion box roughly one hundred feet above the headgate to AMRLAS. Its successor, installed around 1950, still sits there today: a large, three-way, cement diversion structure replete with iron-wheel drop gates held in position by heavy padlocked chains. The two gates on either side of the river divert water along a cement-lined Tenorio ditch to the north and into another ditch on the south, referred to on maps as the "Taos Indian ditch." Roughly one hundred feet below them sits the headgate to the AMRLAS, also a steel and concrete structure controlled by a wheel gate locked into place with a chain and padlock. Locks, keys, and chains went in after the Tenorio Tract case. Only the mayordomo has a key for the AMRLAS headgate, a matter of frustration for some commissioners.

Vecinos say that water loss on the Tenorio Tract dried up the vegas in Upper Las Colonias, further displacing ranchers. World War II and its aftermath led to yet more Hispano out-migration and less agriculture. Another consequence of the ejectment was the BIA's erection of a fence around the Tenorio Tract. The fence blocked customary access from Arroyo Seco to the acequia madre headgate. Parciantes now go the long way around, up the El Salto Road and down a parallel road on what is now pueblo land. The fence also cut off access to the mountains on the Martínez grant, up through the Río Lucero Canyon to Bear Lake, and along the ridge toward the Jaroso and Hondo watersheds, where ranchers used to graze their livestock. The Tenorio Tract boundary line remained a bone of contention through the 1980s. The pueblo claimed that its northern boundary extends to the midpoint of the Arroyo Seco stream. Drawing the line there included the El Salto Road, bordering the south bank of the stream, by which Arroyo Seco and El Salto residents reach their homes and property.

Older parciantes recall that the pueblo initially wanted to put the fence right down the middle of the river, which would have prevented non-Indians from entering lands and homes on the north side. Elizardo remembered that a delegation of elders from Arroyo Seco, including his father, persuaded the Indians to put their fence south of the road, where it sits today (Palemón later added that congressional representatives also were part of the delegation). That agreement hardly settled the matter. Disputes over the El Salto Road erupted at intervals until a 1990 arrangement between the county, US government, and pueblo awarded a large financial settlement to the pueblo.

Parciantes insist that Indians started to irrigate on the Tenorio Tract only after they acquired the extra water. Formerly, they claim, the pueblo irrigated in the middle Río Lucero watershed around El Prado, but not on the upper banks. The general sense among Arroyo Secanos and others seems to be that the Tenorio case and its aftermath contributed to a decline in the intimacy, exchange, and cooperation that formerly characterized relations between Taos Indians and their vecinos.

Despite this lingering sense of loss and resentment over the Tenorio Tract, parciantes in Arroyo Seco typically describe relations between their Pueblo neighbors and themselves as friendly and cooperative. Their sentiments and memories, like those of their counterparts elsewhere in the Upper Rio Grande region, are ambivalent and contradictory. The complex legacy of generations of face-to-face, ditch-to-ditch interaction between these distinct but intermingled peoples cannot be reduced to a simplistic binary reading. The specific incidents over water and ditch management that irrigators recall in tortuous detail reveal an eternal tension between recalcitrance and cooperation, estrangement and intimacy, interdependency and competition.

A rancher with lands north of the El Salto Road, Elizardo recounted an incident years ago when late in the summer the Indians put a *pino* (pine trunk) across the river and blocked the water to Arroyo Seco. The commissioners could not move the tree because it was on Indian land. The mayordomo talked to the pueblo governor, who said, in effect, "We'll see in a few days." The commissioners waited a few days and then went to the compuerta, only to find some men from the pueblo already there, talking among themselves. "And finally they said they would move the tree, and we got our water. But then a week later it happened again. It would not happen at the beginning [of the season] but rather when the water was running out."

Former commissioner Ezequiel Torres recalled that "there were always meetings with the Indians," for example, in 1952–53 when the commissioners wanted to line the acequia madre between Arroyo Seco and the river on the Tenorio Tract with cement, something the pueblo opposed. "We had a hard time for them to agree with us." Ezequiel remembered going to a meeting at a pueblo home, attended by about ten Indians and "three of us [commissioners]." Asked why it was hard, he replied:

> I think they thought we were stealing from them. I don't know. They're hard
> to deal with. When they set their mind they want to do this, they do it, I

mean. And so we finally convinced them to let us do it. Oh, we stayed hours and hours talking to them, you know, and they were talking to themselves. I don't know what they were talking about. Anyway, they finally agreed with us. [May 1996]

Palemón Martínez remembers an occasion in the late 1960s or early 1970s when the pueblo shut off the water to Arroyo Seco completely and gave no response to his efforts to communicate about it. Finally, he drafted a letter to the congressional delegation and got a quick response: the tribal secretary called for a meeting at the diversion point the following morning. Commissioners from both Arroyo Seco and El Prado attended, along with a BIA representative.

Their opening statement was, "What's your problem?" I said, "The diversion has been locked. We want that opened." "Well, why hadn't you said so?" I never knew what had happened, but that was an official doing, because they have the only keys to the lock in place. Now we feel it ought to be a three-way thing. They have total, absolute control since they construct it and keep it, and still do. [July 1995]

Río Lucero irrigators also recount instances every summer when the ditch water is suddenly cut off somewhere upstream by youth who want to fish. These are "renegades," not irrigators stealing the water or tribal officers intending to violate or negate the long-standing diversion agreement among the three communities. The fishing problem is always corrected, but never for good.

Locals attribute recent changes in cooperative activity to the impact of the Taos water rights adjudication, or Abeyta case, in addition to the pressures of population growth and urban development. Today, acequia commissioners must carry documentation of official pueblo permission to tend to ditch business on Indian land. They are rarely stopped, but most mention that written permission was never required until a decade ago—much as locks and keys were not used in the "old," pre-Tenorio ejectment days. Some blame newcomers who trespass on Indian land, but others believe that heightened territorial vigilance and even an increase in irrigation at the pueblo are responses to the adjudication.

What remains constant through the nearly two hundred years of contention over how much water Arroyo Seco gets out of the Río Lucero is the very fact of sharing itself—the fundamental understanding, agreement, and practice that this community deserves, and does indeed always receive, a share of the water. For at least a century, this allocation has ranged specifically and officially between one-third and one-fifth, depending on historical conditions. Before that, Arroyo Seco always received at least one surco. In short, dispute has always been over how *much* Seco should get rather than *whether* it should get any at all.

This simple fact is significant precisely because it is taken for granted. Each river system, along with each acequia community within it, has its own arrangement or custom. Worked out through a process of unending negotiation and conciliation, it operates within the parameters of a sharing instead of a zero-sum paradigm. This basic principle, that no one goes absolutely without water, even—especially—in times of scarcity, inheres in both intracommunity and intercommunity relations, including relations with Taos Pueblo. The entire ragged legal history of the Río Lucero attests to the power and workings of this principle.

At the same time, knowledge of specific regimens, water-sharing arrangements, or customs tends to be narrowly localized. Active parciantes within any given community are always familiar with their own rules but not with those of neighboring communities, unless they themselves use those ditches. Despite their long-standing interaction with pueblo water users, most ditch officers say they know very little about precisely how the pueblo manages irrigation, especially since the federal government constructed many of its outlying ditches in recent decades. Their impression is that pueblo irrigators allocate water less systematically and regulate its use less than the acequia associations do. In Palemón's words:

> I'm not aware of any repartos that they have. I have noticed—and that's not on our ditch [AMRLAS], but looking at the El Prado one—where they tend to divert at any point. [This] may signify that they use a different approach than we do in getting water out of the acequia. Ours are a little more defined. You know, there's a property boundary, and we take it off there. I don't fully understand, but what I've seen, there appears to be that they have some convenience point that they can just divert off the stream. And not a defined system like we have, you know, by property boundaries. [July 1995]

Arroyo Seco's Reparto

Within Arroyo Seco, parciantes are virtually unanimous about the reparto. This system encompasses ditches fed by the Río Lucero via the acequia madre. It distributes the water among upper, middle, and lower zones, rotating the flow among them in two-day cycles. The Linea de Arriba is the easternmost portion, lying between the Alamitos and Torreon ditches. La Linea del Medio extends from a point west of the Alamitos to the Martínez Lateral. La Linea de Abajo runs from the Martínez "on down" to the Rebalse (a Río Hondo ditch). This broad acreage comprises the uplands of Arroyo Seco, extending several miles north and west toward the Des Montes ridge above Valdez. During growing season, the mayordomo and parciantes for each section meet at the main diversion points every 12 hours to change the water in each zone. In years past, they met at midnight; currently, the reparto is scheduled for seven in the evening. One may irrigate by day or by night, much as in the past, when "if you got the water, you went to work. If you didn't, you went back home" (Palemón Martínez, July 1995).

As in all the New Mexico acequia systems, the mayordomo allocates water on the basis of acreage and need. Never within living memory has the water been subject to calls based on priority. Parciantes pay ditch fees assessed at $5 per acre. In times of abundance, everyone enjoys the surplus equally, and the reparto can be a bit lax; in times of scarcity, it is stringently enforced. Need governs the final consideration, and under extreme conditions, mayordomos give precedence to livestock and gardens. This emergency dispensation is known as an auxilio or arcilio. Adjustment is also seasonal. This is Augustín Montoya's summation:

> Everybody attends the reparto—they still do—to each of those areas [the *lineas*]. It's a little bit different when there's plenty of water. Like early spring, if there's enough water, you don't bother with that. Once it becomes more critical or people in the lower end begin complaining, then we set it by lineas. When it gets even shorter, then the mayordomo comes into play, doing a daily allocation. When there was an extreme shortage, of course, the gardens were given a top priority. [February 1996]

Las Colonias

Moving downstream from the Arroyo Seco system, one comes next to Las Colonias, a dispersed string of ranchitos stretching south below Arroyo Seco to west of El Prado in upper and lower clusters. Here one finds an open, rolling expanse of meadowland with a high water table fed by ojitos (small springs). Old-timers recall that it was used to pasture large numbers of horses owned by freighters in El Prado. These freighters operated until the 1920s, when trucks replaced wagons for hauling merchandise. According to Palemón, after the pueblo permanently diverted water upstream on the Tenorio Tract in the 1930s, the vegas in Las Colonias dried up. Despite this setback, some farming continued and evidently still does when conditions allow. Tom Tarleton Sr. noted that cultivation increased in Upper Colonias following a few wet years in the 1980s.

Las Colonias is sustained by sobrante rights to waters from the Arroyo Seco, Río Lucero, and Río Hondo. This water flows down the Lower Arroyo Seco into the branching Upper and Lower Manuel Andrés Trujillo ditches, which go to Upper and Lower Las Colonias, respectively. Infusion from the Río Hondo comes into the Lower Arroyo Seco via the Rebalse (Revalse) and Mariposa ditches, which divert off the Cuchilla ditch near the Des Montes rim above Valdez. The precise locale and form of the diversion have changed through time, as might be expected, and have been the focus of litigation resulting in the arrangement that irrigators presently follow. Today, the diversion structure is a compact, two-door, wood-and-cement compuerta, where one cement-lined ditch continues south and the other veers 90 degrees off to the east. It sits on 140 irrigated acres owned by the late Tom Tarleton Sr., who grew mostly grass hay and some alfalfa.

When I interviewed Tom in the early summer of 1995, he proudly showed me his headgates and told me that he had attended every meeting of his ditch for close to sixty years. He also served as an officer on the Upper Manuel Andrés Trujillo ditch during the 1960s and 1970s. His account of the reparto was as follows:

> The Manuel Andrés Trujillo is in two parts, and the division part is right here on our place. Half of the water goes to Lower Colonias, and half of the water is diverted to Upper Colonias. And there's a compuerta there with a division in it, and it divides the water half and half. [July 1995]

The system and decree by which Colonias divides the waters during times of scarcity on the Lower Arroyo Seco and the Manuel Andrés Trujillo ditch came into being and continue, Tom explained, in the following way:

> The Upper and Lower Colonias…they've had several lawsuits over this water. And right now, when the water gets short, like next week, they will put it all together in one stream, and then it's divided. Now that decree was determined first by Judge Kiker and then another judge—oh, I forgot his name after Kiker…. Anyhow, in 1930 or 1935 along about. And they had a lawsuit, and he determined…and [so]…they built a concrete structure here, where they took the water out for the Upper Colonias people. And the water is divided half and half. Now when it gets very short and there's only enough water for one man to irrigate with, they put it three and a half days on this side and three and a half days for them. And the mayordomos have to get together and do that.
>
> Now what we were interested in—my son was the mayordomo on this ditch, and he wants to get with that mayordomo down there and determine when they want to do that, you see. Then they get the water for three and a half days, and we get it for three and a half days, and it's all in this decree, in the courthouse. At Sunday noon, it says, the people here on the upper part can go and get all of the water. Then that goes on 'til Monday, Tuesday, Wednesday night. At midnight, it's supposed to go to them. Well, they're not to come up here at midnight and change it, so they come up Wednesday night and take it. And then every week or so they adjust the hours. But that's the way…it's three and a half days and three and a half days to each. [July 1995]

"The rest of the time," when water is abundant, Tom said, "it comes and hits that division point, and it's divided two ways" (July 1995).

Lower Las Colonias is also known as Arroyo Secito or Arroyo Seco de Abajo. In addition to the Lower Manuel Andrés Trujillo ditch, irrigators here draw on the Juan Manuel Lucero ditch, which diverts off the Río Lucero about three miles above the Acequia Madre del Prado headgate, both located on the Tenorio Tract. The Juan Manuel Lucero is the longest ditch in the Taos basin; the upper third of its four- or five-mile length lies on Indian land, where it runs closely parallel to an "Indian ditch." Ultimately, it drains into the Anderson ditch near the Río Lucero and Río Pueblo confluence between Lower Ranchitos and Los Córdovas. Unlike its downstream neighbor,

Upper Las Colonias has no rights on the Lucero ditch. Parciantes in Lower Colonias deal directly with the pueblo and Arroyo Seco in getting their water. The Manuel Andrés Trujillo ditch depends on Río Lucero water, but it receives this infusion only as sobrantes or whatever surplus waters flow downstream from Arroyo Seco. It is still the practice, I was told, for people from Colonias to help clean AMRLAS in the spring.

A laborer in his early fifties, Fernando Romo has served as a ditch officer for more than twenty years and irrigates about eighty acres in Lower Colonias. He enunciated a clear set of understandings, practices, and principles that structure water relations with Arroyo Seco, on the one hand, and Taos Pueblo, on the other. He described relations with both communities as harmonious but characterized each side differently. The foremost fact of Colonias's water relations with Arroyo Seco is its limitation to sobrante rights. Still, Fernando described these relations as remarkably cooperative and amicable:

> But even with that [having only sobrantes], we've had no problem in having an ample amount of water for our crops and our livestock. And mainly through the people of Arroyo Seco. They go out of their way to be friendly and to help us with the water situation. They realize we have the sobrantes, but the fact that we run a very close relationship with those people, because they invite us to clean their acequia madre and everything, thinking that the cleaner we have it, the wider they make it, well, they can put more water in there, so they can divert more water to us. And that works real well.
>
> And during times of low, low water, when we figure there's no more surpluses for us down below, we have a tradition also with the people of Arroyo Seco. Not so much on this Juan Manuel Lucero ditch, pero [but] on the Manuel Andrés Trujillo ditch. Now we have a tradition there that when waters get to be so low to where we can't irrigate our crops or anything, but let's say we have livestock or maybe you have a garden or something, well, we can go up and ask the mayordomo of the Acequia Madre de Arroyo Seco for an arcilio. And that means that you basically ask them, "Hey, we need the water for our livestock. No water in the ditches, this and that," or he'll give you an arcilio. He'll say, "Okay, I'll give you so much water for so many days, and fill up your stock ponds or do whatever you're going to do, water your garden," and then they'll take it back, right. They'll give it to you for whatever you think you need it. But that's only during times of real low water levels, you know.
>
> But we do have that with the people of Arroyo Seco, and they honor it, you know. They honor that tradition. They're all aware of it. [January 1996]

The arcilio (a local pronunciation of *auxilio,* or aid), Fernando emphasized, is strictly an emergency measure or "survival-type thing" relating to "food on the table." Even though the auxilio has never actually been invoked within Fernando's personal memory, he is absolutely certain that it would be honored should the need arise, a fact highlighting the customary status of this practice.

The principles by which water is allocated on the Río Lucero are need, availability, and acreage. No officer or parciante claimed priority of ownership as a factor in the allocation of water. In times of abundant flow, people get what they need and there is more than enough. In times of scarcity, the primary consideration is dire need. Fernando explained that the priority under drought conditions is always livestock first, gardens second, and crops and orchards third:

> Here, you know, the ditches, when waters do get that low, real, real low, to
> where's there only a little *chorito* [a small spout of water], you know, there's
> priorities on that *también* [too]. So the priorities would go this way: it'd be,
> first, livestock, first priority. And then the garden. And then if there's plenty
> of water, well, then you irrigate your alfalfas and your meadows, and all that.
> [January 1996]

Parciantes likewise characterize water relations on the Juan Manuel Lucero ditch between the pueblo and Arroyo Sequito as friendly and cooperative. Voicing a widespread sentiment that Indian-Hispano relations were closer a generation ago, Fernando remarked that Indians now farm less. Moreover, he suggested that relations with the pueblo can vary among communities:

> I think that they use less water now, definitely. A number of years ago, the
> old-timers were still around, and they used to grow their big, big corn crops,
> you know. Corn was a big thing up there. And they were all hard workers,
> you know, all the old-timers there, and they got along beautiful with the
> Hispanos, you know. My dad knows all those old-timers by name. They all
> spoke Spanish. And my dad, you know—we, in turn, learned their language,
> through the close relationship they had, you know, not so much our genera-
> tions but, like, my dad's generation. Because they even learned each other's
> languages, you know, because they had a beautiful relationship, you know. I
> like to say that we still do. I mean us, personally, ourselves in Arroyo Sequito,
> through that Juan Manuel Lucero ditch. I can honestly say we haven't had any
> problems at all. I hear a lot of complaints from the El Prado people. They're
> always in conflicts with the Indians, always constantly in battles with them.
> But that's, I think, more personalities getting in the way than necessarily
> waters, you know. [January 1996]

Fernando observed that these days there is more talk about water and less actual use of it. Starting in the late 1980s, as in Arroyo Seco and elsewhere, acequia officers were required to carry a written permit when going on Indian land for ditch business, something they had never done before. He recalled more intimacy and interdependency between Indians and Hispanos when he was a boy:

> No, not so much [talk about] the waters. It was hardly ever brought up. But
> they [his family] used to speak a lot about their friends up there, you know,

how they used to barter. My grandpa, well, you know, he had that land. He had this land there with the ranch, and a lot of his workers on the ranch were from the pueblo. And he would pay them in lambs, cattle, or whatever, you know. So we had many friends up there in the pueblo. I remember as a youngster going up there to visit with my mom's and my dad's friends and never any problems between them. [January 1996]

Fernando believed that there is generally more water in the river these days than many years ago because both Indians and parciantes irrigate less and perhaps because of more runoff in the mountains. He would probably not have made such a claim at the end of the 1990s under worsening drought conditions. Fernando also recalled, with a hint of irony, incidents when the pueblo suddenly shut off the water but eventually restored it. This stoppage would happen where the Juan Manuel Lucero runs closely parallel to an Indian ditch.

The pueblo has a ditch parallel to the Juan Manuel Lucero ditch, and they're, like, a few feet away. And their ditch, at one time, they did a lot of work to it, and they even lined it with cement and stuff. But the pueblo doesn't maintain the same customs the Hispanos do in maintaining the ditches. One of our traditions has been, forever, is go up there in the spring and you clean out your ditches, of course, so you can have a free flow with no obstructions and stuff. And the pueblo is not too up on that. So, consequently, their ditch runs parallel to ours, so they'll sometimes—and it doesn't happen very often—you know, years ago, it used to happen perhaps a little more than now. Maybe different people live around there that don't use the water so much perhaps. But they would block our ditch and then divert it into theirs, you know. And so that would be a form of sharing the water. [January 1996]

Like other parciantes, Fernando professed little knowledge when asked about water distribution among pueblo irrigators: "I really couldn't say. I'm not at all familiar with how they allot their waters. You know, I'm familiar with the Hispano system of allocating waters. I have no idea of how the pueblo would allocate their waters to their members" (January 1996). In his view, El Prado irrigators are more likely than the Indians to cut off Las Colonias's water when it becomes scarce in late summer.

Acequia Madre del Prado

The Acequia Madre del Prado serves roughly 951 acres and about 350 parciantes (Wilson 1978:V-13, T-14). It is the ditch with the most Indian participation, as well as the most disagreement over rights and obligations. Not only does the acequia madre headgate sit on pueblo land, but it also serves tribal parcels interspersed with non-Indian land. These lands include plots acquired by the pueblo through purchase, exchange, and Pueblo Lands Board proceedings during the 20th century. According to

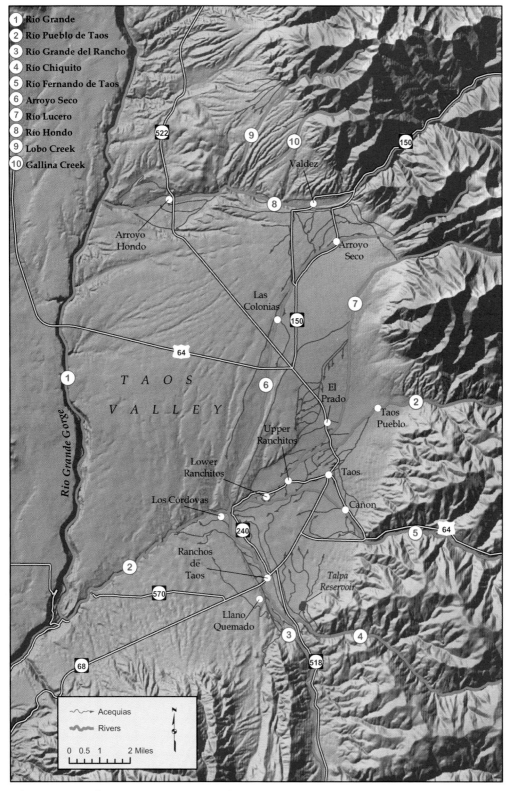

1. Río Grande
2. Río Pueblo de Taos
3. Río Grande del Rancho
4. Río Chiquito
5. Río Fernando de Taos
6. Arroyo Seco
7. Río Lucero
8. Río Hondo
9. Lobo Creek
10. Gallina Creek

Plate 1. Taos Valley rivers, mountains, and acequias. Drawn by Kurt A. Menke.
© Sylvia Rodríguez.

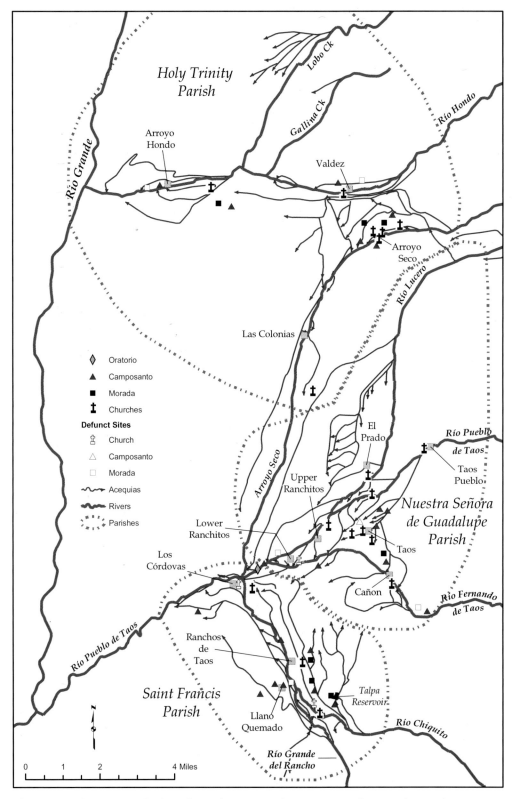

Plate 2. Taos basin watersheds and parishes. Drawn by Kurt A. Menke. © Sylvia Rodríguez.

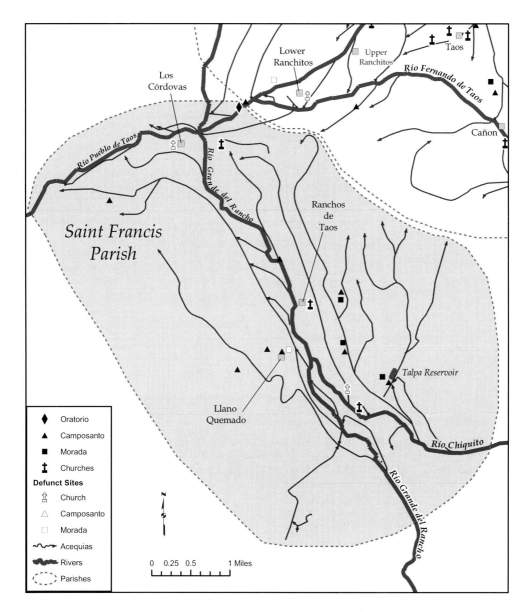

Plate 3. St. Francis parish and Río Grande del Rancho watershed. Drawn by Kurt A. Menke.
© Sylvia Rodríguez.

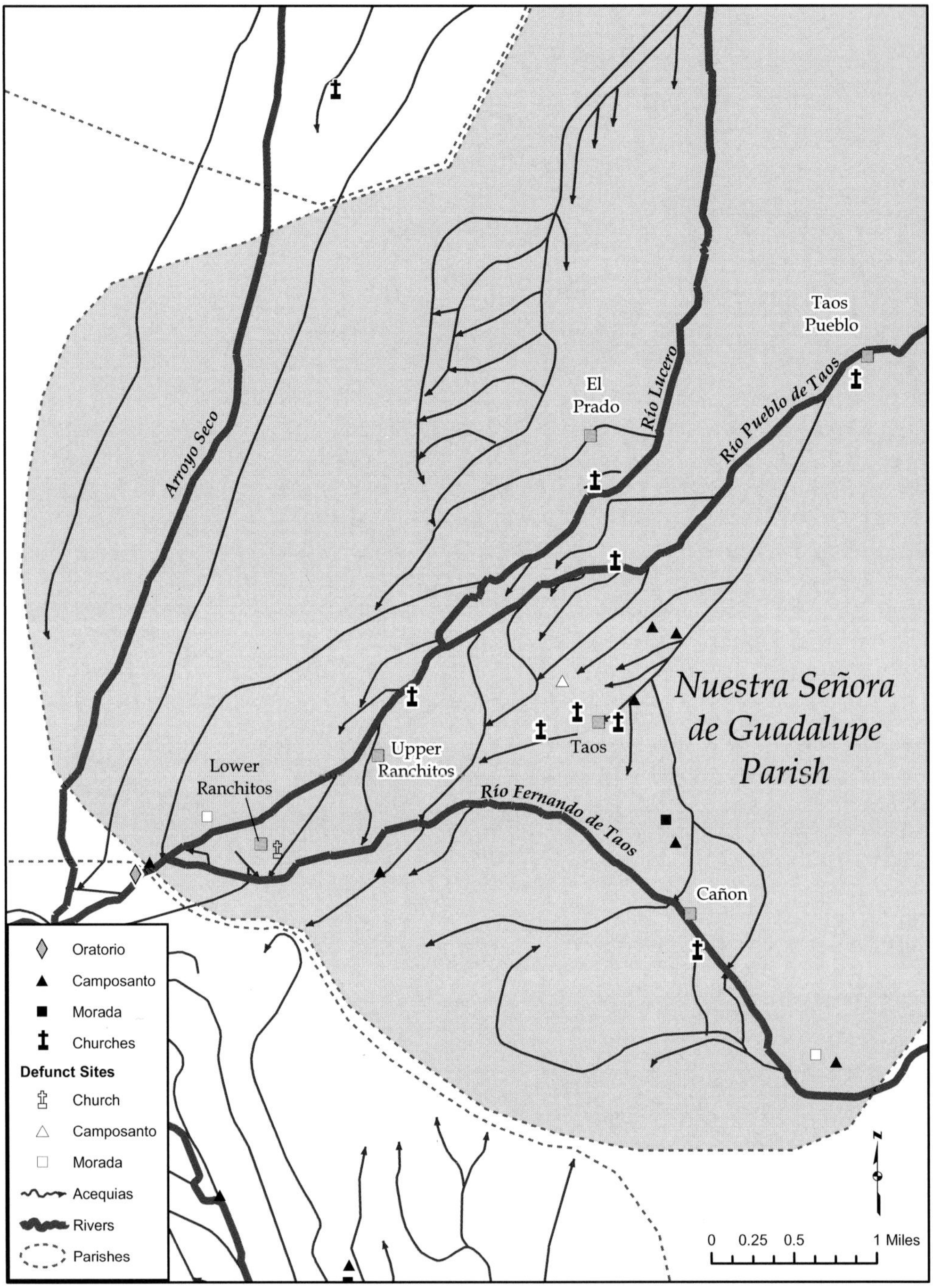

Taos
Pueblo
El
Prado
Río Lucero
Río Pueblo de Taos
Arroyo Seco
Nuestra Señora
de Guadalupe
Parish
Upper
Ranchitos
Taos
Lower
Ranchitos
Río Fernando de Taos
Cañon
Oratorio
Camposanto
Morada
Churches
Defunct Sites
Church
Camposanto
Morada
Acequias
Rivers
Parishes
N
0 0.25 0.5 1 Miles

Plate 4. Nuestra Señora de Guadalupe parish. Drawn by Kurt A. Menke. © Sylvia Rodríguez.

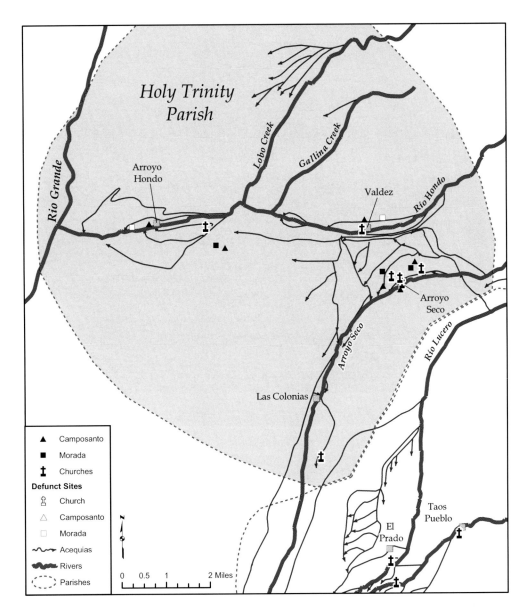

Plate 5. Holy Trinity parish. Drawn by Kurt A. Menke. © Sylvia Rodríguez.

Plate 6. Acequia Madre del Río Lucero before cleaning.

Plate 7. Cleaning the Acequia Madre del Río Lucero.

Plate 8. From left, mayordomo Eliseo García and commissioner Gus García at the Acequia del Medio headgate on the Río Lucero.

Plate 9: Town headgate, Acequia Madre del Río Pueblo.

Plate 10. Felimón Pacheco irrigating his land off the Lovatos ditch.

Plate 11. Día de San Isidro procession in Los Córdovas.

the 1969 hydrographic survey, Taos Pueblo owns 37.7 irrigated acres located in five separate tracts on the acequia madre and owns another 46 irrigated acres off the Acequia del Medio. This acreage is separate from the Karavas Tract, which I will discuss shortly.

The headgate for the Acequia Madre del Prado sits not far inside the pueblo grant boundary, less than a mile below the Juan Manuel Lucero headgate. The acequia madre is about four miles long and runs parallel to and between the Juan Manuel Lucero ditch and the Río Lucero. Cleaning it takes two full days. About halfway down, it sprouts the westward Tanke, Rivera, Varoso, Ciruelo, Gallegos, and Larranaga laterals, which feed pasture and farmlands that extend north and south of Highway 522. At mid-watershed, it is replenished by the Acequia del Medio del Prado, which originates in the Buffalo Pasture east of the old Nuestra Señora de Dolores Chapel (now rededicated to Santa Teresa) or Los Estiércoles placita.

The history of ditch meetings attended by both pueblo irrigators and parciantes, and of the pueblo's sending peones to help clean the Acequia Madre del Prado in the spring, is checkered. Dues, rights, and obligations have become bones of contention on the Acequia Madre del Prado between acequia officers and Taos Pueblo. My account is based on participant observation and interviews with seven past or present officers of that acequia, three of them members of one extended family. I interviewed another four who use the Acequia del Medio. These men ranged in age between 46 and 90 and had spent large periods of their lives irrigating and dividing Río Lucero water with the pueblo and among themselves. Some used the Acequia del Medio, as well as other ditches.

Every man I spoke to agreed on the basic principles of water division when water was scarce and when it was abundant. They all knew by heart the three-way division of the river among Arroyo Seco, the pueblo, and El Prado. Although El Prado farmers had not lost as much as their upstream neighbors in the Tenorio Tract ejectments, they likewise reported that the redivision of Río Lucero water had reduced their own de facto share. This loss occurs, as Ernesto Montoya testily put it, because the pueblo "double-dips" on the Tenorio Tract by channeling water into two ditches located above the Arroyo Seco diversion and then again into what he calls "bastard ditches" lower down, diverting water wherever it (the pueblo) pleases [July 1995]. Gus García, a commissioner of the Acequia del Medio, told me:

> We have not been getting our share, exact share, of water that we were supposed to be allocated.... As soon as the water comes out of the canyon of the Río Lucero, they [the pueblo] divert so much of it to the Tenorio Tract from there. Then, further down, they divert so much to their Beeline ditch, and by the time we, the Acequia Madre del Prado, get our share, there is no 35 percent in the river. [July 1995]

I also spoke to Ernesto's then 99-year-old father, J. J., now deceased, a former commissioner whose paternal uncle had been a mayordomo. J. J. explained that in times of extreme dryness the water alternated between the pueblo and El Prado, either three hours or three days to each in turn. During times of abundance, they let the water run, and it divided automatically at the compuerta. Ernesto's cousin Augustín Montoya, then mayordomo, echoed this principle and elaborated that when water is low, parciantes are allowed four hours per acre and that, in extreme need, people may request and receive an auxilio of temporary emergency water—a custom in which the pueblo has participated. Like others, these men recalled that a decade ago they did not need a written permit to travel on pueblo land for ditch business and there were no locks on the headgates. In the old days, only *palos y piedras* (logs and stones) were used to dam or divert the water.

J. J. Montoya told me that he was a boy when a Taos Pueblo land-claim case resulted in the ejection of some settlers in the El Prado–Ranchitos area. Tribal irrigators, drawing on the acequia madre in El Prado and Ranchitos, subsequently occupied their properties. Indian irrigators came to ditch meetings, and the pueblo governor's office sent workers in the spring to clean the upper ditch located on pueblo property. Although parciantes remembered that Indian landowners participated on the ditch and paid dues in the past, they describe a different situation today. The pueblo occasionally sends peones in the spring but has not paid its dues for several decades and now owes several thousand dollars in delinquent fees.

Acequia del Medio

About three miles south of the acequia madre headgate sits the headgate to the Acequia del Medio del Prado (plate 8), located in the Buffalo Pasture on tribal land, a mile or so southwest of the Pueblo village, northeast of El Prado, formerly called Los Estiércoles (literally, "manure," probably in reference to husbanded pasture). The Buffalo Pasture, with its surrounding marshland, is probably the richest, most extensive and beautiful wetland in the Taos basin. Said to be sacred to Taos Pueblo, this marshland arises from a subsurface, mutual infiltration of waters from the Río Lucero and the Río Pueblo. Their surface confluence is located a few miles to the southwest on the Karavas Tract in Upper Ranchitos. According to Pueblo lore, underground waterways connect the Buffalo Pasture to Blue Lake and the springs that fed the now defunct La Tuatah Pond south of Taos plaza in the middle Las Cruces drainage. The Buffalo Pasture–Los Estiércoles wetland extends west to Wetzel's Pond just above a curve in Highway 522.

I have childhood memories of playing around Wetzel's Pond, where the marshes teemed with frogs, dragonflies, meadowlarks, water snakes, and red-winged blackbirds. Many years later, guided by del Medio commissioners over planks that undulated atop the spongy ground laced with watercress, we grew hushed with reverence at the sheer aquatic bounty of this place. The system of ponds, acequias, and *desagües* (drainage ditches) that the Works Projects Administration (WPA) installed in this marshy area during the 1930s functions as much to contain its prolific surface water and groundwater as to distribute them.

The dual waters of the Ríos Lucero and Pueblo sustain lower El Prado and Ranchitos, both of which lie west of Highway 522. La Loma perches between the town and Upper Ranchitos, also near the interface of both systems. Separate sets of officers and different repartos or customs govern the acequia systems on these two rivers. Yet these systems intertwine because the lands they penetrate are nourished from both streams. Some parciantes exercise rights and hold office on both (and perhaps adjacent) rivers. Each acequia has its own rocky history of cooperation and competition with every neighbor.

Conditions on the Acequia Madre del Prado and the Acequia del Medio differ significantly because of the inter-riverine abundance around the Buffalo Pasture and the fact that the Acequia del Medio is only about 1.5 miles long, takes just one day to clean, and runs constantly.[10] It always has plenty of water, and not much work is required to keep it up. Things are much easier here than on any of the upstream ditches. For the parciantes on the Acequia del Medio, the problem is to contain and control the water rather than try to capture it for a while. Even during the drought of 1996, the water on the Acequia del Medio never stopped flowing. In Gus García's words:

> I think, normally, that we get the water from the springs. It's the overflow
> from the other ditches above us, and sometimes we had to sort of send water
> down the river. So last year [during the drought] we didn't send that much
> water down the river, you know. We just ran it through our system, you know.
> [June 1997]

Nevertheless, the Acequia del Medio, too, has had squabbles with the pueblo. According to the hydrographic survey, the pueblo owns 46 acres of irrigated land located on three separate tracts along the Acequia del Medio, all distinct from the Karavas Tract. Commission secretary Lee Gonzales told me that in the preceding 15 years the pueblo had sent people to clean the ditch four or five times. His records indicate that they paid their ditch fees once, in 1985, and sent eight men to clean the ditch. The following year, the pueblo lawyers sent the commissioners a letter stating that neither state nor federal law requires the pueblo to pay ditch assessments. Acequia records indicate that the pueblo was in arrears from 1977 to June 1995 for $2,828. Still, the secretary told me, they continue to irrigate roughly thirty acres off the Acequia del Medio as they wish, taking the water when they please, without asking the mayordomo as normally expected.

In May 1993 commissioners for both the Acequia del Medio and the acequia madre received a letter from the pueblo requesting a meeting to discuss reopening the ditches to the Karavas Tract. The del Medio commissioners looked into their history and concluded that the Karavas Tract received most of its water from the acequia madre and enjoys only sobrante rights on the Acequia del Medio. The water in the acequia madre does not always reach all the way to the end, but the Medio flows constantly. If they reopened the ditch to the Karavas Tract, it would be getting mostly del

Medio water. The del Medio commission considers itself under no obligation to extend a ditch for sobrantes; therefore, it demurs.

Four additional ditches divert off the Río Lucero south of the Acequia del Medio: the Dan Archuleta in El Prado, the Cortez y Sisneros below it, the Acequia Madre de la Loma, and the South Loma Lateral. Neither the Dan Archuleta nor the Cortez y Sisneros ditch is very long. The first is a private ditch; the second flows south of the river and, according to the Río Pueblo hydrographic survey (1969, vol. 2:310), serves seven parciantes on about twenty-five acres. Historian John Baxter suggests that perhaps either the Cortez y Sisneros or the Lower McClure (Río Pueblo) ditch corresponded to the Acequia de la Isla. In 19th-century documents, La Isla refers to the promontory of land between the Ríos Lucero and Pueblo, just above their confluence (Baxter 1997:63). The Acequia Madre de la Loma headgate sits just above the north boundary of the Karavas Tract. This ditch crosses the tract to arrive at the base of the *loma* (hill), where it continues southwest, serving about twenty parciantes and 433 acres along another two miles. Below the Acequia Madre de la Loma sits the headgate to the South Loma Lateral, inside the southeast corner of the Karavas Tract, just above the southwest corner of the Pueblo league. This ditch is only about half a mile long, irrigating roughly sixty-five acres owned by ten parciantes. Some parciantes on these four ditches belong also to Río Pueblo acequias, including the Molino, the Sánchez, the Lovatos, and Los Molinos.

The Karavas Tract

Lapse in pueblo fulfillment of its obligations on the acequia madre has had dire consequences for the Karavas Tract, a large property located in Upper Ranchitos. The Karavas Tract encompasses the area between El Prado and Upper Ranchitos where the Río Lucero and the Río Pueblo flow together. Their confluence, including La Isla, is located inside the lower end of the tract. A significant number of ditches, not to mention frontage along both rivers, cross or border Karavas Tract land. These ditches include the Juan Manuel Lucero, Acequia Madre del Prado, Acequia del Medio, Acequia Madre de La Loma, and South Loma Lateral. The South Loma Lateral headgate sits just inside the reservation fence, and the Acequia Madre de La Loma headgate just outside.

The precise size, dimension, and plot inventory of the Karavas Tract remain a tangle of confusion in most people's minds, and its boundaries vary from map to map. I have been unable to locate a single, authoritative map of the tract. Gus García estimated the size of the tract to be 460 acres, but the 1942 warranty deed lists it as 773.786 acres.

The tract is named for two Greek brothers who came to Taos in the early 1900s and ran the Columbian Hotel and its successor, La Fonda Hotel, located on the south side of the Don Fernando de Taos plaza. In 1936 they acquired two adjacent pieces from Epimenio and Anna Martínez, land from the former Cristóbal Mares estate and the former Vicente Mares ranch. The brothers irrigated part of this land and used it to grow wheat, apparently *a medias* (sharecropped out to locals), in addition to growing produce for the hotel restaurant. In 1942 they sold the entire tract to the pueblo for $20,000.[11] The local story goes that the tribe gradually stopped farming and irrigating on the Karavas Tract, let it go fallow and become overgrown, and ceased to maintain the ditches. Later, the pueblo put wells on the land.

By the early 1970s, acequia madre commissioners were fed up with the pueblo's failure to help keep the ditch usable. They saw no need to continue maintaining the end of the ditch up to the Karavas Tract, because the pueblo had stopped paying dues and sending peones for the spring limpia. They rerouted the tail of the ditch eastward into a desagüe so that the acequia madre no longer reached into the Karavas Tract. Francis Quintana, whose land sits at the end of the acequia madre, told me that he gave the commissioners permission to drain the ditch into the desagüe just north of his property line.

Recently, the pueblo complained that its members cannot use the acequia madre to irrigate their land and requested that it be reopened for their use. Commissioners countered that the pueblo may own water rights but it has forfeited its ditch rights through disuse, nonmaintenance, and nonpayment of dues. Despite the large number of acequias that cross the Karavas Tract, parciantes say that the lands were irrigated only from the Acequia Madre del Prado and the Acequia del Medio and that the tract enjoyed only sobrantes on the latter. Commissioners on both these ditches insist that the Karavas Tract has forfeited its ditch rights on the acequia madre. The mayordomo and a commissioner on the Acequia Madre de La Loma likewise assert that the former Mares lands never had rights to their ditch.

Although unclear about the exact size or shape of the Karavas Tract, Ernesto Montoya does know the number of acres for which the tribe is assessed on the acequia madre:

> See, we have them assessed for 108 acres on our ditch, and I don't know how
> many acres they claim out there, because they have a bunch of acreage all
> through…I don't know exactly how much acreage they have in the Karavas
> Tract. [June 1997]

Showing me a letter the commission received from the pueblo in 1997 (dated April 9), which asserts that as a political subdivision of the state of New Mexico, the ditch association has "no authority or jurisdiction to assess ditch fees to Taos Pueblo," Ernesto commented:

> And I think that there's where they're wrong, because of the fact that they're
> using our ditches, okay, and we're not doing it on *their* ditch. We're doing it
> on *our* ditch, and they have water rights on our ditch, for that's the only thing
> that we are doing, just like any other peon. We are assessing them just like
> any other…I mean, any other parciante. [June 1997]

From the commissioners' standpoint, the pueblo wants it both ways: use of the acequias without being subject to their rules and obligations, by virtue of tribal sovereignty. The shiny new locks and chains on the headgates of the Río Lucero thwart tribal as much as non-Indian water thieves. Physical and symbolic measures taken on both sides to constrain the other's water use coexist with genuine cooperation and judiciously calculated gestures of mutual compliance. Recently, the pueblo started requiring ditch officers to carry permission forms in order to enter the Karavas Tract to tend the ditches. Parciantes say that they accede to this stricture "as a courtesy" but privately regard it as legally spurious because these ditches have always been theirs.

Custom and Drought

The ultimate test of the power of custom is drought. Old-timers agreed that the summer of 1996 was one of the driest in living memory, and it only grew worse in subsequent years. By early May, US Geological Survey computers showed that the cubic flow in the Rio Grande was one-tenth the normal amount for that time of year. There had been two major forest fires in the Río Arriba (one above San Cristóbal), and the air was yellow with dust devils. On June 3, ditch officials met with tribal representatives at the Taos Pueblo governor's office to work out a plan for water sharing on the Ríos Pueblo and Lucero under these dire conditions.

The acequia associations and the pueblo agreed on several points that demonstrate how living custom is tacitly understood and overtly practiced. First and foremost, they agreed to share the water as always, which is exactly what they ended up doing. They agreed at the outset that this drought summer was "not the time or place" to debate the legal decrees for these rivers but rather to work out the pragmatics of how they would share the sparse amount of water then in the river. They did not discuss instituting a system of priority calls that would automatically privilege the pueblo.[12] They did consider going to a two-day rotation of the water among the three Río Lucero communities, but as it turned out, they did not have to.

In the end, they simply followed the system already in place so that, ideally at least, everyone would suffer alike and no one would be denied. Toward this end, the pueblo decided for the first time to employ two monitors to oversee internal use and work with acequia mayordomos and commissioners to ensure that things went smoothly. The acequias and pueblo also agreed to cooperate on the installation of new culverts on Indian land to improve delivery of Río Lucero water.

Acequia officials saw the novel use of pueblo monitors as a positive sign of cooperation. Palemón Martínez, the president of the TVAA, also took it as evidence that the pueblo regulates internal water management less systematically than do the acequia associations:

> Well, the pueblo was the one that appointed some monitors, you know. We
> didn't change. We've always had a mayordomo and commission. But they
> never had one, and they appointed somebody to kind of oversee their opera-

tions and the total system to minimize problems. And I appreciate the fact
they did that.

Q: And these monitors were to monitor their internal system as well as their
external system in relation to the acequias?

PM: Well, they were to monitor the whole system and to make sure it
wasn't tinkered with, and how they managed, I don't know. The one recollection I have of walking the acequia with a Taos Pueblo official is that he was
interested in knowing how we operated in our system, the matter of assessments, and the monitoring of the water situation once it gets into our system.
So I got the impression that maybe he thought we may have some ideas that
he might use here, because their system apparently has been different, less
controlled, I think. [June 1997]

All suffered from the drought, some more than others, partly by virtue of their
location on the ditch. One Arroyo Seco grower reported that he lost about 80 percent
of his alfalfa crop. The loss meant that he ended up having to buy about 1,200 bales
of hay at $3.50 each to feed his cattle. Those who could not afford hay had to sell their
cows. There and in El Prado, mayordomos resorted to daily, ditch-by-ditch repartos.
Still, no one ever got enough water, and there were days when livestock in El Prado
went thirsty. Irrigators in Upper Ranchitos probably felt the least impact because of
the infusion from springs upstream in the Buffalo Pasture, although the amount of
water was less than usual. Because the water never reached that far, those at the end of
the ditch in Lower Colonias got none at all.

A predictable view in Arroyo Seco was that the pueblo ended up getting more
than its share, at Seco's expense, because the pueblo fills two diversions at the upper
headgate it controls and then it takes "another third" at the headgate for the acequia
madre. There were the usual incidents of unknown individuals cutting off the water
on Indian land to fish. Twice, they cut cables on the headgate, which the commissioners quickly replaced.

The drought of 1996 was likewise a test of the basic principles of water sharing
under extreme conditions on the lower river. During the drought year, Ernesto
Montoya took over as acting mayordomo of the acequia madre when his *primo* (cousin)
Augustín had to step down because of work demands at the Moly Mine in Questa.
Afterward, Ernesto reported on the state of the upper system and explained how he
handled his task as mayordomo:

> The Tenorio Tract ditch takes water *above* the compuerta, so they [the pueblo]
> were really taking water there. Actually, they're the only ones who had any
> fields to cut, because my people down here didn't have any. And then Arroyo
> Seco took their part of the river. It automatically goes to them. And by the
> time it got down over here [El Prado], all we had was water for…well, at the
> start of the season, we had for about, oh, I'd say eight or ten parciantes to

irrigate one irrigation for a few days. And I limited them to the time that they could irrigate.

The rest of the season, I concentrated on bringing water for the livestock and having a little water and tried to have as much water as possible on the ditches. And coming past Ben Wheeler, I put the water in there, and it wouldn't go, it just wouldn't go down. It didn't reach. It was just seepage. It just seeped down into the ground. It all went in. So I concentrated on having water in the Ciruelo, and in the Varoso, and also on having it in the Rivera because the Rivera ditch is where most of the cattle were. Because starting up on top, the pueblo had some horses up there in the pasture, and they didn't have any water. When they took it off, they didn't have any water. So I wanted to have water in that one for all those horses and all that. And then have water for the people I rented our pasture to and Mr. Rumsfeld—well, it wasn't Torrence. It was Mandy and Rumsfeld both. And then all the way down the acequia to the people that needed water for their livestock. So gardens, nothing. This year [the summer of 1997] is different. This year, there's *plenty* of water. [June 1997]

Ernesto acknowledges the pueblo take above the Arroyo Seco diversion on the Tenorio Tract, and his narrative illustrates the core principles at work in the living practice or custom of water sharing on the Río Lucero. To begin with, under conditions of extreme scarcity, water is allocated according to need, with priority given to livestock and then gardens. The mayordomo's concern that horses on tribal land also receive water through the Rivera Lateral highlights the centrality of need to the system's operation.

The crisis-induced appointment of two ditch monitors by the pueblo to assist the mayordomos in distributing the water in 1996 demonstrates that water sharing animates interaction between acequia associations and the pueblo and sketches the parameters within which such interaction takes place. The joint effort resulted in a novel situation in which the pueblo monitors protected the acequias against the usual renegade blockages improvised by youths fishing on tribal land. The acting mayordomo voiced his appreciation for the pueblo's cooperation during the drought:

The pueblo hired two what they call "ditch monitors." We call them "mayordomos." And these ditch monitors were Steve Archuleta and Tommy Lefthand, and they really helped me out there. It was really something that I was really appreciative to the pueblo for doing, because without them, I don't know how I would have done it. Because about four times we went up there and some of the people up there [above the Arroyo Seco headgate] had blocked the river completely, completely blocked it. And about three or four times they helped me to take off that blockage. And finally, Mr. Lefthand just got so doggone mad that he took a bulldozer, and up at where we call the picnic grounds, he took that blockage off and made it permanent that they wouldn't be able to cut it off anymore. And I think these were youngsters or somebody that was trying to fish or something and get the fish out of the river. But it still caused a lot of big problems. [June 1997]

Ernesto summarized their mutual accomplishment and then, like other parciantes, remarked that the pueblo seems to have no established system for allocating and monitoring irrigation water on tribal land:

> Well, we tried to make it fair, especially having Steve and Tommy help me monitor it and taking off those blockages and everything. But they understand now the way that we do our sharing in our ditch, and they were going to see if they would implement it in theirs. Because I understand that at the pueblo anybody that wants water goes and gets it, or whatever.... There is no system or mayordomo. There wasn't anybody till last year. [June 1997]

Startling or unlikely as this presumption may seem, it might shed some light on the discrepant and contradictory record of acequia-pueblo relations on the Río Lucero. On the one hand, the pueblo claims in writing neither to participate in nor to be subject to acequia law and custom. On the other hand, the governor's office does, in fact, participate in established practices and principles of water sharing, division, and allocation with the acequias along Río Pueblo tributaries. This contradiction suggests that the pueblo operates according to its own method of dividing and distributing irrigation water inside tribal boundaries. At the same time, it has a sporadic history of accord with acequia customs, rules, and principles when dealing with neighboring communities and ditch officers. The pueblo's fluctuating participation on the acequia madre and Acequia del Medio reflects how its allegiance to both internal and external systems is situationally responsive to opportunity and risk. Taos Pueblo's short- *and* long-term survival strategies always require a fluid mix of resistance and opposition, cooperation and conformity. These long-standing yet constantly renegotiated agreements and associated diversion structures together constitute the very means by which Taos Pueblo and its neighbors have managed to survive four centuries of competition and coexistence. Without these agreements, practices, or customs and the physical structures that concretize them, no multicommunity of villages would have evolved along the tributaries of the Río Pueblo and Rio Grande during the 17th, 18th, and 19th centuries. Without their ongoing operation, there would be no Taos as we know it.

Conclusion

Several findings emerge from this bittersweet story of how water is shared on the Río Lucero. Like the Río Pueblo repartos, this system seems a hybrid of Syrian (proportional) and Yemenite (rotational) models. A theoretically fixed, three-way, proportional partition among Taos Pueblo, Arroyo Seco, and El Prado divides the river as a whole. Yet within each local acequia system, the rotational model obtains, on either a regular or scarcity-determined basis. Some places depend on sobrantes, yet all must conform to ditch rules. In emergencies, one may ask for an auxilio. When there is not enough to go around, water goes first to animals, then to vegetable gardens and orchards. These rules evoke the Islamic Right of Thirst and Right of Irrigation.[13]

Pueblo-acequia conflict in the upper watershed is over how much water Arroyo Seco gets—not, significantly, over whether it gets any at all. El Prado likewise chafes under the loss of water it believes should come to it. On the middle ditches of the Acequia Madre del Prado and the Acequia del Medio, acequia-pueblo dispute arises over the pueblo's failure to comply with acequia rules. Here, pueblo and acequia irrigation associations seem to operate according to different sets of rules and obligations. In some instances, their interaction goes smoothly, for example, on the Acequia Madre del Río Pueblo, where tribal and acequia ditch-cleaning crews work up to their common boundary and everyone accepts the three/four-day division. As another example, the pueblo hired special monitors to oversee its Río Lucero ditches during the drought. At other times, pueblo-acequia cooperation breaks down, as on the Karavas Tract.

The division and allocation of water under all possible conditions (abundance, "normal" limited flow, extreme scarcity) follow a set of clearly understood, well articulated, universally agreed-upon principles. Individual temperament and situational variation notwithstanding, the guiding principle at work here, as well as on the Río Pueblo, is that no one must go entirely without as long as there is any at all to be had.

"When [the flow] is low, nobody has any. When it's high, everybody has some. That's the way it was too. If there's a cup of water there, we will share it" (*State of New Mexico v. Eduardo Abeyta and Celso Arellano et al.*, testimony of Esequiel Trujillo, transcript, May 20, 1991, 233). These simple words express a moral economy of water adapted to a specific place. The tripartite division of the Río Lucero exemplifies for some scholars the interaction between custom and law, as well as a fundamental principle of water allocation in Spanish colonial and Mexican New Mexico.[14] The repartos on the Río Lucero and Río Pueblo offer lessons about how to balance the needs of individual communities for a limited but shared resource, based on the principle of equity. The relationship between what people say that they (should) do and what they actually do may not be conscious or problematic to the actors in question, but it tells the ethnographer something about how they put ideals into daily practice. Therefore, the ethic of water sharing shapes far more in the lives of parciantes than simply the way they manage irrigation water.

part two

RESPETO

f i v e
Respeto and Moral Economy

Honor, therefore, provides a nexus between the ideals of a society and their reproduction in the individual through his aspiration to personify them.

—*Pitt-Rivers*, "Honor and Shame"

An old custom among Nuevomexicanos, less practiced today but still known to the post–World War II generation, involves an adult requesting a drink of water from someone younger, typically a child. The spoken request is, "Hijo [or Hija], tráeme agua" [Child, bring me water]. The youth is supposed to stop whatever he or she is doing, obediently fetch a glass or cup of water, and stand attentively before the elder, arms folded, until the vessel is drained and handed back. The elder then blesses the junior. Those familiar with this practice often comment that it has become rare, because as everyone knows, young people today "ya no tienen respeto" or "les falta respeto"; they lack this kind of respectful attitude. Nonetheless, responding to a request for water in such a manner is still considered the hallmark of good upbringing and of proper comportment between juniors and seniors and among peers. This custom and the ideal it embodies illustrate that aridity, reverence for water, and a patriarchal, risk-aversive moral economy are connected in Nuevomexicano culture.

I defined moral economy earlier as a system of principles and values that supports and guides cooperative, interdependent economic practice. E. P. Thompson (1963) coined the term in his monumental history of the transformation of the English peasantry into the working class. Political scientist James Scott (1976) elaborated on the concept in his study of why peasants in Southeast Asia might or might not rebel. Scott was interested in how the peasant subsistence ethic, as part of a risk-averse adaptation to conditions of scarcity, might give rise to rebellious sentiment or action under certain circumstances. The relationship between moral economy—or its violation—and themes of resistance emerge in the final chapter. Anthropologist Paul Trawick, drawing on fieldwork among indigenous irrigators in the Peruvian Andes, defines the moral economy of water as follows:

> A concrete ethic based on a well-defined set of practices, rules, and norms, and corresponding material relations. These have to do with the proper use of vital resources—land, water, and labor—and the ways that individuals should relate to each other, through the central reality of work, and to the community as a whole. Although the moral economy is inward-looking, focused on internal social interaction, it is also a "political" economy, as any such ethical system must be by definition, and of course it does not exist in isolation. [Trawick 2003:292]

Parciantes construct the social meaning and purpose of their lives as members of a community out of sacred and secular acequia practices. This community identifies itself as historically continuous, genealogically connected, territorially placed, and socially enacted through the interrelated practices of irrigation, ditch management, water sharing, reciprocity, and religious celebration. Ritual observances (*funciónes*) are woven into a larger cultural fabric. This culture is a dynamic, ever-changing process or field, not a static, bounded, or finite entity. It is a process whereby the ditch-based population inscribes itself, through time, upon the topography or landscape of the Taos basin. It is a process that produces local subjects and shapes them into moral subjects. The ditches and the practices that maintain their functionality and communal meaning represent the historical process through which the natural topography becomes a cultural landscape. Religious teachings and rituals are parallel processes through which children learn moral comportment and gain membership in a devotional community.

The idea of *respeto* surfaces often in conversations about acequia and religious matters, as well as other aspects of everyday life. Like ditch cleaning, the novena (described in chapter 6) serves as a venue for inculcating key values, such as respeto, through the custom of *la bendición* (blessing). Today, it is clear that adults' old-style authoritarian power over children is a thing of the past—to the regret of elders but the relief of the young. Although children at the San Isidro novena in Las Córdovas complied with the practice of kneeling to be blessed and kissing the hand of an adult, their embarrassment was often acutely apparent.

Virtually none of my midlife generation practices the once routine bendición except on special occasions like the novena. One *viejita*, watching children slouch around on armchairs before the prayers began, remarked that in the old days they would not have dreamed of taking a chair before every adult was seated. Indeed, many older individuals display a distinctive type of reserve and politeness; the rare younger person who does so is said to be raised "in the old way." This demeanor embodies the normative ideal of respeto or personal honor.

Agnes García, who is younger than I, is unmistakably such a person. When I asked Aggie what respeto means to her, she paused, then said that respeto is something she connects to her grandparents and to being on the land, farming it, and honoring God the way her ancestors did. Agnes and her husband, Andy, have served as mayordomos for the novena of San Isidro three times, including the year I attended (1996). They are doing so again in 2006. Her family is very active in the St. Francis parish and the San Isidro tradition in Los Córdovas. Although Andy and she are not farmers and both have jobs in town, their fathers are irrigators involved with their respective acequia associations. Indeed, Andy's father is Gus García, the commissioner of the Acequia del Medio who escorted me through the middle Río Lucero watershed and wondered aloud whether there had been a master plan for the Taos Valley acequia system. Gus has worked for many years as a baker at a popular downtown restaurant. Like other parciante-parishioners, the Garcías negotiate a daily world that spans the local, emplaced parish and the electronic, postmodern city.

The parciante moral economy represents a northern New Mexican variant of what anthropologists call the Circum-Mediterranean Honor-Shame Complex. Introduced by Julian Pitt-Rivers in his ethnography of an Andalusian town, *People of the Sierra* (1971; also see 1966), the honor-shame complex has been the subject of many scholarly conferences, volumes, and recent critiques.[1] The honor-shame complex also lies at the heart of Ramón Gutiérrez's (1991) analysis of social inequality in 18th-century colonial New Mexico. Proponents consider honor-shame diagnostic of a circum-Mediterranean culture complex that encompasses Christian and Muslim variants, whereas critics deconstruct regionalism as either a strategy or an artifact of containment.

Honor refers to the social worth of a person and is analytically differentiated into two kinds, honor-status and honor-virtue. *Honor-status* refers to social standing by virtue of birth; *honor-virtue* refers to personal comportment. An individual's honor and social worth are measured according to these two axes of value. Honor is gendered and can be described as a system of social reproduction based on male control over female sexuality. The honor of men in this system depends on the chastity of women. The infamous double standard results: men compete for honor, and women, as its embodiment, are subordinated and sequestered. Honor-status differentiates people vertically through gender, class, and ethno-racial caste. In both the Iberian and colonial Latin American contexts, its epitome was *limpieza de sangre* (purity of blood). Honor-virtue differentiates individuals horizontally within a moral community. Whereas honor-status serves to stratify men and women, honor-virtue equalizes the morally deserving (Pitt-Rivers 1966; Gutiérrez 1984).

The absence or loss of honor is shame. Shame is both anathema and integral to the maintenance of honor. In New Mexico and probably northern Mexico, the key native constructs in this system are *respeto* and *vergüenza* (shame, disgrace, modesty). English translation does not convey the full, nuanced range of meanings connoted by these two terms. An honorable man shows respeto for others and, in turn, deserves respeto from those who know him. Only by having an internalized sense of vergüenza can he avoid shameful behavior and thereby preserve his honor and receive respect. Respeto is central to one's sense of dignity and worth. It is both a personal and a public virtue, and its embodiment is always gendered.

Sociologist and Mora native Facundo Valdez (1979) describes the vergüenza concept in northern New Mexico in terms of ideal male conduct. According to Valdez, the ideal man in rural northern New Mexico is helpful to his neighbors, is moderate and self-controlled, and has *firmeza*. A combination of traits, firmeza indicates that a man is reserved, independent, trustworthy, and willing to challenge capricious or arbitrary authority (Valdez 1979:100–101). He is stoic, reliable, and strong.[2] Most significantly, the cornerstone of this ideal is the ownership of land:

> Let us set up, as an ideal type, a man *con mucha vergüenza*. He is a rancher and a farmer who owns his own land, and rights to common land. In the traditional village there are not many other occupations available, and in ranching and farming a man is his own master, who neither is dependent on a boss nor taking advantage of others as a merchant or someone else providing services. He would feel that working for wages was demeaning. It is not that he objects to working for others, but his attitude toward such work is, *es difícil trabajar por otro* [it is hard to work for others]. It is better to exchange labor between two independent landowners. [Valdez 1979:100]

This construct poses a balance between vertical and horizontal differentiation. On the one hand, land ownership amounts to a class division; on the other, rights to common land, or membership on a ditch, imply egalitarian and communitarian values. This balance, and the tension it entails between individual autonomy and community cohesion, is a pivotal theme of rural Hispano life. One must own land with water rights to be a parciante. Households and individual holdings are linked through kinship, the acequias, ejido lands, and collective religious practice. These activities and the principles they enact simultaneously divide and unite people. They create an inside and an outside, prescribing norms by which internal and external distinctions are sustained. For the interval of its duration, religious ritual symbolically resolves these distinctions and their underlying contradictions.

Rather than exaggerate a Mediterranean source for local norms of intergenerational respect, let me note that the custom of asking a junior for water is also practiced in some Indian pueblos, including Taos, Laguna, and Santa Clara. At Taos Pueblo, a child's traditional household duty is to fetch water for his or her elders from the river that flows through the heart of the village. Dining one evening in town with me and other friends, a 34-year-old woman who was raised by her grandparents at Taos Pueblo referred to the custom in passing. She described exactly the same routine, down to waiting with folded arms until the cup is drained. The elder's request, she said, is always for "real" water, meaning the water that flows from Blue Lake.

Anthropologist Elsie Clews Parsons (1991:75) describes the same custom at Laguna Pueblo, noting that when handing back the vessel to the junior, the senior says, "Shetunii" [May you grow tall], and the junior responds, "Tauwa" [Good, i.e., Thanks]. Colleague and Santa Clara Pueblo native Beverly Singer confirms this practice and relates it to the custom of kneeling before an elder for a blessing. Ethnographer Deidre Sklar (2001:75) mentions a variant of this custom among Mexican Americans in Tortugas, New Mexico, not far from the US-Mexican border.

To further complicate the question of origin, a colleague, Mohamed Ali, who teaches Arabic at the University of New Mexico, tells me that this custom is universal in Muslim culture, where it may occur not only between an elder and a junior but also between any two people. Such a request must always be honored, and the spoken blessing that goes with it is mutual (personal communication, August 8, 10, 2005). One historian offers a solution: "In the Southwest Borderlands, diverse social traditions of honor and shame, of violence, kinship, and community met, merged, and regenerated in new expressions" (Brooks 2002:9–10).[3] Still, the more answerable, important question is not whence this practice diffused, but rather why it exists among such diverse peoples, who nevertheless have one thing in common: they all dwell in arid or semiarid environments.

Anthropologists theoretically associate an honor-shame moral economy with a larger political economy of scarcity. Drawing on fieldwork in Sicily, Jane Schneider pinpoints this connection:

> The problem of honor becomes salient when the group is threatened with
> competition from equivalent groups. It is especially salient when small, partic-
> ularistic groups, such as families, clans, or gangs, are the principal units of
> power, sovereign or nearly so over the territories they control. Concern for
> honor also grows when contested resources are subject to redivision along
> changing lines, when there is no stable relationship between units of power
> and precisely delineated patrimonies, i.e., when the determination of boundary
> lines is subject to continual human intervention.[4] [Schneider 1971:2]

The New Mexican context has always been one of scarcity. Water scarcity or aridity set the environmental parameters within which subsistence farming and pastoralism could take root and flourish in the Upper Rio Grande Valley. Societies that survived in this setting adapted by devising ways to capture, preserve, and organize access to water. These techniques and practices were sustained by a moral economy and religious worldview. Even though the Old World provenance of acequia organization is certain, indigenous and Iberian water-management traditions flowed together on the colonial frontier in ways that preclude the tracing of some elements to one or the other source.

Whereas honor-status determines one's position within the social order, including family and community, honor-virtue (or respeto) is always a matter of individual, personal comportment. Moral and religious instruction, as well as everyday secular practices, produces individual subjects. Local subjects are produced also through practices of place. Place making is a process whereby "feelings of belonging to an imagined community bind identity to spatial location" (Gupta 2003:321).

Place making involves both narrative and practice, or words and deeds (Gray 2003:227). Drawing on critic Raymond Williams's (1977) concept, anthropologist Arjun Appadurai (1995:204) calls it the production of locality as a structure of feeling. This process involves not only the inscription of a situated community upon a particular locality but also "the inscription of locality onto bodies, or the production of local subjects" (Appadurai 1995:205). Seen in these terms, secular practices such as irrigation, water sharing, and acequia maintenance, in addition to religious practices such as the novena or processions (which I examine next), "are ways to embody locality as well as to locate bodies in socially and spatially defined communities" (Appadurai 1995:205).

s i x
Honoring San Isidro

Oh, they still believe in that. They still believe in their, well, it's part of their religion and…San Isidro is the patron saint. Even though he's not, he might not be, the patron saint for as much agriculture, he is still remembered as the patron saint of all workers. And we might not be working farms and fields as much, but we're doing many other things, you know. These days we're doing carpentry more. We're doing more construction, plumbing, electrical, you know. That's all labor, and he's the patron saint of all those people.

—*Gabriel Chávez*

The connection between secular acequia practice and religion is that religion, in the form of doctrinal belief and community ritual, is what keeps many people going. Family and parish locate every individual, and repeated acts of procession, like repeated acts of irrigation, identify a people and tie them to their place. In the town and surrounding placitas, Taoseños engage in a constant round of saints' days and other holy days in the Catholic calendar. Ritual participation is both personal and public. It openly commits the individual to a devotional community and to the church.

Each of the communities in Taos that predate the American era identifies itself in terms of its patronal chapel, camposanto, morada, acequias, fields, and procession routes. In some cases, local identity also includes a land grant.[1] My focus here is on the celebration of San Isidro performed in Los Córdovas. The chapel, Capilla de San Isidro, belongs to the St. Francis parish, which is more or less coextensive with the Río Grande del Rancho watershed. Los Córdovas is the lowest placita on the river, located just above its confluence with the Río Pueblo. It also sits just below confluence with the Río Pueblo of three more streams: the Fernando, Lucero, and Arroyo Seco.

The Los Córdovas celebration is of interest for several reasons. In Catholic iconography, San Isidro Labrador appears as a man guiding an ox-drawn plow with an angel at his shoulder; alternatively, the angel is doing the plowing (plate 11). Devotees take a saint as a protector and a spiritual role model. Because San Isidro is the patron saint of farming, the feast day celebration held in his honor reveals how parciantes are equally parishioners. The texts of the hymns and prayers give eloquent voice to the moral economy by which local Catholics believe that they should live. These precepts also guide irrigation practices and water sharing.

Seventy-four-year-old Candido Valerio is the mayordomo of the Tío Gervacio and Los Córdovas #1 ditches. His wife, Anita, belongs to the extended family that owned the original *oratorio* (oratory or private place for prayer) *de San Isidro*. They have served as mayordomos of the chapel several times. Candido explained the San Isidro tradition simply: "Well, it's a tradition that has gone on for many, many years. And I think it will keep us together. I think it will help us understand each other and, I think, live peacefully" (May 1996).

San Isidro and Los Córdovas

Los Córdovas has celebrated the feast day of San Isidro on May 15 for as long as anyone can remember. Sixty-four-year-old Gabriel Chávez, who irrigates off the Río Pueblo in Los Córdovas using the Anderson–Spring–Drake ditch, explained why he and his neighbors continue to celebrate the patron saint of farming:

> That's what I believe in. That's the way I was brought up, and I consider it to be very valuable to my heritage and myself, you know. It's part of me. I traveled. I was away for a long time, but it's never left me. It's always remained a part of me. And I consider that whatever success I had in my career, I had it because of my upbringing in this regard. I believe in it. It does me a lot of good. [May 1996]

A career air force retiree, Gabriel has participated in novenas and other parish funciónes and has served as mayordomo in both the chapel and the main church (St. Francis de Assisi in Ranchos). He continued:

> The fact that they went out and paraded their patron saint through their fields, and all that was just a reflection of their belief in, well, their belief in their God and religion and Christ. And that nothing was going to get done without that belief, you know. And I believe that's why. And it's still done. Yeah, we still take our patron saint out through the fields. [May 1996]

May is the month when farmers prepare their fields for cultivation, and some parciantes are still involved in the annual cleaning of their acequias. May is also the month of Mary, a time of intense religious activity for Catholics. Within the same parish, in the neighboring community of Llano Quemado, people hold rosaries throughout May in the Chapel of Nuestra Señora del Carmen. Observances to the Virgin occur in other parishes as well. For Mother's Day, May 12, 1996, the Guadalupanas (a women's prayer group devoted to the Virgin of Guadalupe) rose at 3:00 a.m. to begin the 17-mile pilgrimage from the village of Las Trampas to the Santuario de

Figure 6.1. San Isidro, Patron Saint of Farmers, by Horacio Valdez. Reproduced by permission of Vincente Martinez. Photograph © Sylvia Rodríguez.

Chimayó. About three hundred people from all over the state participated, including individuals active in the San Isidro novena in Los Córdovas. Forty-five-year-old María Medina made the walk and then rushed back to attend the novena. A few days later, she and her husband, Joe, hosted an evening of novena prayers at their home.

Several extended families are active in and closely identified with the Los Córdovas San Isidro tradition. All include active parciantes. Mayordomos of the acequia come from more or less the same families as mayordomos for the parish, so the same families who irrigate are those who carry the saints in procession along the fields, ditches, and circuits to sacred sites. Occasionally, the roles of acequia mayordomo and parish mayordomo are concurrently filled by the same individual. Usually, though, this is not the case because both jobs are so demanding.

Institutional distinctions exist between these two kinds of mayordomos. The mayordomo of the acequia is elected annually by parciantes along an acequia madre, and the same individual may fill the role for many consecutive years. Parish mayordomos volunteer for a year, usually dating from the feast day of their local church or chapel's patron saint. The parish mayordomos are often a married couple and perform their duties as a pair. Throughout the year, they tend their own chapel and serve in the mother church or parish seat, rotating with mayordomos from other chapels in the parish. Not unlike service on the ditch, being a mayordomo in the church involves responsibility and sacrifice that confer authority during the year of service and enhanced status afterward. Lifelong parishioners may end up serving as church mayordomos more than once, at intervals of several years.

Mayordomos for the San Isidro chapel maintain the premises year-round and assume primary responsibility for organizing the feast day celebration, which requires much work and some expense. They clean the chapel, tend the saints' statues, prepare the altars, and organize the vespers, processions, and mass, as well as the nine-day lineup of hosts (including themselves) for the novena. They print and distribute the song and prayer booklets and take care of the countless other details involved. In 1996 two married couples in their forties, Mabel and Steve Pacheco and Agnes and Andy García, were serving as junior and senior chapel mayordomos. Also involved were their children, parents, and other kin. Their term of office had begun the preceding Día de San Isidro and was to end on the evening of May 15, 1996.

The "new" Chapel of San Isidro, located on Road 240 between Los Córdovas and Cordillera, was built in 1951 by community labor on a plot of privately donated land. It is a modest, flat-roofed, brown-stucco building surrounded by pastureland. The altar holds two *bultos* (statues) of San Isidro, as well as statues of other parish saints. On the inside back wall of the chapel hang more than 70 plaques bearing the names of all the mayordomos who have served over the years, going back to the construction of the building. Mass is held every third Thursday in the San Isidro chapel.

Before 1951 the celebration took place in a private family oratorio located inside a corner of the original enclosed placita of Los Córdovas, roughly a mile to the southwest. Candido and Anita Valerio recall that because people prayed the rosary every day during the months of May and June, there was no novena, just a morning mass, an evening procession, and a community fiesta.[2] Joseph Krumgold's children's book, *And Now Miguel* (1953), depicted this fiesta and later became the basis for a Cold War–era State Department film of the same title, starring some of the people of Los Córdovas. Because the oratorio hosted a parish function, the Catholic Church sought to claim the property. Anita's family was faced with the choice of either closing the oratorio to community use or surrendering it to the church, so the community built a new chapel.

Today, the celebration involves a novena that culminates on the feast day with an evening mass in the chapel and a procession of the saint's bulto along the road to bless the fields. A vespers (*vísperas*, an evening prayer service) and procession may be held at the chapel on the penultimate night as well. According to Corina Santistevan from Cordillera, a lifelong participant in her seventies:

We always have a novena for nine days before the fifteenth of May. We usually have it at different homes of the different members of the parish and particularly of the community of Los Córdovas and Cordillera. They host the novena for one night. And then we have San Isidro stay with us at night. And the next night, he goes to another home to be honored and to be there for the novena the next night. And that continues for nine nights. The tenth night, of course, we celebrate in the Chapel of San Isidro, in between Los Córdovas and Cordillera. [Personal communication with the author, April 1996]

Parishioners host the evening prayer sessions in their homes and serve a buffet dinner to the congregation afterward. Each host family keeps a chapel bulto of San Isidro for a night and a day and then transports the saint to the next household. Feloníz Trujillo, Corina's neighbor and also a lifelong participant in her seventies, helped lead the novena prayers for many years with her husband, Ruben, who is now buried next to the chapel, right across the road from their home. She explained:

Yeah, well, nine days before the fiesta, we pray the novena each night. We get together in different houses, each one. They offer the homes for that. And we go to different houses. My husband and I pray[ed] the novena for them for 12 years before he died. And we go to the mayordomos. We go to different people. I've had it here at home a lot of times too. And then the last day, we pray it for eight days out, I mean, that's nine days. Then the vísperas we do here in the church. That's the day of the novena.

We get together at the church, and then we go out in the procession with the santos on San Isidro's eve. And then the day of the fiesta. The years before, they used to celebrate the mass in the morning about 10, 11 the latest. But now they always do it in the evening 'cause a lot of the time the mayordomos, a lot of the people work, you know. Almost everybody nowadays work[s], so they do it in the evening and it's real nice.

We also go out in procession and the mayordomos are honored, the outgoing mayordomos and the incoming mayordomos. They present a gift to Father and to the Sisters or to whoever helps, to the "prayors," you know, the ones that pray the novena and all that. They always presented us with a little something. It was, it's nice. I like it. I like it a lot. I didn't do it last year. My heart was too broken to do it. I had just lost my husband, and it was bad. And it's been sad. So I don't know. [Personal communication with the author, April 1996]

Feloníz described how long the prayer sessions lasted:

Maybe about half an hour to pray it, and the singing and all that, and then we ask, you know, the intercessions. We ask for God to bless the people that offer their home, and we ask for all the people who have died, and things like that. And then they sing the San Isidro song, and that's it. And then we just get together and have a party, have the eats. Some houses, they go all aboard. They go more than others. [April 1996]

The 1996 Novena

The 1996 novena began on Wednesday, May 8, and concluded on Saturday evening, May 18. It lasted an extra day, I was told, because the visiting priest was available to conduct the mass only on Saturday the 18th. On each of the nine evenings of the novena, a prayer session of roughly 40 minutes followed by a potluck buffet dinner was held at a different home between 6:00 and 8:30. Vísperas on the tenth evening and mass on the eleventh took place in the chapel, with processions from there on both nights.

During the celebration, participants used two bultos of San Isidro, both residing in the chapel: an older, raw-cedar statue that shows an angel looming large to the right of San Isidro at his plow and, gessoed and painted, a newer statue that shows the angel plowing to the left of a much larger San Isidro. The celebrants took these bultos out of the chapel on the first day and housed them for 24 hours at the home of each host family. Each night after the service, the new hosts transported the bultos to their home, where the family prepared an altar with candles to be used the following evening. On the final evenings, the saints returned to the chapel for the vísperas and the mass, where they were *entregados* (handed over) from the outgoing to the incoming mayordomos. A tradition not observed that year was the *limosna*, a ritual in which the mayordomos go door to door asking each household for *seis reales* (about 75 cents) to help pay for the mass.

The mass was followed by the *entrega*, or *entriega del santo*, a ritual procedure in which the outgoing mayordomos hand over the saint to the incoming mayordomos. This occurred inside the chapel, where the two couples walked toward each other along the aisle. They met, and the old mayordomos gave the saint to the new ones and placed medals around their necks. In turn, the old mayordomos received little *retablos*, which are two-dimensional reproductions of San Isidro. The entrega was sung throughout.

On the 10th and 11th nights came the procession. It emerged from the chapel and went along the road perhaps a quarter of a mile to the east of the chapel on the tenth night and about the same distance west on the last night before returning to its starting place. Each night, an altar girl and boy alternated in leading the procession, bearing a cross. The senior mayordomos carried the modern painted bulto of San Isidro, followed by the junior or novice mayordomos carrying a banner inscribed with "San Isidro Labrador de Cordillera," the neighboring community where they live. Next came the two pairs of incoming mayordomos carrying bultos of San Francisco and the Virgin. Family and community members followed, singing *alabanzas* (hymns of praise) and praying. A priest swung a censer and chanted alongside them (plate 10).

A combination of formal ritual, informal conviviality, and commensality marked each evening session. The mood gained intensity over the ten-day period. At moments, a petitioner would be overcome by emotion, for example, during prayers *del hogar* (for the home). Overall, a warm, upbeat mood of Christian community and mutual engagement accompanied the serious business of group devotional practice. The event generated its own momentum.

The spring of 1996 was extremely dry and windy, and the region was plagued by wildfires that filled the air with dust devils and acrid yellow smoke. The San Cristóbal (or Lama) fire started on May 5 and burned throughout the novena. Everyone was worried about the fires and drought. These difficult conditions were a frequent topic of conversation, and parishioners and clergy offered many special prayers for rain.

Devotional Community

Each person who participated in any aspect of the celebration was known to the others and embedded within larger kinship networks that extend through Taos and beyond. Almost all the families who hosted an evening prayer and meal were related by blood or marriage (or both) and were also neighbors. They came from communities on the Río Grande del Rancho and from the nearby Río Fernando and Río Pueblo watersheds; the waters of all three flow together not far from Los Córdovas. About two hundred people actively participated in these events.

The evening groups ranged from a dozen adults and eight children to more than twenty adults and a dozen children. On most nights, one or two parish nuns also participated, and one evening the popular young priest from the Holy Trinity parish, Father Vincent, attended. Parishioners from neighboring communities might come to one or two sessions. On the final night for the mass, it was standing-room only in the chapel.

Depending on who the mayordomos are, a different combination of personal kin networks are activated in any given year. In 1996 the senior mayordoma, Agnes García, her parents, Agapita and Tony Santistevan, her sister Sylvia Torrez, and her cousin Corina Santistevan hosted on four of the nine nights. Sylvia, who lives next door to Aggie, hosted the first night of the novena. Aggie's elder prima (female cousin), Corina, a leader in local parish/watershed traditions who led the prayers, hosted on the third night. Aggie and her husband, Andy, were hosts on the fourth night, and her parents hosted on night six.

Doña Corina, whose account of the novena appears above, took charge of lay liturgical aspects of the celebration, including selection of the hymns and prayers, and supervised their proper execution during the prayer services. Her 91-year-old brother-in-law Polito Valerio, now deceased, mentioned to me almost in passing that the novena was largely a women's concern. Perhaps this circumstance relates to Aggie and Sylvia's claim that mayordomas frequently become pregnant during their year of service. Indeed, Aggie's second son was born on Día de San Isidro during her preceding time as mayordoma.

Candido and Anita Valerio hosted the fifth night of the novena. Prominent in the extended custodial network of this tradition, Anita's family of origin, the Chávezes, was featured in the 1950s children's book and film *And Now Miguel*. Mayordomos from the preceding year hosted on the eighth night. Many men in these parish families have served as ditch officers over the years and still do, just as some belong to the moradas in Ranchos or Talpa.

All but one session took place in Los Córdovas or neighboring Ranchitos. The community of participation exhibits extreme social density because the people involved are interrelated in multiple ways through time. But it is not exclusive. The single novena session held outside the Río Grande del Rancho watershed took place in Cañon, at the home of an Anglo couple, Leslie and Skip Pedlar. Members of the St. Francis parish, they were scheduled to serve as the incoming junior mayordomos for the coming year.

The 1996 Novena Prayers and Hymns

The booklet or missal prepared by Doña Corina and distributed and collected again each evening lists 15 prayers and hymns for the evening service. All adults and older children alternately stood and kneeled in a circle around the home altar, where the two bultos of San Isidro stood with a few flowers and one or two lighted candles. The altar was usually set up on a coffee table in the center of the living room. People knelt to pray and stood to sing. Kneeling during roughly half of the prayer service is hard on the knees, depending on how much carpeting covers the floor. The repetitive shift between kneeling and standing is especially taxing on older individuals, who are nonetheless the most devoted kneelers. Before and after the prayer service, people sat around informally in chairs and couches, chatting, eating the buffet dinner.

Throughout the 11-day event, Doña Corina played a directive role in overseeing and explaining the protocol. She advised the mayordomos in arranging for the processions and mass. On the first few nights, she opened the service with a tale from the life of San Isidro or about his patronage of Los Córdovas. She invited special prayers and encouraged continuous prayer. On the tenth night, she spoke briefly from the pulpit in the chapel. I entered the circle through Doña Corina's tacit sponsorship.[3] Her interpretation informs mine below because she guided my participation and played a major role in selecting and transmitting the texts used in the novena.

The program outlined in the missal for each evening was as follows:

> Por la señal de la Santa Cruz (By the Sign of the Holy Cross)
>
> Abrid, Señor nuestros labios (Lord, Open Our Lips)
>
> Acto de Contrición (Act of Contrition)
>
> Tres Padres Nuestros, tres Ave Marías, Y tres Gloria al Padre (Three Our Fathers, three Hail Marys, three Glories to the Father)
>
> *Cántico—Santa Inez del Campo (Song to St. Agnes of the Fields)
>
> *Segundo Oración Diaria, Omnipotente Señor (Second daily prayer, All Powerful Lord)

*Gozos del Glorioso San Isidro (Verses of Glorious San Isidro)

*Cántico—Dios te Salve, Luna Hermosa (God Save You, Beautiful Moon)

Oración para el día Noveno (Prayer for day nine)

Tres Padres Nuestros, tres Ave Marías, Y tres Glorias al Padre Petición del
   Hogar (Prayer for the home)

Peticiónes de la Gente (People's prayers)

Bendición (Blessing)

*Alabanzas a San Isidro (Hymns of praise to Saint Isidore)

Each of these elements involved a collective speech event in which all adults (including me) prayed, sang, and read aloud from the missal. To illuminate key themes, I discuss only the five texts addressed to San Isidro and two female saints (indicated above by asterisks). Parishioners who recite prayers and sing hymns do not necessarily stop to ponder the deeper meanings of each and every word. Yet, through time, these messages do sink in. In addition to the clergy, lay specialists such as Doña Corina perform oral exegeses of such texts.[4]

The fourth prayer on the program, Oración de todos los días, dedicated to San Isidro, invokes the patron's grace to aid and bless the novena dedicated to his glory:

> Glorioso San Isidro Labrador, a quien Dios puso en este mundo, para que en el nos sirvieses de ejemplo de todas las virtudes, y en el cielo para que alli fueras nuestro patrón y venerado protector; alcansadme Señor, las gracia que os pido en esta novena, si es para gloria suya, honra vuestra y bién de mi alma, y si no, tal conformidad con la divina voluntad, que por medio de ella logre las felici-dades de la gloria, Amen. [Glorious San Isidro Labrador, whom God put in this world to serve as an example to us of all virtues, and in heaven so that there you will be our patron and revered protector; extend to me, Lord, the grace that I ask for in this novena, if it is for your glory, your honor, and the good of my soul, and if not, in obedience to divine will, by means of which achieve the joys of glory, amen.]

After three Our Fathers, three Hail Marys, and three Glories to the Father, all in Spanish, the participants sang a canto to Santa Inez. Doña Corina said that she picked this hymn for gender balance and because it praises Santa Inez *del Campo*, that is, of the field or country, the domain of irrigation and farming. She noted references to blessed rain and protection against storm phenomena.

Santa Inez del Campo	*Saint Agnes of the Field*
Tus milagros bellos	*Your beautiful miracles*
A los te aclaman	*Are acclaimed*
Ruega a Díos por ellos	*Pray to God for them*
Tus milagros bellos	*Your beautiful miracles*
A mil voces canto	*A thousand voices sing to*

Libra al que te aclama	Liberate who acclaims you
Santa Inez del Campo	Saint Agnes of the Field
Con solo tu nombre	At merely your name
El Demonio espanta	The Demon takes fright
Con tu gran poder	With your great power
Santa Inez del Campo	Saint Agnes of the Field
A los caminantes	Over the travelers
Cubres con tu manto	You cover with your cape
Y aclaman tu nombre	And they acclaim your name
Santa Inez del Campo	Saint Agnes of the Field
Gentiles y Fieles	Heathens and Believers
Te obedecen tanto	So obey you
Por ser Virgen Pura	For being a pure virgin
Santa Inez del Campo	Saint Agnes of the Field
En una cubierta	Under cover
De esa agua Santa	From this blessed water
Virten tus milagros	Your miracles spill forth
Santa Inez del Campo	Saint Agnes of the Field
Angeles y Santos	Angels and Saints
Que os merecen tanto	Who so deserve you
Son tus compañeros	Are your companions
Santa Inez del Campo	Saint Agnes of the Field
Aguaseros, truenos	Downpours, thunder
Los sujetas tanto	You subdue
Con tu gran poder	With your great power
Santa Inez del Campo	Saint Agnes of the Field[5]

Jesuit scholar Father Thomas Steele has this to say about the significance of Saint Agnes for New Mexican farmers and herders:

> Saint Agnes…is a sort of Diana figure, a patroness of purity and the outdoors, and especially of sheep and shepherds (because of the likeness of "Agnes" to the Latin word for lamb, agnus). Santa Inés is shown in santero art with some lambs in the background, and thus resembles Our Lady as a Shepherdess, Nuestra Señora como una Pastora. [Steele 1974:131]

Until recently, sheep herding was an important subsistence practice on the rich vega surrounding Los Córdovas. Note the reference to travelers or pilgrims and also to "heathens" and "believers," terms that suggest a chosen people identified in contrast to others who are not. Both are familiar themes in northern New Mexico. The protector chases away evil with her great power, and her devotees revere her for her purity. Santa Inés guards the purity of young girls. The norm of virginity aligns male control over female sexuality with the protection of class and ethno-religious boundaries. All these elements define the honor-shame complex or moral economy.

Next is a second Oración del Día addressed to the Lord, which mentions San Isidro. Then a devotional hymn titled, "Gozos del Glorioso San Isidro" (Verses in Praise of the Glorious Saint Isidore), is sung to the patron saint:

De un humilde Labrador	*Of a humble Laborer*
Implorémos esta día	*We this day implore*
Con la mas santa alegría	*With the holiest joy*
La intercesión y favor	*Your intercession and favor*
La caridad más ferviente	*Fervent charity*
Tu sencillo pecho inflama	*Inflames your innocent breast*
Y ardiendo en su pura llama	*And burning in your pure flame*
Al mundo fuiste ejemplar;	*For the world you were an example;*
Por eso el necesitado	*For this the needy*
Y el míserio desvalido	*And miserable helpless*
Acuden con su gemido	*Cry for help*
A la puerta de tu hogar	*At the door of your home*
Se los simples pajarillos	*The innocent little birds*
Carecen de su alimento	*Need your nourishment*
Suministras el sustento	*You provide the sustenance*
Que calma tan grave mal;	*That calms grave ill;*
Y si tu amo aquejado	*And if your master complains*
De sed, un día se ve	*Of thirst, one day will be seen*
Por tu oración y tu fé	*By your prayer and faith*
Brota fresca manantial	*A fresh spring burst forth*
De la oración mas perfecta	*Of the most perfect prayer*
Isidro, fuiste modelo	*You, Isidore, were a model*
Pos eso del alto cielo	*So from the highest heaven*
Recibiste el galardón;	*You received the reward;*
Y tu fé sencilla y pura	*And your simple and pure faith*
Con el mayor alborozo	*With the greatest delight*
Obtiene sacar del pozo	*Brings forth from the spring*
A tu hijo sin lesión	*To your unblemished son*

De la tierra y sus labores	*Of the earth and your labors*
Te llegas quizá a olvidar;	*You may forget;*
Más Providencia divina	*So that divine providence*
A quién tu plegaria sube	*To whom your prayer rises*
Remite alado querube	*Sends alongside you a cherub*
Para tu campo labrar	*To work your field*
En vano Satan agita	*In vain Satan agitates*
Las más perfidas pasiónes	*The most perfidious passions*
Pues en nobles corazones	*Because in noble hearts*
Nunca su fuego prendió;	*His fire never lights;*
Así pues tu Santa esposa	*Such is your blessed wife*
María de la Cabeza	*Maria de la Cabeza*
Por su virtud y pureza	*For her virtue and purity*
Como estrella aparecío	*She resembled a star*
Pues Dios premiando tu celo	*God rewarding your zeal*
Y tan viva caridad	*And such ardent charity*
En vista de tu humildad	*In sight of your humility*
Hasta el cielo te ansalzó;	*Hooked you to heaven;*
Sobre tu patria querida	*Above your beloved country*
Tiende benigna mirada	*A benevolent gaze extends*
Pues a tus plantas prostrada	*Prostrate before your plants*
Siempre tu ámparo invoco!	*I invoke your protection always!*

This text, along with the concluding alabanza, reveals the core meaning that San Isidro Labrador holds for Spanish-speaking farmers in northern New Mexico. It extolls the saint's charity, faith, purity, and humility, as well as his miraculous power to make a spring gush forth in time of drought. The hagiography of this beloved saint is as follows:

> St. Isidore was born near present-day Madrid, Spain, around 1070, and he died there in 1130. He is recognized as the city's patron saint. A humble agricultural laborer, St. Isidore is said to have neglected his duties in the fields in order to attend mass and to pray. An angel was thus sent to plow in his stead. [Briggs 1981:36]

San Isidro protects all farmers and field laborers. The hymn refers to several well-known events from his life, including God's sending the angel to help him plow. We will see below, however, that New Mexicans have their own extremely telling variant of this story. A miracle occurs when Isidro strikes his staff to the ground and a spring bursts forth. Another incident involves his mistrust of his wife, María de la Cabeza. She left the home each day allegedly to go pray. Suspicious, Isidro followed her one day

and was humbled to find her, indeed, transfixed in prayer. This event may be fc
tional to women's claims to the great outdoors and reveals the centrality of religious
observance to women's claims to authority.[6] The signature tale, depicted in all icons of
San Isidro, is the plowing incident.

In New Mexican versions, however, rather than Isidro's being too absorbed in
church to plow, it is the other way around. And the only divine admonition sufficient
to dissuade him from his labor is the threat of a bad neighbor. The following is a version recorded by anthropologist Charles Briggs in the village of Córdova less than 50
miles from Taos:

> He was very manly, a very good farmer, and he adored our Lord a great deal.
> One time it was Sunday, and his wife made him work. Once he was working,
> the Lord spoke to him, telling him that as it was Sunday he should not work.
> St. Isidore responded that he had to work. The voice then said that if St.
> Isidore did not stop working, God would send him hail. But St. Isidore said
> that he wasn't afraid of hail, that he was going to keep working. Then the
> voice spoke to him again, and said that if he didn't stop working, God was
> going to send him a plague of locusts. But St. Isidore was not afraid, and he
> kept working. Then the same voice spoke to him again, saying that if St.
> Isidore did not leave his work, God would send him a bad neighbor. St. Isidore
> replied that this he couldn't stand, and so he left his work and went to mass.
> When he returned from mass his wife was not angry, because an angel had
> planted his fields. You see, he wasn't afraid of a storm or a plague of locusts,
> but he couldn't stand a bad neighbor. [Briggs 1980:184]

Social relations, among immediate neighbors and between husband and wife,
weigh more heavily on the daily scale of survival than relations with the church or
perhaps even God. These are not abstract social relations; they involve everyday, face-
to-face interaction with people who depend on one another to survive. In this relation
of intimacy is a formality, a kind of honorable restraint or respeto. This ideal is not
unlike, these texts show, the personalistic relationship one has with a saint: intimate
yet regulated and reciprocal, wherein devotion elicits blessing and protection. Good
neighbors are everything in an arid land where no one rules with undisputed power
and where survival requires cooperation, especially to irrigate. Irrigation was the
supremely cooperative activity by which colonial settlement succeeded. It persists
today, perhaps no longer the economic mainstay but still at the heart of who people
are and of their connection to their land and to one another.

At the same time, the role of María de la Cabeza is striking. She is pious but prays
outdoors and, in the New Mexico version, makes Isidro work on Sunday. She is both
taskmaster and moral exemplar, a bit like Doña Corina. In the novena, the hymn to
San Isidro is immediately followed by Dios Te Salve Luna Hermosa (May God Save
You, Beautiful Moon):

Dios te salve, Luna Hermosa	God save you, beautiful moon
Dios te salve, Luz del Día	God save you, light of day
Dios te salve, Sol y Estrella	God save you, sun and star
Dios te salve, María	God save you, Maria
Los angeles en el cielo	The angels in heaven
Y los hombres en alabanza	And men in praise
Te invocan llenos de amor	Full of love invoke you
Virgen, llena eres de gracia	Virgin, full of grace
Muy rendidas a tus plantas	Surrendered to your plants
Reina, merced te pedimos	Queen, we pray for mercy
Cocédenos, Gran Señora	Grant us, Great Lady
Pues el Señor es contigo	For the Lord is with you
Más hermosa que la luna	More beautiful than the moon
Y más linda que sol eres	Prettier than the sun you are
Desde el principio del mundo	From the beginning of the world
Señora, bendita eres	Lady, you are blessed
Pues tu fuiste escojida	Since you were chosen
Virgen Sagrada, bien puedes	Holy Virgin, you can
Tenerte por la mejor	Be foremost
Entre todas las mujeres	Among women
Los ángeles y los santos	The angels and saints
Tengan gloria con gran gusto	Take glory and joy
En el nombre de Jesus	In the name of Jesus
Digamos, bendito el fruto	We say, blessed the fruit
Del oriente sale el sol	In the east the sun rises
Dando al mundo clara luz	Giving clear light to the world
De tu boca nace el alba	From your mouth the dawn is born
Y de tu vientre Jesús	And Jesus from your womb
Quién dichoso merciera	What lucky man would deserve
Ser tu esclavo, Madre mía	To be your slave, my Mother
Con un letreto en el pecho	With an inscription on one's breast
Diciendo, Santa María	Saying, Holy Mary
Desde que te coronaron	Since they crowned you
De diamantes y de flores	With diamonds and flowers

Te suplicamos, Señora	*We beg you, Our Lady*
Ruega por los pecadores	*Pray for us sinners*
En fin Divina Señora	*In the end, Divine Lady*
Ten piedad, gracia, y luz	*Have piety, grace, and light*
Misericordia pedimos,	*We beg for mercy,*
Diciendo, Amen! Jesús!	*Saying, Amen! Jesus!*

This hymn to the Virgin Mother invokes mostly celestial imagery, along with plants, fruit, diamonds, and flowers. Here, in the realm of the holy, Our Lady reigns supreme.

It was followed by a third Oración del Día offered in the name of San Isidro, read from a special book containing prayers for each of the nine days. Again, people recited three Our Fathers, three Hail Marys, and three Glories to the Father. Then the evening's host performed *la petición del hogar* to invoke a blessing for his or her home and family. Short prayers and blessings followed, invoked by anyone on behalf of specific individuals (the ill, distressed, striving, and deceased; for firefighters) and specific situations (prayers for rain). The final song was another alabanza to San Isidro:

San Isidro Labrador	*Saint Isidore the Plowman*
Patrón de los labradores	*Patron of farmers/workers*
Que nos libre tu favor	*May your favor free us*
De langostas y temblores	*From locusts and quakes*
Por la gran misericordia	*From the great mercy*
Con que te ayudó el Señor	*The Lord helped you with*
Derrama paz y concordia	*Peace and harmony spread*
Entre todo labrador	*Among all who labor*
Pues que fuiste designando	*Because you were designated*
Por patrón de la labor	*patron of work*
Siempre serás adorado	*You will always be adored*
Del devoto labrador	*By the devoted worker/farmer*
Cuando el Señor por castigo	*When the Lord for punishment*
Nos manda mal temporal	*Sends us bad weather*
Con tu bondadoso abrigo	*With your kind coat*
Nos vemos libre del Mal	*We find ourselves free of Evil*
Del ladrón acostumbrado	*From the accustomed thief*
Que nunca teme el Señor	*Who never fears the Lord*
Nos libres nuestro sembrado	*You free our sowed fields*
Te pedimos por favor	*We ask you please*

El granizo destructor	Destructive hail
Que no nos cause su daño	Not to cause us damage
Te pedimos con fervor	We fervently pray
Tener cosecha este año.	To have a harvest this year
En tus bondades confiando	Trusting in your goodness
Te pido de corazon	I pray from my heart
Le mandes a mi sembrado	That you send my sowed field
Favores y bendicíon	Blessing and favors
Adios, os santo glorioso	Farewell, glorious saint
Escogido del Señor,	Chosen by the Lord,
Hasta el ano venidero,	Until next year,
San Isidro Labrador	Saint Isidore the Plowman

Participants also sing this alabanza on the last two nights in the chapel, before and *during* the procession. It is always included in the novena and víspera booklets and is *always* associated with either a procession or the memory of one. Therefore, it comprises the oral component of the act of procession.[7]

In 1996 they sang the following entriega del santo, composed by Frank Gusdorf. As always, it names the mayordomos:

O San Isidro Bendito	O Blessed Saint Isidore
Te acabamos de servir	We complete our service to you
Y los mayordomos nuevos	And the new mayordomos
Te vienen a recibir	Come to receive you
Se ha llegado el día	The day has arrived
Esta primavera fría	This cold spring
Hoy celebramos toditos	Today we all celebrate
A San Isidro Bendito	Blessed Saint Isidore
Aqui esta tu santuario	Here is your sanctuary
Con gusto te lo cuidamos	With gusto we care for it
Te lo entregamos cantando	We deliver you singing
Con Steve y Mabel llorando	With Steve and Mabel weeping
San Isidro Labrador	Saint Isidore the Plowman
Cuidanos nuestra labor	Take care of our labor
Siempre siendo guía	Always being guide
De Agnes y Andy García	To Agnes and Andy García

Los mayordomos salientes	The outgoing mayordomos
Te entregan su corazón	Deliver their heart to you
Te entregan tu capillita	Deliver your little chapel to you
Con humilde devoción	With humble devotion
Los mayordomos entrantes	The incomimg mayordomos
Te vienen a recibir	Come to receive you
Hoy te entregamos a ellos	Today we surrender you to them
También te quieren servir	They also want to serve you
Ahora les entregamos	Now we deliver to them
Nuestro patrón San Isidro	Our patron Saint Isidore
Cuidenlo que es un buen santo	Take care of him our good saint
Con much gusto le canto	With great gusto I sing to him
San Isidro Labrador	Saint Isidore the Plowman
Ayudeles aprender	Help them to learn
Para que ellos te sirvan	So they may serve you
Con devoción y placer	With devotion and delight
A ustedes peregrinos	To you pilgrims
Pidemos su bendicíon	We ask for their blessing
Esperamos seamos dignos	We hope we are worthy
De nuestra salvación	Of our salvation
Adios santito bendito	Goodbye blessed little saint
Te pidemos por favor	We ask you please
Que nos ayudes este año	Help us this year
A cuidar nuestro labor	To take care of our labor
San Isidro Bendito	Blessed Saint Isidore
Te acabamos de servir	We finish serving you
Ya los mayordomos nuevos	Now the new mayordomos
Te vienen a recibir	Come to receive you

A delicate balance of intimacy and formality stands out in this text. As in other hymns, the singers address the saint directly, using *tu*, the familiar form adopted with an equal or junior. Inflected with a diminutive, this form of address evokes the saint as holy child. At the same time, the singers revere and petition the saint as a superior—as if the saint-mayordomo relation wavers eternally between parent and child. The mayordomos take care of the saint, who takes care of them. The last phrase of the third stanza, which refers to the new mayordomos weeping, signals the emotional intensity of this relationship. Many times have I witnessed weeping during the entri-ega del santo.

The San Isidro novena, like other saint's day celebrations, models an ideal of reci-procity: between saint and devotee, between generations, between the genders, between kin, and between neighboring parciantes. It elevates and sanctifies these everyday bonds through ritual and posits a saint as the behavioral ideal or model. We see the complementary relationship between Isidro and María de la Cabeza; the defer-ence and responsibility that inhere between juniors and seniors; the selfless service and shared authority that move from one set of mayordomos to another. In its entirety, the novena can be summarized as one big lesson in respeto. This is why the novena occa-sions the blessing of children by their elders. Thus one generation is instructed by another about who they are and how they should comport themselves in this, their place.

The intergenerational nature of the celebration is crucial to its transmission and definition as tradition. At least three generations are actively involved at any given time. Members of the current midlife adult generation serve as mayordomos; their par-ents and other elders offer moral and spiritual guidance to ensure maintenance of the proper tone and procedure. Preadolescent children and some teenagers are also present at every function, and some assist in small tasks. The role this tradition plays in per-petuating core cultural-religious values was illustrated by the fact that each prayer ses-sion ended with a ritual blessing of the children by their elders.

The bendicíon consists of the once widespread practice of children kneeling before a parent or grandparent to be blessed, usually before taking leave. The elder pro-nounces a blessing in Spanish: "En el nombre del padre, del hijo y del espíritu santo, que Dios le bendiga" [In the name of the Father, Son, and Holy Spirit, may God bless you]. The elder makes the sign of the cross on the younger person's forehead. Elders performed this rite on most nights of the novena. Sometimes, only the oldest person present performed the blessing; other nights, all the adults, including me, joined in. I felt uneasy in conferring the blessing, just as some children looked uncomfortable in receiving it. Yet despite whatever doubt or turmoil any of us felt privately, the simple act of compliance confirmed our public submission to the power of this ritual gesture.

Ritual Power

In New Mexico, there is an ancient tension between local and ecclesiastical control over what some call paraliturgical traditions. This surfaced during the novena in con-versations about precisely how the participants should conduct the vespers, mass, and procession. Clergy come and go over the years in every parish, and some prove more sympathetic and compliant than others when it comes to local feast day and other cus-tomary celebrations. A priest's personal popularity depends partly on the degree to which he encourages, promotes, and accedes to the particulars of local paraliturgical practice. For example, according to Doña Corina, it is "customary" for the priest to preside not only over the mass but also over the vespers, procession, and blessing of the fields. The regular pastor normally fulfills this role, but it happened this year that he would be on vacation in mid-May. There was some concern about whether his replacement would be willing to comply with the tradition.

As it turned out, everything went as prescribed, but during the novena I became aware that Doña Corina and a parish nun were having a disagreement about whether a priest was actually necessary to carry out the blessing of the fields. A recent transfer to the St. Francis parish, Sister Mary Elizabeth (a pseudonym) suggested that a deacon or even the people themselves could do it. She further asked why so many of the prayers and hymns needed to be in Spanish when everyone spoke English. This question provoked Doña Corina to remark that "people who lack their own story too often fail to understand those who do have one."

Sister Mary Elizabeth confided her amazement at the rigid insistence that things be done just one way. She told me that this parish has the reputation among clergy for being difficult and demanding. The congregation was wearing out its priest. The sister admired the devotion she witnessed, but she wondered privately whether in Ranchos, people's "culture was really their religion." In addition to the unselfconscious entitlement of linguistic domination, this backstage skirmish illustrates the tenacious defense of local practice in the ongoing negotiation between Catholic clergy and the rural laity over ritual control.

During this period, I attended the novena in the evening and by day interviewed parishioners and parciantes about acequias and about religious belief and devotional practices. I also toured acequias, escorted by commissioners, and observed irrigation and ditch cleanings. The mere fact that I could interview different individuals from the same extended families about these seemingly separate domains of activity seemed to underscore their deeper connection.

Despite my familiarity with Taos, the intensity and magnitude of local religious activity dawned on me slowly. Active parishioners all over Taos and the surrounding region are constantly engaged in an endless cycle of masses, rites of passage, feast days, and other ritual observances that mark the Catholic calendar. This commitment entails a substantial number of processions centered on the network of chapels and churches that comprises the three parishes of the Taos multicommunity.

Tension between the pressure to convert and resistance to surrender may be intrinsic to the ethnography of religious experience. Every ethnographer must deal with these contrary sentiments somehow. As the ten days wore on, I was riven between my empathy fueled by shared devotional practice and my role as an "objective" observer unable or unwilling to embrace Catholic belief. Even in faith's absence, the somatic power of ritual participation can easily drown out the thin voice of skeptical reason. Parishioners met my awkward presence with simple kindness. Most placed me within the genealogical context of my father's extended kin network in Taos. They knew my grandparents, my parents, my own generation, and, in some cases, the next one as well. One evening, Doña Corina singled out my participation, and the project it represented, for a special prayer and blessing. People raised their hands toward me as they sang a hymn to Mary. A mixed wave of embarrassment, gratitude, guilt, anguish, and exultation washed over me.

My inner schism reached its climax when on the night of the víspera I broke away from the congregation to photograph the procession, an act that gave clear spatial expression to the sin of ethnographic objectification. Even though I had permission to photograph and the priest consented to bless my camera, my sense of guilt was acute. My action troubled me more than it apparently did most parishioners, who had known from the start that I was there doing some kind of research "for the acequias." The excruciating exception occurred when a man who had not attended the novena took me for a tourist and irately accosted me before others could intervene. I had photographed processions before and have since. In none have I experienced the kind of inner crisis induced by participation in the novena. I attribute this to the somatic power of progressive ritual.

Today, a decade after I took part in the novena, I can still feel its power and the intensity of the inner conflict it evoked in me. In some way, the experience changed me. I still feel a bond of gratitude and obligation to the devotional community that graciously allowed me into its midst, requiring that I participate fully and not merely observe and, in the process, conferring blessings on me. Some conflicts have no resolution. Probably, I will always oscillate between the seductive power of communitas and the distancing, objectifying gaze of an ethnographer.

Dance scholar Deidre Sklar, who studied a devotional dance community in southern New Mexico, advises anthropologists to recognize the irreducible somatic dimension of religious experience: *"Symbols cannot be separated from soma without robbing religion of its power"* (Sklar 2001:193–194, emphasis added). A progressive ritual such as a novena requires a sustained organizational and cooperative effort that, by virtue of its format, promotes an intensifying and ultimately cathartic sense of immersion in religious experience and community. Participation on any single evening, whether a prayer session, the vespers, mass, or a procession, can be a compelling experience. Participation in multiple sessions, and especially the entire sequence, requires a significant commitment of time and engages each participant at a personal level. The cumulative effect has powerful and important psychophysical, emotional, and social dimensions. It is a primary mechanism by which Catholicism and all other organized religions entrain devotees from an early age.

Group prayer emphasizes the social nature of religious activity and promotes bonding and reciprocal commitment among participants. A ritual event such as the San Isidro celebration engenders interpersonal connection and social solidarity, linking this immanent sense of community to a larger moral-religious purpose. The act of procession, moreover, simultaneously traces and inscribes a connection to place—one particular place.

s e v e n
Procession, Water, and Place

In the old days most chapels and moradas had a drum which hung on the wall of the chapel. These drums were home made, sometimes made from a large lard pail or from a burned out log, with goat skin over both ends. They were laced so they could be tightened. There was one in the Durán [also known as Our Lady of Talpa] Chapel. Durán said that when there was a drouth, the neighbors would gather at the chapel for a religious procession through the fields. One would carry a bulto of Mary and another the Crucifix, sometimes two men would carry the large black cross. Durán said he led the procession beating the drum to attract God's attention. Also, they wanted Mary and her son to see the condition of the farm lands. They would stop now and then for prayers. He said many times they brought rain.

—Harry Garnett, unpublished reports on the Durán Chapel, 1951 and 1952

Water is pervasive in folk Catholic religious symbolism and practice in northern New Mexico. It is the source of life and the medium of blessing and baptism. When farming was universal, the religious significance of water was perhaps more pressing than today, although drought is presently leading to heightened water consciousness in the regional media. New Mexicans pay homage to the centrality of water and weave it into their community ties through religious processions. Every church has its saints, and the saints travel around. The processions assert community identity and express interconnection and interdependency of communities. By physically transporting sacred objects from one locale to another and according them great reverence, processions resacralize the space through which they pass, an agricultural landscape defined by water sources, ditches, and built structures, including holy sites.

Processions belong to a genre of human ritual behavior that involves symbolic discourse. Like dance, this genre is spatial and kinesthetic. But these movements of linearly ordered bodies and artifacts through culturally mapped space differ from dance in that they tend to be more "indexical," with reference to context, than expressive. They imply a relationship between those in the procession and the geography through which they move. Even while promoting communitas, processions also embody a division between those who walk and those who do not. In procession, there is no middle ground: either you join in, or you stand apart and watch. Many take this activity for granted, but a procession is nonetheless a special and observable public event with a cultural text. It unfolds in space and enacts a place. Such cultural texts are about those who perform them. They symbolically encode people's relationships to one another and to the places where they dwell.

Anthropologists have paid less attention to procession than to pilgrimage (Turner 1978; Morinis 1992). The two ritual practices have much in common but differ in terms of distance, effort, and duration. Pilgrimage is an arduous journey that takes one far from home, whereas procession is a short, devotional circuit.[1] The spiritual transformation wrought by pilgrimage implies a return, but the destination, sublime and remote, is foremost. Pilgrimage ventures into the unknown; procession circumscribes one familiar place. Recession is an equal part of procession. Procession symbolically encloses a specific terrain. Catholic procession usually leaves from and returns to a chapel or a church, often pausing to pray at stations along the route. A procession has vocal, auditory, olfactory, visual, and kinesthetic components. Processants pray, sing hymns, and may carry sacred objects such as a rosary, a candle, a censer, a cross, a banner, and a statue or an image of a saint.

Processions therefore confer and enact meaning in relation to a specific territory, both acceding to and exceeding the boundaries of mutual distinction that participants share with their neighbors. Every procession is a kind of topographic inscription rite. Procession makes place and sacralizes space. Sacred sites, their settings, and the ritual activity with which people animate their environment correspond to architectonic space.

Anthropologist James Fernandez coined the term architectonic to refer to culturally constructed or animated spaces that can be perceived by means of ethnographic participant observation. Fernandez writes:

> Participation enables us to feel something of what our informants feel in the spaces they occupy and in which they act. It is essentially a method aimed at the experience of place. For me the term "architectonics" raises the question of the feeling tones that activity in various constructed places evokes and that makes them places. Sacred places have an additional quality—an additional evocativeness that is symbolic in nature. [Fernandez 2003:187]

Architectonic refers to a structure of experience or feeling evoked through long-term interaction between people and a place. The term signifies an ethnographer's version of a folk model that expresses a people's relationship to the landscape and architectural space they inhabit, cherish, and symbolically own.[2]

A procession traces a specific path in space and gives meaning to the particular territory it traverses. The material transformations wrought by human habitation mark this territory. An annual procession reinscribes its pathway of spatial extension through a mapped cosmos. The coordinates of this map (the features by which correspondence is established between the physical geography and a cultural model of it) are the infrastructural artifacts of human occupation: acequias, roads, fields, houses, placitas, cemeteries, kivas, chapels, shrines. Many such archaeological and architectural structures are visible in the Taos basin, and many are still used as ritual space. Their architectonic formations have coalesced primarily around or in relation to water sources: streams, springs, lakes, meadows.

Water sources are the key foci in the sacralized cultural landscapes of aboriginal, historic, and contemporary populations. In Pueblo and folk Catholic cosmologies, these landscapes include some of the same features: springs, lakes, streams, ditches, reservoirs, fields, burial grounds, and shrines. Chapels, churches, and graveyards are found in Indian pueblos and Hispanic villages alike. Kivas are uniquely Pueblo, and moradas uniquely Hispanic.

Sacred Landscape

Taken as a whole, the Taos Valley constitutes a sacred landscape-hydroscape for those who have endowed it with symbolic meanings through generations of cultural discourse and practice. The term *sacred landscape* usually invokes an image of site-specific Indian religious belief and practice. But not only Indians find religious meaning in landscape. Although the ways in which Pueblo and Spanish-speaking peoples sacralize their environments do differ, over the centuries both have endowed their habitats with meanings and have inscribed their landscapes with structures, subsistence practices, and ritual actions. Those who perform religious rituals believe that their actions promote harmonious relations among community members and with the divine power that controls nature, life, and death.

The folk Catholic nexus of holy sites and hydraulics is one of the cultural systems that inscribe and animate the Taos Valley. This sacralized topography corresponds to the agricultural and community landscape of irrigators. The aboriginal system of ritual topography, belonging to Taos Pueblo, is based in the upper Río Pueblo watershed and also extends throughout the basin, differentially mapping the same geographical terrain. These two architectonics are distinct but historically interactive systems. Each relates waterways and water sources to a network of holy sites, including outdoor shrines. I focus only on the folk Catholic system because the pueblo's sacred geography is esoteric and carefully shielded from outside inspection by a rule of secrecy.

The greater Taos basin encompasses a mix of past and present, attenuated as well as current—and therefore ever-changing—ritual practices and physical structures. The folk Catholic multicommunity constellation or architectonic is both persistent and plastic. Today's parish seats, boundaries, and procession routes undoubtedly differ from those of the 18th and 19th centuries. Yet a complex of ritual practices linked to holy sites persists in vital and resilient form. Folk religious practices change through time but continue to express very localized attachments to specific places.

Two distinct but interrelated landscape structures, the acequia system and the folk Catholic nexus of holy sites, define the sacralized landscape of the Río Grande del Rancho or any other watershed. The acequia infrastructure includes all the ditches, headgates, desagües, ponds, *canoas* (flumes), and other human-made hydraulic devices that shape the habitat. These are oriented to and inseparable from the natural hydrology of streams, springs, lakes, and meadows. The nexus of folk Catholic holy sites includes all churches, chapels, moradas, oratorios, camposantos, *calvarios* (hilltop crosses), and procession routes. Comparatively ephemeral features include altars set up for specific processions and *descansos* (roadside crosses that mark where someone has died). Color plate 2 (Taos basin watersheds and parishes) illustrates the mutual coextension and interpenetration of these two structures into a single architectonic, wherein the sacred landscape is the irrigated landscape.[3]

I do not claim that that these two systems were originally planned or laid out in conscious, deliberate relationship to each other or even that parishioners or parciantes would articulate or confirm such a relationship. Yet the act of procession attests to the spatial codistribution of hydraulics and holy sites in any given parish-watershed and throughout the Taos basin as a whole. Much as Fernandez suggests, ritual participation makes perceptible the sacred architectonic space these hydraulic and holy sites together compose.

Parishes and Watersheds

The Taos basin contains three Catholic parishes: San Francisco, with its seat at Ranchos de Taos; Nuestra Señora de Guadalupe, in the town of Don Fernando de Taos; and Santísima Trinidad, based at Arroyo Seco. All three mother churches are located in or near old plazas. The valley's original parish was San Gerónimo at Taos Pueblo, serving as parish seat until 1826, roughly twenty-five years after the Guadalupe Chapel was built in town. The Ranchos Church, completed by 1815, first belonged to the San Gerónimo parish and then to Guadalupe. It became a separate parish in 1937. Each parish contains a mother church and several chapels located near camposantos and moradas. These serve the populations of the nucleated and dispersed communities that crystallized into a multicommunity during the 18th and early 19th centuries.

The Río Grande del Rancho watershed is more or less coextensive with the St.

Francis parish (see color plate 3). The modern Guadalupe parish extends across the Río Pueblo, Río Fernando, and lower Río Lucero watersheds (see color plate 4). Holy Trinity parish embraces the Arroyo Seco, upper Río Lucero, Río Hondo, and San Cristóbal valleys or watersheds (see color plate 5).

The Río Grande del Rancho valley opens out below a mountain canyon several miles southeast and upstream from Los Córdovas, just above the village of Talpa, into the ample expanse that drains northwest into the meadows of Los Córdovas. The old placita of Talpa sits on the upper banks of the Río Chiquito near its confluence with the Río Grande del Rancho. These streams are the two arms of the upper or mountain reaches of the Río Grande del Rancho watershed. West of Talpa and south of Ranchos along a ridge lies the settlement of Llano Quemado, served by the southernmost and second-longest ditch in the Taos basin, the Finado Francisco Martínez.[4]

Five communities, each with ditches, chapel, camposanto, and procession routes, now occupy the Río Grande del Rancho watershed. The parish seat and mother church—the famous and much photographed mission church of San Franciso de Asís, which parishioners proudly replaster with *zoquete* (mud plaster) every spring—dominates the Ranchos plaza in the middle part of the valley. Talpa has the Chapel of Nuestra Señora de San Juan de los Lagos, and Llano Quemado has Nuestra Señora del Carmen. Cordillera, strung along a ridge that cuts across Los Córdovas, shares the latter's San Isidro Chapel. There are two moradas in Talpa and one in Ranchos.

Two "sister" chapels were established in Talpa during the second quarter of the 19th century. They were named for the shrines and the then-famous Mexican pilgrimage sites of Our Lady of Talpa and Our Lady of San Juan de los Lagos, both located in Jalisco state (Wroth 1979:26–30). The former, the Durán Chapel, has fallen into ruins.[5] It was dedicated to the Penitente Brotherhood and served as an important site along the parish's Good Friday procession. Wroth (1979:26–30) suggests that the chapel was built on an indigenous sacred site, because under the altar were two small holes containing a moist holy dirt believed to have curative properties, much like the famous *pozito* (little hole) in the Santuario de Chimayó. He notes that the chapel was involved in a San Isidro Day procession. This suggests that the upper and lower portions of the Río Grande del Rancho watershed each had a San Isidro procession or else that the Los Córdovas procession once reached into the upper valley.

The Chapel of Nuestra Señora de San Juan de los Lagos is still active and remains an important site along the Good Friday procession route, which starts and ends at the St. Francis Church and includes the chapel, both Talpa moradas, and the Ranchos morada. The Good Friday procession I joined in 2000 traveled south from the main church along back roads and various acequias to the Chapel of Nuestra Señora de San Juan de los Lagos and then east and north to the upper Talpa (Río Chiquito) morada and camposanto. The two are right next to the Talpa *depósito* (reservoir), built in 1929–30 to store water from the river for irrigation in the dry months.

At the upper morada, bultos of the Madre Dolorosa (Sorrowful Mother) and Cristo Crucificado (Christ Crucified) were carried outside for the traditional enactment of the final *encuentro* (encounter) between Mary and Jesus. Attended by a prayer group of Hermanos (Penitente Brothers) and two Verónicas (young girls dressed in black), the line of roughly 150 penitents (Good Friday processants are called *penitentes*) proceeded up the embankment from the morada, past the stations of the cross set up around the southeast corner of the reservoir, to a calvario on the bank.[6] After kissing or touching Christ's cross, each processant descended the bank and followed the road, along other acequias, to the Nazareno (Nazareth) morada.

At the Nazareno morada, the procession circulated past a wooden cross in its camposanto. The processants then moved westward to the Ranchos morada and camposanto, which sit right next to a water storage tower built by the local mutual domestic water association. From there, the processants returned to the Ranchos placita and St. Francis church, where a service continued for hours.

The St. Francis parish also observes the Las Posadas novena, a ritual reenactment of Mary and Joseph's search for shelter in Bethlehem, culminating on Christmas Eve. Each of the preceding nine evenings starts with a prayer service at the St. Francis church or one of the parish *capillas*. The subsequent procession includes a man and a woman—chosen each night on the basis of who in the congregation comes from farthest away—who represent Joseph and Mary and carry their statues. Singing, praying, and bearing lighted candles, processants walk to the homes of hosts, who offer pastry and hot drinks to the crowd. By Christmas Eve, several families have given overnight *posada* (lodging) to the bultos and have served a repast to the devotional community.

Parishioners from Llano Quemado walk in procession for Nuestra Señora del Carmen's feast day, celebrated July 15 and 16. On the first evening, the procession moves east toward the mountains, and on the second, to Ranchos for a communal feast (Hooker and Santistevan 1996:102).

The San Isidro procession in Los Córdovas inscribes the lower zone of the Río Grande del Rancho watershed, just above its confluence with the Río Pueblo de Taos. This area holds pasturelands with a high water table fed by springs. Sitting in what amounts to the "delta" of the Taos basin, below the confluence of the Arroyo Seco, Lucero, and Fernando streams with the Río Pueblo, Los Córdovas constitutes the topographical vortex of the larger Taos drainage. Below the Río Grande del Rancho confluence, across the Río Pueblo, there is an old oratorio and camposanto known as Peñas Negras.[7] The oratorio is a three-sided adobe structure inside the graveyard, where coffins could be sheltered before burial. This area marks the boundary between Lower Ranchitos and Los Córdovas.[8]

The original Los Córdovas placita, which included a torreón (defensive tower), was established in the 18th century along an old road to Don Fernando de Taos now known as the Middle Road. Before 1951, when vísperas were held in a family chapel in the old placita, the procession crossed through fields and over acequias in this older neighborhood. The modern procession takes place roughly a mile to the east of the old placita. It extends in both directions from the new San Isidro Chapel, which sits on Road 240 about halfway between Los Córdovas and Cordillera. Even though the precise location and route of the San Isidro procession has changed over the years, the landscape it inscribes still contains the same elements: road, fields, springs, ditches, homes, corrals, yards, a chapel. Like all parish processions, it symbolically encircles natural and cultural features of the environment, linking built structures with bodies of water in a tracery of community-family-parish-*campo* (countryside) sacralized space.

Altars and Traveling Saints

Each church, chapel, and morada has its own patron saint and bultos, which congregants carry in processions. Each capilla hosts at least one annual celebration, or función, for its patron's feast day, following the format of vísperas, mass, procession, and community repast. Each chapel has its own mayordomos, who take care of the saints and the chapel and serve on a rotating basis in the mother church as well. For some celebrations, such as San Isidro or Las Posadas, the saint visits or stays overnight in someone's home. On the parish feast day, mayordomos carry the bultos from their respective chapels in a procession based at the mother church. The statues are often placed on altars set up along the route. Bultos from each chapel within a parish may also be carried or used on Good Friday to accompany the encuentro between Jesús and María Dolorosa.

Altars, built for a procession or as a permanent part of a chapel, home, or landscape, figure prominently in sacralized space. Catholic altars come in several forms: permanent, consecrated altars inside churches, chapels, and moradas; permanent altars in private homes, known as house shrines; and temporary indoor and outdoor altars constructed for special ritual occasions. Because temporary or calendrical lay altars can be set up inside homes, as well as outdoors, they embody a link between private or interior domestic space and public or exterior community space.

Altars can be both individual productions and contingent ephemera. Every altar is dedicated to a specific saint or miraculous event. Each represents an arrangement of symbols, objects, and meanings consecrated through prayer. Every altar is a ritual offering, an aesthetic composition, a symbolic text. Temporary or ritual altars usually stand on tables. Their basic elements include a white lacy cloth, candles, a cross, flowers, and two- and three-dimensional holy images.

Outdoor altars are smaller, more transient, and more personal artifacts than the buildings and cemeteries that sacralize the landscape through which all processions pass. They are both creatures and coordinates of procession. Processions take place in relation to these sacred sites, which, whether permanent or ephemeral, are located in places that always merit attention. Religious associations usually sponsor outdoor altars. Therefore, in 2000 the Guadalupanas erected the first Arroyo Seco Corpus Christi altar, the Sacred Heart Society created the second, the Hermanos Penitentes the third, and the San Antonio Society the fourth. Each hosted the procession with its own prayers and hymns, or alabanzas. The three altars in the 2001 town Corpus Christi procession were sponsored by the Altar Society, the Guadalupanas, and the parish Marriage Program.

Other sacralized constructions of a semipermanent nature include yard shrines, grotto or rock shrines, calvarios, and descansos. A yard shrine is usually a stone *nicho*, a rounded niche (mortared; but sometimes wood or even an upright bathtub end) placed in the yard of a family residence to contain a statue or an image of the Virgin or the patron saint. Rock shrines—featuring low rock walls (unmortared) that encircle small crosses, statues of the Virgin Mary, candles, and other offerings—may be found on hillsides or in grottos, often near calvarios. Several stand on the hillside in Talpa above the morada and nearby depósito. Every active morada maintains a calvario, typically a large white cross on the nearest hillside. Private individuals can erect and use calvarios and rock shrines; some families maintain them for generations. Descansos are another common feature of the folk Catholic sacralized landscape. In recent years, these have sprouted by the dozens along the roadsides of northern New Mexico to commemorate where someone has died in an accident. In the late 1990s and early 2000s, roadside descansos became increasingly elaborate. Some between Albuquerque and Santa Fe are decorated according to season.

Processions through Time

Accounts of Catholic ritual practiced a century or more ago attest to the long-standing importance of processions and their frequent relationship to water in Taos. In the summer of 1896, Merton Miller saw Indians and Mexicanos join together in procession to pray for good crops, carrying an image of the Virgin Mary through their fields and shooting rifles. At the 1898 procession for Nuestra Señora de Guadalupe in Don Fernando de Taos, newcomer art colonist Bert Phillips and another observer, Lester Myers, were told by a parishioner to remove their hats when the bulto of the Virgin passed. When they refused to perform this simple gesture of respeto, an altercation ensued in which the sheriff, Luciano Trujillo, was shot and killed (White 1994: 43–47).

More bucolic accounts from the same period describe processions to pray for rain. Blanche Grant reports that processions to petition for rain were held in the Taos area as late as 1904:

> One of these took place a short distance from La Loma, as the small hill in the western part of town is called. The people of Talpa, Ranchos, and Ranchito set up three stations for their saints and brought images which were put in a row under the shelters, in front of a background of white sheets and bright colored ribbons. At each of the stations was held a "velorio"—a sort of wake for the saints, with much low singing and praying. The first day passed and the fields remained parched. The second night, the heavens opened and the rain fell in torrents so that on the following day the good folks were plowing through deep mud carrying their santos back to church and home. [Grant 1983 (1934):179]

Grant cites John G. Bourke on similar practices witnessed around 1880, including one at Taos Pueblo and one conducted in town by Mexican women:

> They marched around the parched fields, praying for rain. Sure enough the rain came but in such torrents that it washed all the crops away. One of the men explained, in all seriousness, that they must have inadvertently made the rounds of the field once too often! [Grant 1983(1934):80]

These processions may have been undertaken specifically to pray for rain, as Protestant observers reported, or performed as part of the regular feast day calendar, when supplicants would also offer special prayers. Doña Corina recalled that when she was a child, people in Los Córdovas planted peas and corn on May 3 (Día de la Santa Cruz [Holy Cross]) and carried the baby Jesus to the fields to bring rain. One year a deluge followed, and a few days later they brought the Virgin out to see the damage done by her son. People often pray to mitigate the effects of violent weather. To protect their plants during a hailstorm, some still burn a piece of the palm frond handed out in church on Palm Sunday.

Processional traditions currently thrive throughout the Taos Valley. All three parishes maintain active processions. Each chapel holds at least three processions a year, one at home for the patron feast day and two at the mother church on the parish feast day and Good Friday. Three per chapel adds up to around fifty processions a year among all the local chapels in the three parishes. The shortest route that all chapels and churches maintain is a quick, usually counterclockwise circuit around the church-yard. Some processions—for example, in Ranchitos, El Prado, and Los Córdovas—go out and return along a road in one or another direction up to a specific landmark. During winter, evening procession routes may be lined with *luminarias*, which are burning stacks of ocote (pitchy pine). Longer, daytime processions such as Good Friday or Corpus Christi can extend as much as two miles, with celebrants pausing to pray along the route at a series of chapels, moradas, or altars.

Ritual traditions wax and wane through time. For example, before the 1960s the biggest procession in the Guadalupe parish in Taos was for Corpus Christi during June. Little girls in white dresses scattered rose petals before the path of the Blessed Sacrament, borne in a monstrance by the priest. Participants visited several altars set up outside the churchyard. This practice lapsed after the old Guadalupe church burned in 1961 and the parish built a new and bigger one a block to the north. In 2000, however, after a lapse of 40 years, an energetic new priest, Father Terry Brennan, encouraged parishioners to revive the town's Corpus Christi procession. The new event incorporated three of the original stations or altars, in addition to six new ones, along a two-mile circuit.

A look at this procession route reveals that a variety of secular and sacred sites is meaningful to contemporary Taoseños. Processants left the church northwest of the Taos plaza and made a large, clockwise circuit around the downtown area. They went west to the school, north to the city government and police offices, south to a mall, t to a hotel on the plaza, and then to the San Antonio chapel on La Loma plaza. rmally, they returned eastward to the church via the historic homes of the Trujillo, Padre Martínez, and Romero families, all three of which served as altar sites in the old days. The altar at the Padre Martínez house was reconstructed by a descendant, Vicente Martínez, who consulted old family photographs and provided objects used on the old altar.[9]

In 2001 processants performed a smaller circuit around three altars situated inside the churchyard. Starting north, they moved counterclockwise from the steps of the parish office to the old St. Joseph's school doors and around to an altar under the south portal of the church. At the Holy Trinity parish in Arroyo Seco, on the very same day at the same hour, another Corpus Christi procession walked from an altar on the steps of the newly renovated adobe church to four other altars. The second stood in a private yard almost a mile east up the El Salto road, which runs beside the Arroyo Seco Creek. The procession returned southwest through irrigated fields to the morada and nearby oratorio of San Antonio. Beside these structures stood altars erected by members of the respective associations. The last was a children's altar, located at a statue of the Virgin near the new church back at the placita. Recall from chapter 4 (about the Río Lucero) that the El Salto road parallels the Arroyo Seco stream, as well as the boundary with pueblo land containing the Tenorio Tract. Another mile or so above the second altar site sits the headgate of the Acequia Madre del Río Lucero de Arroyo Seco, the canal whereby Arroyo Seco's ditches receive their vital infusion of water from the Río Lucero. The name El Salto refers to a series of waterfalls located up the hill.

Water and Sanctity

Out of 15 active churches and chapels in the Taos basin, at least 9 are dedicated to holy patrons associated in one way or another with water. These include San Isidro, San Antonio, and manifestations of the Virgin Mary. San Isidro is linked to water not only because he is a farmer but also by his miracle of bringing forth a spring. Therefore, the San Isidro procession performed by Atrisco Holy Family parishioners in Albuquerque's South Valley travels along an acequia behind the church, where the priest blesses the water.

San Antonio de Padua is one of New Mexico's most beloved saints. Portrayed iconographically as a Franciscan carrying the Holy Child, he is considered a protector of animals and is commonly petitioned for help in finding lost things. Processions in his honor are often made to water sources. In Valdez, for example, parishioners walk from the chapel to a bridge that spans the Río Hondo, where the priest blesses the water. In the East Mountains outside Albuquerque, Matachines dancers lead their feast day procession for San Antonio to a spring and community water source (Rodríguez 1996:123–131).

Symbolic association of the Virgin Mary with water is a prominent theme in Mariology. Three Taos basin chapel sites (Cañon, original El Prado, and Arroyo

Hondo) refer to her manifestation as the sorrowful mother (Nuestra Señora de los Dolores), which, besides attesting to the centrality of Holy Week in the religious cycle, evokes water in the form of tears. Water association is explicit in the case of Nuestra Señora de San Juan de los Lagos in Talpa and La Pura y La Limpia, or La Purísima (Immaculate Conception), in Upper Ranchitos, where water is abundant and the imagery joins female chastity with aquatic purity. The Guadalupana's blue mantle symbolizes both water and sky. The claim that the Chapel of Our Lady of Talpa was established over an old sacred spring makes another water connection.

Narratives about the old days express the view that people were more respectful of water and of one another than they are now. According to Polito Valerio:

> La gente de nosotros de española en los tiempos más antes cuando yo 'staba pequeño tenían mas fé y más respeto, que la plebe, que la plebe que tenemos ahora. Mire ese agua la cuidaban que era una bendición, oiga. [Our Spanish people in times long before when I was little had more faith and more respect than the youth we have today. Look, they took care of this water that was a blessing—listen!] [Personal communication with the author, May 1996]

Elders also recall that people prayed while planting their fields. Polito continued:

> En aquellos tiempos sembraban con caballos y arado no más de mancera no, se ponían las riendas acá y agarraban el arade y hay va, y cuando iba a desparramar el grano decía, "En el nombre de Dios, para de vos, y para Dios, menos pa' el diablo." Y esas eran las palabras que usaban. [In those times they planted with horses and a plow, they'd just put the reins here and grab the plow handle and, when scattering the seed, would say, "In the name of God, for you, and for God, less for the devil." And these were the words they used.] [May 1996]

First Holy Communion field masses were sometimes held near a stream bank. Outdoor prayer could be a private matter as well. Gabriel Chávez remembered seeing his father kneel in the fields. Polito described how the sight of a spring might move believers to pray:

> Pues cuando ven el ojito la cosa más precioso que Dios nos hizo a nosotros, dice, para tomar esta agua tan fina y tan clara, y se santiguan. Otros tienen otro sistema me entiende. [Well, when they see the little spring, the most precious thing God has made for us, it's said, is to drink such fine and clear water and bless themselves. Others have a different system, you understand.] [May 1996]

Traditionally, people bathed in the streams, ponds, or ditches early on Día de San Juan Bautista (John the Baptist), June 24, when all the waters were said to turn pure at dawn. Some say this is no longer done because the waters are polluted, but 90-year-old Polito told me otherwise and recalled his own experience:

Si bañan. Si se bañan. Todavía algunos se hacen. Pero en aquellos tiempos más antes era lo primero que hacía uno. No más se levantaba y se iba uno a la 'cequia o al río y se metía y eso, eso era uno de los sistemas que tenía mi padre y yo y mis hermanos. Y mis tíos la misma cosa, y 'onde quiera, aqui mismos en La Cordillera; yo vivía en Talpa. [Yes, they bathe. Yes, they bathe themselves. Some still do it. But in those times long ago, it was the first thing one did. One arose and went to the ditch or river and got in, and this, this was one of the systems my father had, and me and my brothers. My uncles, the same thing, wherever, the same as here in Cordillera. I lived in Talpa.] [May 1996]

The less well-known San Juan, Nepomuceno (May 16, the day after San Isidro), is the patron of silence and secrecy for Penitentes and also, interestingly enough, the patron of irrigation (Steele 1974:188). Water and blood are linked in the popular saying *Agua es la sangre de la tierra* (Water is the earth's blood) and by the very term *sangrías* for acequias (laterals). For parciantes, this water is *la sangre de Cristo* (the blood of Christ). The sacramental transformations of water into wine and wine into blood in the Christian tradition attest to a ritual equivalence between water and blood, as in the mingling of water and blood flowing from Christ's fatal wound during the crucifixion. The earliest use of the term *sangre de Cristo* as a place-name in the Upper Rio Grande Valley occurred during the colonial period with reference to a body of water (Wroth 1983:283–292). Thus the mountains above Taos are named not only for their ruddiness at sunset but also for the holy, life-sustaining waters that run down from them.

Conclusion

Roy Rappaport (1999) proposes an anthropological theory of religion that attempts to synthesize ecological and interpretive perspectives on the role of ritual in human adaptation. He suggests that ritual evolved as the means by which humans communicate to themselves about themselves and about their relation to their environment. Traditional and nonliterate societies use ritual to encode information and an ethic that adapts them to their environment. Sacred rituals are the medium or setting for the transmission of core values and regulatory messages of this kind. Every cultural system represents an adaptation evolved over generations by people who occupy or move across a particular habitat and territory.

Most of human history and prehistory is the story of what happens when these systems come into contact and conflict with one another. Conditions of contact create boundaries of difference. Boundaries may persist, harden, dissolve, intensify, and fluctuate through time. Primordial systems are purely hypothetical because there is no people, culture, or ritual system whose relation to its environment is not, in some sense, deterritorialized and mediated by the global forces of capitalism. Indeed, the human face of these myriad processes of deterritorialization, diaspora, and mobility are what many anthropologists now study.

The Taos Valley is a dynamic human ecosystem, historically constituted by the construction and operation of an ingenious, gravity-driven hydraulic infrastructure. The primary subsistence base for more than three centuries, this infrastructure is still maintained through the practices and discourses of the population that built, owns, and uses it. Religious beliefs, moral values, and ritual practices are integral to the operation and maintenance of this system. Even though the subsistence pattern of the people in question has changed dramatically over the past century, the entire acequia culture complex remains integral to their social cohesiveness, economic welfare, sense of historical continuity, and moral-spiritual understanding of who, what, and where they are.

e i g h t
Water and the Future
of Intercultural Relations

Si lo perdemos, se perdería, la tierra quedaría muerta. Sin derechos de agua.

[If we lost it, if it were lost, the land would be left dead. Without water rights.]

—*Telesfor Eliverio García*

Farmers in the Taos Valley have been negotiating and managing the division of river water for more than three hundred years. This involves customary agreements, or repartos, between Taos Pueblo and the acequias on the Río Pueblo and the Río Lucero and also among the acequias on these rivers and every other river in the basin. Despite the uniqueness of each custom, all the agreements come down to a common principle of water sharing. By definition, water is always shared, sometimes simply and sometimes in more complicated ways. The tacit, underlying premise is that all living creatures have a right to water. Every custom involves a specific combination of proportional and rotational methods for allocating scarce water. When water is abundant, the mayordomo allocates it on a first-come, first-served basis; the amount is proportional to acreage. Several communities, including the town of Taos, were founded on the availability of sobrantes, extra water left in the river during or after other diversions.

On the Río Pueblo, the acequia madre went from sobrantes to regular rights to nearly half the river, an arrangement that ultimately became rotational with the pueblo (3 to 4, or more precisely 2.5 to 4.5, days every week in times of limited flow). Ditches downstream in Ranchitos also use the river, supplemented with water from springs and the ríos Lucero and Fernando. On the Río Lucero, repartos were worked out between the pueblo and the acequias in Arroyo Seco and El Prado, as well as among the acequias themselves. Here, the major three-way division is proportional instead of rotational, but internal rotations among acequias apply when needed, as on other rivers.

The principle of water sharing belongs to a larger moral economy that promotes cooperative economic behavior through inculcating the core value of respeto and gendered norms of personal comportment. Religious beliefs and practices sanction these norms, promote communitas, and enact a devotional community's relationship to its traditional irrigated land base. Ephemeral and more permanent holy sites define the folk Catholic sacred landscape, which is oriented around its water sources and a network of ditches. Religious procession reinscribes or resacralizes this landscape and simultaneously reinscribes the meanings of identity and attachment to place upon the persons or bodies of processants.

All of this adds up to the fact that the New Mexico acequia or irrigation communities involve a moral system, a way of life, a social and cultural identity, and an attachment to place.[1] This is why acequia associations resist the loss or transfer of water rights away from the ditches to nonagricultural use: it threatens the integrity of the whole, by removing not only water from the system but also labor and participation from the ongoing communal effort to maintain the ditches. The Abeyta case, specifically, and gentrification, in general, threaten to remove water rights from the acequias on a massive scale through a "thousand cuts," one parciante at a time. Like the other adjudications, Abeyta opposes pueblo and acequia interests and intends to replace the ethic of sharing on the basis of equity and need with a zero-sum system of allocation based on prior appropriation.

In the minds of parciantes in the Taos Valley, the hope for a fair and negotiated settlement to the case battles daily with the fear of major water loss threatening the acequias. The TVAA officials therefore agreed that I should ask the stark question at the heart of cases like Aamodt and Abeyta: What will happen if the acequias lose their water? They considered the question relevant because of Taos Pueblo's claim, filed in the Abeyta case, to all the water in the valley.

The parciantes who addressed the unthinkable foresaw ecological devastation and social conflict and disintegration. Whether terse or elaborate, their answers address the entire range of impacts a hydrologist, an economist, an environmental biologist, a sociologist, or an anthropologist would likely posit as possible consequences of massive water loss. All agreed that the acequias would come to an end.

The commonly narrated scenario starts with the land drying up along the waterways and the greenbelts that border them. Farmers and ranchers will be unable to irrigate, so their animals, trees, fields, and gardens will die. The land will lose its value, so people will have to sell it and move away. They will lose their culture. Taos will become like Los Angeles or Las Vegas. Each individual elaborated a bit differently on this basic narrative.

Several answers focused on the biological and ecological effects of water loss to the acequias. Telesfor García's terse summary provides the epigraph above: "Si lo perdemos, se perdería, la tierra quedaría muerta. Sin derechos de agua" [If we lost it, if it were lost, the land would be left dead. Without water rights] (July 1995). Gus García (no relation) said:

> I have flown over Taos, and I've flown from Taos to Albuquerque. And the only greenbelt there is, is along the rivers and where the acequias flow. And I'm afraid that if the acequias do not flow, the terrain would all of a sudden, the greenbelt, would get smaller and smaller down the river. And that's where it means the only ones who would benefit would be the down[stream] users. Because the rivers would only carry the water down and…the greenbelt would get smaller and smaller, and it would hurt everybody. Eventually, it would dry up, this area, tremendously. [July 1995]

The practical consequences were foremost to Luís Martínez:

> If the acequias lost their waters, we'll be completely out of everything up here because we need the water for irrigation. We have some fruit trees that they need the water. Even if we don't plow but if we do make a nice garden, well, you need a lot of water to bring it up, especially when it's hot days, you know…. Oh, the water is very essential for everybody, for everybody. [July 1995]

His downstream neighbor, Felix Miera, elaborated:

> There'd be a lot of property that'd be just wasteland. Without water, land cannot survive. It'll become a desert. And that would happen with all these people who have property, who depend on water from the ditch to irrigate. They would lose everything they have. I have all these trees up here, with flowers and lawns all around my home. Without water from the ditch, I wouldn't be able to keep all of these, because from the well I wouldn't have enough water to irrigate all my trees. Those trees have been there for almost 50 years. I would say that without that water, we would lose most of them. I would lose everything in the back. My pasture would be dried out, so that thing would be worthless. [July 1995]

Land will lose value, and parciantes will be forced to sell and move away. In the words of 74-year-old Elizardo Pacheco from Arroyo Seco:

> Que pasará? Los terrenos nuestros no valdrán nada…. Y con la gente, pos uh, posible que vendan y se vayan a otro la'o, a las plazas que hay mucha gente de aquí que se ha ido a las plazas y a otros la'os, Los Angeles. [What would happen? Our lands would be worth nothing…. And with people, well, it's possible they would sell and move somewhere else, to places where there [are] lots of people from here that have gone to other places and parts, Los Angeles.] [May 1996]

Eliseo García, the 77-year-old mayordomo of the Acequia del Medio in El Prado, said:

> Pues, pienso que estará muy triste, muy mal que si íbanos a perder nojotros derechos que hemos tenido en de que vinieron nuestros antepasados. Tenemos los derechos hay. Si nos íbanos a perder, pues, sería una cosa, las propiedades de nosotros no servieron muncho pa' muchos porque necesitamos la agua a beneficio de la propiedad. [Well, I think it will be very sad, very bad, if we will lose our rights we have had, which came through our ancestors. We have the rights there. If we were to lose them, well, it would be a thing (that) our properties would not serve for much of anything because we need water to benefit from property.] [July 1995]

Asked what would happen to people, Eliseo replied:

> Sería una cosa muy triste y muy mal porque sabemos que sin agua no podemos hacerle muy bien. Y hora pa' nuestros animales que uno cría y todo, pues que iba a pasar, yo creo que tendría una cosa muy, no tendría valor para nosotros. [It would be a very sad thing and very bad because we know that without water we cannot make it very well. And now for our animals that one raises and all, if that were to happen, I think it would be a thing very…it would have no value for us.] [July 1995]

TVAA president Palemón Martínez outlined economic ramifications:

> I guess it could be something like other people are facing, you know. If you look at Santa Fe, for example. My impression is that there were three thousand acres of irrigated land in 1918. The readjudication in 1975 listed about six hundred acres of water right. So there was a change. There was a new player, you know. A public water company supplying the domestic needs—industrial, to a certain extent. Then another element that creeps in is assessments to maintain the infrastructure. Rate changes like occurred in Santa Fe during the past maybe fifteen years, where it has probably the highest water rate in the state, in the region. So that type of thing takes place when there's change, I think. The one thing is…we have probably the cheapest water rate because of the way we do things. The more infrastructure development that occurs, the more complicated, and investments, management, come into play. [July 1995]

Fermín Torres from El Salto elaborated on another theme, loss of culture:

> Pues, si las acequias pierden su agua, se pierde también toda la cultura, se van a secar los terrenos, tal vez norias también. Se van ir pa'bajo. Tal vez la gente tendrá que comenzar a salirse si no tienen agua. Tendrán ir a buscar lugar 'onde puedan vivir más, 'onde hay agua. Será una cosa triste. [Well, if the acequias lose their water, the culture is also lost. The lands will dry up. Perhaps wells, too, they will go down. Perhaps people will start to leave if they don't have water. They will have to go find a place where they can live more, where

there is water. It will be a sad thing.] [Personal communication with the author, July 1995]

Orlando Ortíz from Cañon echoed Fermín's sentiments:

> It would be a very tragic situation, I think. Because, well, it's very much a part of the culture, as you're aware, for the acequias to carry water, to be available to the people who do want to continue cultivating their lands. It's been a very strong part of community existence in our area from the time of the early Spanish settlers. And, I don't know, it would be a bad situation. And, of course, it might happen eventually, that the acequias are abandoned if development continues and fewer and fewer people continue to cultivate their lands. It could be a very serious result, I think. [July 1995]

Fifty-one-year-old Augustín Montoya encapsulated the eco-social impact scenario outlined above most articulately:

> I think it'd be really devastating to all of the Taos Valley if the acequias would lose their water. I believe that the lands around would certainly dry up. Our aesthetics would really suffer a terrific loss. I believe we would lose a lot of trees, we would lose a lot of the greenery, perhaps some of the *ojos* would dry up. We would lose a lot of our culture and tradition with it. [February 1996]

Asked to explain, Augustín added:

> We would lose our culture and tradition just by losing the practiced way of life that we have been enjoying—being neighbors, having to share something with a real need for it. That would certainly be a great loss. I believe that that's what has held the acequia system together—people having a common need and a common goal, which would keep that water flowing. [February 1996]

Retired high school coach Rudy Pacheco stated the problem in terms of justice, history, and principle:

> That would be a great injustice because in this world there is land, there is water, and land becomes useless without the water. In historical practices, we have a right as citizens of this nation, because in the Treaty of Guadalupe Hidalgo the only issues raised were when the treaty came into force with an agreement with the United States—either sell everything you have and possess and go down to Mexico, which the settlers here didn't want to do because they were here, very little recognized by a nation that was born and we were under them for 24 years. So the practices of over two hundred years under Spanish rule were in place. This was their home for many generations. And they didn't want to leave, so they accepted being part of the United States and petitioned by a petition of statehood to be part of the United States. And under the

treaty, they promised to protect all our rights but also practice the responsibilities. So those are rights we have historically. And to deny us those now would be a gross violation not only of historical practice but also the Treaty of Guadalupe Hidalgo and also the treaty of us accepting membership under the United States, under the constitution of New Mexico. [July 1995]

Asked what might follow from this injustice, Rudy articulated a theme of resistance: "I think everybody is 'sue-crazy.' But I think if we didn't fight for our rights, we'd be violating our own principles. So I'm sure we will pursue" (personal communication with the author, July 1995). Roberto Martínez from Lower Ranchitos believed that resistance would ultimately keep the water from being lost: "No no podemos perderlos de ninguna manera porque les vamos a pelear" [No, we are not going to lose them anyway because we will fight them] (personal communication with the author, July 1995).

Often associated with this note of resistance, three more themes emerge from parciantes' answers: ethnic resentment, the hope for an alternative solution to water loss, and social conflict. The first is made clear in Elizardo Pacheco's reference to the loss of land value forcing people to sell and move away: "O sí [sería mala cosa para la gente]. Y logo la, los, la gringada es lo que 'sta esperando que la gente venda sus terrenos pa' embocarse ellos" [Oh, yes (it would be a bad thing for people). And then the "gringotude" is waiting for people to sell their land so they can swallow them] (personal communication with the author, May 1996).

More frequent, however, is reference to Taos Pueblo as an—or the—adversarial party in the matter of water loss. For example, Telesfor automatically perceived the acequias' loss as the pueblo's gain:

Po'los indios la agarrarían y nos la vender a nosotros pa'trás. A según parece. Y—lo cree. Al rumbo que parece que quieren ellos. Agarrar posesíon de la agua y luego vendersela al que la necesite.... A según nos ha dicho el tratado que han hecho los Indios reclamando su *aboriginal right*, pues parece que ellos quieren agarrar el poder de toda la agua y vendersela a las demás gente que 'stá allá fuera, aunque ya haiga salido de los propriedad de ellos, tendrán el derecho vendernosla, a nosotros y los demás que la necesiten. Y el *livestock* también necesitará el agua lo misma cosa que necesitan las tierras, pero si la agarran el "pueblo" pues será imposible poder usar el agua para regadío o para animales, para casas, y ellos lo que quieren es agarrar el poder de todo el agua, para podernos la vender a los demás después. Y se me hace a mi sería una cosa muy mal hecha en que le dieran todo al "pueblo" y dejaran a los demás a morir de sed. [Well, the Indians will get it and sell it back to us. So it would appear. And—believe it. That appears to be the direction they want—get possession of the water and then sell it to who needs it. According to what the treaty has told us, the Indians have been reclaiming their aboriginal right. Well, it appears that they want to get the power of all the water and sell it to the rest of the people who are outside of there, even if it has come from their property. They (the Indians) will have the right to sell it to us and others who need it. And the livestock will also need the water the same as the lands do, but the pueblo will get it and so it will also be impossible to be able to use the water for irrigation or for animals, for houses. And what they want is to be able to sell it to the rest of us afterward. And it seems to me this would be a very bad thing to do, to give it all to the pueblo and leave everyone else to die of thirst.] [July 1995]

This scenario illustrates the violation of an implicit "law of thirst" that ordains sharing the last drops of water. Asked whether this really could happen, Telesfor, who lives in Arroyo Seco, alluded to the never forgotten Tenorio Tract ejectments and water loss, the role of the federal government, and his view of Pueblo and attorneys' motives:

No sé. Pero siendo que los Indios los ha reconocido y protegido el gobierno tanto pues no se puede dudar tampoco. Porque a las cargas los han echado afuera de sus casas para dejarselas a los Indios para que caigan ay las casas. Nunca han hecho uso del terreno. Ellos reclaman, todos los reclamos son que, *sacred water and sacred properties. That's what they've always used as an excuse for getting it.* ¿Verdad? Y me parece que con eso, les han aconsedido todo lo que les han dado. Porque eso es lo que hacen. Toda, todas las sierras esta se han dado al Pueblo dicen que es *sacred lands and sacred water that's there and they have to go over and do their ceremonies over there. That's all they have used it for.* Pero no sé lo que pueda pasar pero se me hace a mí que ya quitarsela a los que riegen con ella y hacen su vivir de ella, del agua, diciendo que por tantos años la han tenido, nunca se han conformados ellos con la decisión del corte, y entre más, más parece que nos están poniendo más oposición, si no ellos los abogados son los que 'stan haciendo la vida. Lo que hay es que ya se impusieron a que los mantengan del todo y ya no quieren hacer nada ellos. Y los abogados que 'stan haciendo la vida, pos ellos no los van a saltar. [I don't know. But being that the government has recognized and protected the Indians so much, one cannot doubt it either. Because under orders they have thrown people out of their houses to leave them for the Indians so they could let them fall down. They have never made use of the land. They claim, all their claims are, sacred water and sacred properties. That's what they've always used as an excuse for getting it. Right? And it seems to me that they have taken all the advice they have been given. Because this is what they do. All, all of these mountains have been given to the pueblo (because) they say it is sacred land and sacred water that's there and they have to go over and do their ceremonies over there. That's all they have used it for. But I don't know what could happen, but it seems to me they already took it away from those who irrigate with it and make their living from it, from the water, saying they have had it for so many years. They have never complied with the court decision. And it seems they are now putting up more opposition to us, or if not them, then their lawyers, who are making a living at it. What it is now is that they are used to being supported for everything and they don't want to do anything themselves. And the lawyers are making a living from it, and they are not going to cut them loose.] [July 1995]

Noteworthy is Telesfor's opposition of sacred and secular uses of the water, as well as his implicit judgment that it is not okay for Taos Pueblo to claim that the land and water are sacred if the pueblo is going to dispossess others and not use the water to farm.[2] The fear of unilateral control over the water by Taos Pueblo is common among many parciantes. Palemón was especially attentive to the managerial aspects of such a scenario: "And who would be the owner? Taos Pueblo? Then they become the marketing structure, and everybody would be at the mercy of whoever owns the water" [July 1995]

Asked about impacts, he continued:

I guess you could assume scenarios that could be from minor to major if they owned it and had total control of it. They could say, either you could pay whatever they request, or otherwise, could be, say, we no longer service you. I don't know. I don't think that could ever happen, you know. Somehow, hopefully, there's justice throughout the whole system, to them and to us. It's not a new ball game, you know, for however developments occurred. They were here, at one point. I presume somebody else might have been here before them. And then the Spanish settlers came in and certain developments occurred, and then things evolved. Others came. Things are changing. And that's the nature of life, I guess. So, hopefully, we can work things out. I'm still hopeful we can do something from a negotiated standpoint if we're willing to recognize that there are other people, and that's not unique to this area. It happens everywhere, I guess. But if they own it, I guess we would be at their mercy. Either from a supply standpoint or from a rate standpoint, and management. [July 1995]

Some men insisted that it is impossible for the acequias to lose their water. First, when it flows, too much water comes down those rivers for anyone to hold back, with plenty for everyone. Second, it would be unjust and in violation of parciantes' customary principles and historical rights. Third, they will never allow it to happen. Some refused even to address the possibility and tersely answered, "I don't know," or "I just haven't thought about that," or "I wouldn't know," period.

After emphasizing the impossibility of water loss, several reluctantly arrived at a prediction of social conflict and physical violence. Their comments are worth noting. Fernando Romo of Las Colonias combined a certainty that the extreme scenario cannot happen, with a sympathy for the Indians, on the one hand, and with what every irrigator knows, on the other:

I don't think we will. I think that's a far-fetched possibility, you know. I don't think the Indians want that kind of animosities between us. The fact that we've been neighbors for five hundred years and these water traditions have run so smoothly. Like I said, about the only people I hear complaining about the Indians are the people from El Prado. You just hear it all the time. You hear them complain about the Indians this, the Indians that. So sometimes I believe, more so now, you know. Some of those guys that are there now—I don't want to mention names—*pero* [but] they have hard heads, man, you know? They're constantly, constantly at battles with them. Also, finally, I think the Indians are getting pissed off and they're saying, "Well, look, we're going to show these guys, you know. Let's just lay claims to those waters, period." You know, I mean, everything originates on their watersheds, you know. The Río Lucero, everything comes through their [inaudible], you know. They're the ones up above. *Y los de arriba son que friegan siempre* [and those above always have the advantage], you know. [January 1996]

Pressed to consider the possibility, Fernando responded:

Well, you know, if it was because of the pueblo keeping the waters and drying up our lands and our acequia, hey, we're not going to sit around and let this happen, you know. We're all warriors, you know. We'll fight for our water rights, I mean, to the point of killing each other, I guess. Because the Hispanos, the people that are close to their land, I mean, you'll die before your...I mean there's been deaths before over waters, you know. And if something this drastic ever came, I mean, I think there'd be war, all-out war, you know. I really do. But I don't think that would ever happen. Like I keep repeating, and I know, I think there's more problems to worry about, you know. Not so much the Indians taking so much water or this or that, you know. Because, like I say, when there's water, there's enough for everybody. When there isn't, *los de más abajo son perdidos, los de más arriba son los que logra* [those below are lost, those above are the winners]. That's plain fact, you know, and why fight it? *Pero* [But] you know the things that I'm more worried about, you know, and I think it concerns us and it concerns the Indians just like it does us. And there are these environmental restrictions that they want to put on the waters. A good example would be that minimum flow, you know. They're trying to keep that minimum flow on each. [January 1996]

Steve Trujillo, an investment banker and commissioner on both the Acequia de Los Molinos (Río Pueblo) and the Acequia Madre de La Loma de Ranchitos de Abajo (Río Lucero), gave a variation on the theme:

I haven't even thought that way because I don't think the acequias are going to lose their water. You know, but if they were, and for cause, or for what reason, I hate even to think of that...if, in fact, we're discussing the question of adjudication.

You're talking about a question of Taos Pueblo and their claims and all. If the acequias were to lose their water, I think you would have a polarization of the community, I think, at extremes. I mean, it's not a matter of saying, "Well, you closed off my road to get to my place. Now I have to build a road." But without water, I think you'd have—I'm not a radical, but I could see some radical movements. And I don't know to what degree, but I would hate to see that day come. Because I don't think it's going to be something that law enforcement or the law is going to come into a man's way of thinking. I mean, it's a matter of survival. You need nourishment. It's basically, you can deal without that, but longer than you can without water. So same thing with the earth. It's no different. And I think you're playing with people's lives. Not the land itself but with the life of a person, and I don't think that's going to be acceptable to anyone. And so I don't think that the system or anybody can see it any other way. I mean, maybe that's the way it is in New York City, Chicago, Los Angeles, whatever. That's an extreme. This is not, you know. It's a different custom. It's a different way of living. It's a different mentality. I think you would really see a polarization of the community, that you would have some very ill feelings, beyond just the soul and mind. I think it may come to some physical stuff—it would be my concern—needlessly, right or wrong. I don't know. [July 1995]

Finally, Roberto Martínez, the last of his family to be born in the Severino Martínez hacienda, foresaw the local eruption of violence as part of worldwide behavior:[3]

Vamos hacer lo mismo que estando en Rusia, lo mismo que están haciendo en otros lugares, lo mismo que hacieron en las Islas Filipinas, pelear la gente uno con el otro. Matarse unos a los otros hasta que quedan los que mandan más. Por eso ahora mismo hay tanta fración en diferentes esta'os, que no saben la nación, en Washington DC que es lo que 'sta pasando, que tiene ganges, con rifles y con todos ese, como Mafia, que van a pelear, que 'stan listos ya pa' pelear en diferentes 'sta'os, en este 'sta'o no tenemos todavía, *back east*, hay 'onde 'stan peleando, 'stan peleado el, los Cuclanes, *you've seen on television* de Cuclán. Y otras clase de clubs o sociales o *rifle clubs* o cosas asina. Y aquí se va volver asina. [We will do the same thing they are doing in Russia, the same thing they are doing in other places, the same thing they did in the Philippine Islands—one people will fight with another, kill each other until those who command most will remain. Because of this, right now there is so much friction in different states that they don't know the nation, in Washington DC. This is what is happening. They have gangs with rifles and all that, like Mafia. They will fight. They are ready to fight in different states. In this state, we still don't have this, back east where they are fighting as you've seen on TV, the Kuklan (KKK) and other kinds of clubs or social groups or rifle clubs, and things like that. And so will it happen here.] [July 1995]

These conservative men, all over 40, are farmers, ranchers, workers, businessmen, and retirees. None is a radical, hothead, or politician. None was the least strident in his answer to my provocative question. Their allusions to resistance, ethnic resentment, social conflict, and violence command attention. What do they tell us? The scenario they paint represents a hypothesis one hopes will not be tested. Yet it merits consideration in its own right because it represents the standpoint of a major player in the grand game—or war—of water rights adjudication. It will affect how the game or battle plays out.

The fundamental axiom that emerges from parciantes' accounts of customary practice in water sharing is that, in times of need, no one goes entirely without so that another may have it all. In times of drought, they share what water there is, and animals get theirs first. The zero-sum solution is anathema to an ethic and adaptation forged under conditions in which the power over water must be shared cooperatively. To such a sensibility, the imposition of an absolute zero-sum regime would violate the basic subsistence ethic and pose a direct threat to survival. In predicting that social polarization and violence would erupt, these parciantes are not threatening to promote division or commit violence. Rather, they are voicing their intuition of what massive water loss would mean to the moral economy of acequia practice. It would represent a violation of the fundamental right to subsist—not to mention the final destruction of long-standing reciprocal, cooperative relations with Taos Pueblo. Significantly, this response seems to corroborate James Scott's hypothesis that a perceived violation of the individual right to subsist, which lies at the heart of the peasant moral economy, was precisely what would drive them to revolt.[4]

Agricultural economist Clyde Eastman (1998) has argued that a conventional economic analysis of commercial operations is not appropriate to the study and explanation of small-scale agriculture. Small-scale farming and ranching operations such as those owned by parciantes in northern New Mexico are not producers of profit but rather proponents-sustainers of savings. Parciantes' small-scale operations are a means of maintaining rather than expanding their wealth, of passing it on to their offspring through a way of life. Yet with escalating real estate prices, this savings accrues inherent interest, so the value of this wealth does grow. Eastman correctly considers their wealth and way of maintaining it as rational behavior. As long as farm operations do not create debt, they are operating successfully from the farmer-rancher standpoint, especially given the range of material and social benefits participants derive from these activities.

Understanding the intrinsic use-value of small-scale farming in its social dimensions is crucial, but we must acknowledge the fact that in real market terms the water rights and land collectively owned by the acequias and therefore by individual parciantes are worth millions of dollars and potentially much more. On the rising scale of the dollar value of water rights in the 21st century, aboriginal rights and acequia rights are the priority blue-chip stocks. They are the sine qua non of all future development in the scenic Taos Valley and downstream as well. The acequias and parciantes stand to lose a cherished and defended way of life, beautiful irrigated land, a stake in its bioregional future, and potentially millions, perhaps even billions of dollars as a result of the water rights adjudication. The quantification of a water right makes it easier to sell, and the monetary value of every water right will be determined ultimately by its seniority. Although economic and social values are distinct, they are also ultimately inseparable, just as social and cultural values are distinguishable but inseparable.

Another way to approach the complex interpenetration of economic and social values is to ask why parciantes who no longer subsist primarily by agriculture so tenaciously defend acequia ownership and persist in acequia practice. They certainly do not say that they do it because it is worth millions of dollars to them. Likewise, neither do the Taos Indians protect their annual religious pilgrimage to Blue Lake because it is worth millions of dollars to them. On the contrary, every reason they, as well as their voluntary and hired advocates, are likely to offer in explanation explicitly rejects the commercialization of these resources. Instead, parciantes and pueblo residents explain the significance of these resources in terms of cultural, social, moral, and spiritual values—in terms of religion and identity. The power of their arguments lies in the premise that dollar value and humanistic values are fundamentally incommensurate. In short, one cannot put a monetary or otherwise quantifiable value on cultural-religious identity, ancestral-genealogical attachment to place, spiritual and moral community, or a shared sense of meaning, belonging, and social purpose in the world. These are the things that people collectively prize but that money cannot buy—even though capital and the state have irrevocably cast these in monetary or rational terms.

Rather than further reify ethnic difference, let me ask how such difference is produced or established and why. After all, Indians and Mexicanos have cohabited for so many years in the Taos Valley that one has to wonder how and why they remain separate people. Are the differences locals assert and the identities they enunciate and perform artifacts of the anthropological imagination? Are they strategies of containment imposed by forces like the state? Do they mask economic inequality or class? As a self-identified entity that has struggled to remain culturally autonomous and geographically separate from its assimilationist external surroundings since the so-called start of history, Taos Pueblo, first and foremost, asserts difference in the Taos Valley. The pueblo stakes its identity on ownership and control of its aboriginal resource base, including the upper Río Pueblo and Río Lucero watersheds. Parciantes who live in the same and adjacent watersheds stake their identity on their acequias, land, family, and parish.

The state underwrites difference by conferring trust status on the Pueblos and other tribes and by ordaining who is or may become a citizen of the nation or province and what that involves. Modernity promotes difference, through tourism and art (Rodríguez 2003). Water rights adjudication exploits the difference produced by the pueblo, the state, the tourist market, and individual actors.

Yet Pueblo and Hispano societies probably have more in common than not. The "not" part, the diacritica of difference, is geographic and spatial, explicit, accentuated, self-referential, and public. Difference is the basis for people's proprietary claims to the watersheds they inhabit in the Taos basin. Within the specific context of the Taos basin, the acequias and parish-based sacred landscape are implicitly juxtaposed to the hydrologically related sacred landscape of Taos Pueblo, which differently maps the same terrain. The two are distinct yet historically interactive and interpenetrating architectonic systems that, arguably, constitute a larger inclusive system, traceable through time.

Taos Pueblo and its parciante neighbors have in common a kind of structural parity, both internally and vis-à-vis each other, with respect to access and control over river water. Within this scheme, "each community tends to be a bounded social universe mapped onto a bounded territorial unit" (Kearney 1996:175). A moral economy ideologically guides their internal relations. Both groups are subject to minority or subaltern status inside the United States but occupy very different categories or niches within the world ethno-racial order. In anthropological terms, these categories correspond to "primitive" or "tribal" or "indigenous," on the one hand, and "peasant" or "folk," on the other. The scholarly predilection is always to study these two peoples separately, just as the adjudication of water rights opposes them as adversarial entities.

The legal, political, and social consequences hinging on this classificatory distinction are immense. Both populations assert traditional cultural identities expressed in language, religion, kinship, and attachment to place. Ritual action powerfully enacts community identity and can give participants' lives a sense of spiritual, social, and moral purpose. The elaboration and defense of cultural difference is a strategy that promotes community solidarity and asserts a claim to place. "Thus it is that cultural resistance becomes integral to differentiation. The person seeks to become desired (to be valued) according to the ideals that define personal value in his or her community" (Kearney 1996:162).

The irony is that the unitary, univocal, essentialized identity articulated through such resistance serves also to entrench participants' subaltern status (Scott 1985; Kearney 1996:162–163). By reifying these categories of difference, anthropologists, political activists, and others participate, however unintentionally, in reinforcing their power to contain. "Central to this theory of containment," Kearney (1996:167) writes, "is the proposition that subalterns themselves participate in the construction of the univocal identity." Moreover, "standing behind all of these interlocutors and creating corresponding official categories and projects of and for peasants is the state" (1996:167).

Instead of an ossified relic from the past, the self-conscious Nuevomexicano or Hispano identity of the kind Taoseños display is an emergent phenomenon that incorporates the residual and the local in an effort to resist the dominant, diasporic pull of globalization.[5] The residual and the local include the scarcity-based moral economy of respeto, reparto, and familial attachment to an irrigated land base. These elements give meaning to parciantes' lives in a postmodern world where powerful forces constantly promote the fragmentation and dissipation of a stable sense of self or of an enduring common attachment.

The lesson to draw from New Mexico's acequia associations is that water is a resource best shared in a community of mutually responsible and accountable stakeholders. This may well be the lesson of all autonomous irrigation communities. The dilemma facing modern policy makers is the difficulty, if not impossibility, of implementing such need- and equity-based communal models within modern technological and demographic contexts. In Veronica Strang's (2004) ethnography of the meaning of water in the Stour Valley of Dorset, England, she acknowledges this discrepancy of scale but nevertheless concludes that such models can offer important guidelines for urban water policy:

> What is feasible, with a little creativity, is to consider how the qualities and values which characterised earlier arrangements might be carried into a modern context to inform policy decisions and thus enable more collaborative and ecologically sustainable arrangements of water ownership, use, and management—arrangements that would flow with, rather than against, the meaning of water.[6] [Strang 2004:252]

I conclude with two points about the contemporary context of local water scarcity. First is the fact that the causes of scarcity are no longer merely microclimatological conditions and competition among users. According to most estimates, acequia irrigators use less water today than a generation ago, but the demands on surface water and groundwater are escalating because of development and gentrification. Urban and population growth are expanding at a rate projected to exceed the extant regional water supply by mid-century. Forest growth in recent decades has reduced mountain runoff from winter and summer precipitation into the streams, according to some. In this millennium, New Mexicans appear to be entering a period of severe drought, part of a natural cycle that global warming will exacerbate, even if it did not trigger it.

The water crisis in the North American desert borderlands is just one of many in the world. Scarcity and the preservation of clean freshwater supplies are global and transnational issues because borders affect water rights, access, and liability. Moreover, water has become an international commodity, and a limited one, for sale to those who can pay. The New Mexico water rights adjudication is a manifestation of the worldwide conflict over who owns what water, how it should be used, and whether it should be treated as a human right or a commodity. In this context and in similar situations, local moral economies struggle against the hegemonic zero-sum, winner-take-all ethic of global capitalism. Acequia culture combines the sharing of river water with secular and ritual practices that unfold in space and require mutual respect: irrigation and procession. Such practices make place and self. People cherish and defend the surviving acequia systems of New Mexico not because they are a dead artifact from an archaic past, but because they continue to function, in ever-changing yet persistent form, fulfilling a range of contemporary material and social needs.

Epilogue

On March 17, 2006, Taos Pueblo, the Taos Valley Acequia Association (TVAA), the town of Taos, twelve mutual domestic water associations, and the El Prado Water and Sanitation District reached a negotiated settlement of Pueblo water rights claims in the Abeyta case. The New Mexico Office of the State Engineer (OSE) announced the settlement 14 days later and held two public hearings during the month of April. The sparsely attended hearings took place at the Taos Convention Center. Then, on a hot, windy afternoon at the end of May, the agreement was signed at Taos Pueblo in an outdoor ceremony attended by New Mexico governor Bill Richardson, Attorney General Patricia Madrid, many state, city and county officials, the press, and all the parties to the case and their attorneys, as well as family members of the men who participated in the negotiation. The negotiation process had taken 17 years, so the individual and collective sense of accomplishment and relief was immense and palpable. Echoed by the press, Pueblo spokespeople called the agreement historically momentous for the tribe. Some even compared it in importance to the return of Blue Lake.[1]

The signing ceremony on May 30 took place in the north plaza of the pueblo, not far from the banks of the Río Pueblo, set against the spectacular backdrop of Taos Mountain. Tribal elders sat in beaded finery beneath a ramada shaded with freshly cut green branches. The pueblo governor's canes of authority lay on the long, brightly blanketed table where the signing would be performed. White awnings erected on either side shielded audience members from the blazing sun, and beside the podium, US, New Mexico, and Taos tribal flags flapped wildly in the wind.

The two-hour event featured a succession of speakers, including the pueblo and New Mexico governors, state and local officials, and representatives of all the local parties. Each affirmed the magnitude of the agreement and extolled the spirit of cooperation that produced it. All pledged commitment to the next stage: gaining congressional approval and funding from the federal government. Governor Richardson promised that the state would do its part. Having finally reached a settlement, the parties resolved to present a united front in Washington, where their representatives would travel in June to inaugurate the federal phase of the project. Implementation of the agreement would secure a sustainable future for Pueblo and non-Indian water users in the Taos Valley.

After the document was signed, everyone joined in a round "friendship dance," circling a core of drummers. The dance was followed by a generous feast, prepared by Pueblo women and held at the tribal community center across the river. Dessert included two large, decorated cakes commemorating the historic agreement.

Public statements by all the parties confirmed that the terms of the compromise would protect their most fundamental water needs for the future. In a March 31 press release, State Engineer John D'Antonio said that the agreement "will resolve the water claims of the Taos Pueblo and bring certainty to thousands of water right claimants in the Taos area, while still protecting the main stem of the Rio Grande" (OSE 2006).

Pueblo governor James Lujan Sr. called the settlement fair and said that "when it is completed, it will resolve the pueblo's water rights claims, as well as long-standing disputes between the pueblo and non-Indian irrigators. It will provide the basic rules for groundwater production in the valley without injuring surface water supplies or overburdening the aquifer" (OSE 2006).

TVAA president Palemón Martínez said, "We are pleased that a settlement agreement was finally developed which we feel adequately protects the acequias' rights as well as the rights of other parties to the settlement. Long-standing customs of surface water sharing will continue in the future" (OSE 2006).

The scope of the complex, 100-page agreement far exceeds the subject matter of this book. At this writing, I have barely begun to study it. I can report that the settlement preserves the 1893 water-sharing agreements for both the Río Pueblo and the Río Lucero and provides for the acquisition of water rights by Arroyo Seco. It provides for the protection, preservation, and recharge of the Buffalo Pasture, as well as the restoration of acequia rights to the Karavas Tract, and ensures Pueblo cooperation in the maintenance of numerous acequias in the middle and lower Río Lucero and Río Pueblo systems. It also guarantees that priority calls will not be made on the Río Pueblo or Río Lucero in times of scarcity.

These represent a fraction of the issues that the settlement covers and that have perdured for generations between Pueblo and acequia irrigators. The total cost of the settlement is said to be $133 million, $100 million of which would be for infrastructure, acquisition, offset, and mitigation costs of the proposed Taos Pueblo Water Development Fund. Praising the achievement of a settlement that avoids costly, divisive litigation, state representatives to the US Congress and Senate nevertheless cautioned that it would be an uphill battle to secure funding in George W. Bush's Washington. Total costs for New Mexico, including the Aamodt settlement and other cases, reportedly amount to $1 billion (de Bruin 2006). Like every other plan for development along the Rio Grande, the Abeyta settlement relies heavily on the importation of San Juan–Chama water. The grand irony of the San Juan–Chama Diversion Project is that, by introducing "new" water into a fully allocated system, it purports to remedy the very crisis it has caused for the acequias.[2]

Some individuals gave compelling personal testimonials during the public hearings and signing ceremony. One Pueblo Water Task Force representative spoke about how difficult and fraught with conflict the negotiation sessions had sometimes been, recalling times when individuals walked out thinking that they would never return, saying things they would later retract. At the first hearing, tribal negotiators' children spoke movingly about how the long years of their fathers' involvement, hard decisions, self-doubt, sacrifice, and frequent absences from home had affected their family life. One young man, who had earned a degree in hydrology, spoke of how he had been a small boy when his father began attending the negotiation sessions. Another said that he felt as though he was walking in the footsteps of his grandfather, who had devoted decades to the struggle for Blue Lake.

Negotiators explained how, over the years, they had grown to appreciate individuals on the other side and, in the end, realized how much they had in common. One man remarked that he came to trust his parciante counterparts because, like him, they wore jeans, not suits, and after their endless meetings would go home to feed their livestock or clean out a ditch. Eleven individuals who had contributed significantly to the effort but had not lived to see this day, including Eduardo Lavadie and Geoff Bryce, were named and remembered.

In all these public venues, the major player who said the least and commanded the least attention was Palemon Martínez, the president of the TVAA. Palemon comported himself in his usual reserved, taciturn manner, operating with the slow, quiet care of someone carrying a vial of nitroglycerin. Not once did a newspaper article about the settlement quote him or mention his name. I was struck by how little the press made of the TVAA's vital role in instigating the negotiation so many years ago, the significance of the water-sharing agreements that the TVAA had managed to preserve against the threat of an externally imposed system of priority calls, or simply what it means to represent and be accountable to what by then numbered 55 acequia associations in the Taos Valley.

Despite my dismay at a seeming pattern of occlusion, I must admit that this laconic, unobtrusive, low-key, publicity-aversive approach proved extremely effective at the local, face-to-face level. After all, this was exactly how a man *con mucho respeto* should behave. In the national arena, however, where people sell their souls for a few moments of glory in the spotlight, such a strategy might not work so well. Perhaps this is why Eduardo wanted me to write a book about the case.

Notes

Prologue and Dedication

1. On June 6, 1967, Reies López Tijerina and some twenty members of the Alianza land grant movement attempted a citizens' arrest of the state attorney general at the Río Arriba county courthouse in Tierra Amarilla. The plan went awry, resulting in gunfire and violence, the Alianzas' flight into the hills, and a police manhunt and quasi-military occupation of the area that drew national attention, becoming a milestone in 20th-century New Mexico history (see Nabokov 1970). When I testified there, the courthouse appeared much the same as it had at the time of the raid.

2. In retrospect, this intense, internecine division seems more a dispute over tactics than intent, given the common goal of preserving water rights and traditional land use.

3. There is no universally acceptable nomenclature for Mexican Americans. Some refer to themselves by that term, and others use *Mexicano*, *Chicano*, or *Latino*. Eduardo probably used the term *Mexicano* in this particular context, but in other contexts he might have used *Raza*, *Chicano*, *Nuevomexicano*, or *Hispano*. As someone who identified himself politically as Chicano, he would not have used the terms *Spanish* and *Spanish American*, although many in Taos still prefer these terms without necessarily denying their mestizo heritage. I use the term *Mexican American* here to evoke the nonlocal perspective that Eduardo and Geoff wanted to transform. Throughout the rest of the book, I employ the terms *Hispano*, *Mexicano*, and *Nuevomexicano* more or less interchangeably to refer to native, Spanish-speaking New Mexicans.

Preface

1. According to the wishes of the TVAA board, all individuals mentioned in this book are referred to by their actual names. The one exception is in chapter 6, where a pseudonym is used.

2. The term *coyote* in New Mexico is a linguistic vestige of the colonial casta system of ethno-racial ranking. Today, it usually refers to a biethnic Anglo-Hispano but can apply to any mix between categories of identity. Its connotations range from neutral to negative or are made affectionate with a diminutive, as in *coyotito/coyotita*. My mother was an upper-middle-class Anglo from Austin, Texas, and my father, an upwardly mobile Hispano-Mexicano from Taos who ran a drugstore on the plaza. They each had their own hybrid set of parents, who were variously rooted in the contested and ever-shifting soil of the greater United States–Mexico borderlands. I grew up just outside the bosom of my father's extended family, which was concentrated in La Loma; I did not know any of my Austin kin well. According to my late grandmother, Otília Trujillo Rodríguez, at least six generations of Trujillos preceded mine on La Loma. Before that, some of them came from Pojoaque.

3. The principal players in the Abeyta case include Taos Pueblo; the TVAA, with more than seventy-five hundred individual parciantes; the city of Taos; the El Prado Water and Sanitation District; 12 mutual domestic water users associations; the New Mexico Office of the State Engineer; the US Department of the Interior; and the US Department of Justice.

4. Secrecy is a powerful Pueblo norm. It is a mechanism or an adaptive strategy Pueblos have long used to maintain internal stratification, as well as external boundaries vis-à-vis outsiders (see Brandt 1980).

Chapter 1, Introduction

1. Royal land grants, *mercedes reales*, were grants of land made by the Spanish crown to individuals (private) or a group of heads of household (community) as a reward for service or an incentive to settle on the colonial frontiers of New Spain. Westphall (1983:276) lists 13 land grants issued for the central Taos basin between 1702 and 1815.

2. New Mexican acequia systems resemble the Iberian and Moorish traditions whence they sprang. Historian Thomas Glick summarizes:

> The Spaniards brought with them to the American Southwest a constellation
> of arid-land techniques, including both the technology and institutional
> framework for irrigation and the distribution of water. These customs and
> techniques represented, in turn, a prior diffusion of Near Eastern culture intro-
> duced into Spain by the Muslims in the early Middle Ages. Although custom
> differed from place to place and that of eastern Spain was distinct from that of
> southern and western Spain, the Islamic substratum lent to the entire penin-

sula a basic homogeneity of water-distribution institutions. Thus, whether irrigation communities were autonomously administered or controlled by town government, or whether water was considered public or private, attached to the land or alienable (the typical juridical distinctions made by legal scholars), actual practice was based upon a number of suppositions common to all: the irrigators of one canal (or water source) received water in proportion to the amount of land irrigated and subscribed to maintenance costs in proportion to the amount of water used; administration, whether elective or appointive, was entrusted to officials, usually irrigators themselves, who knew the local custom. For this reason, irrigators tended to have substantial power to regulate their own systems, whether formal control was vested in a higher authority or not. [Glick 1972:4]

3. José Rivera's book *Acequia Culture* (1998) provides the most comprehensive overview of New Mexico acequia history and organization. It contains a wealth of documents pertaining to the rules, regulations, and records of various acequia communities in the state.

4. Based on a review of hundreds of documented water cases from the 17th, 18th, and 19th centuries in Mexico and the Hispanic Southwest, M. C. Meyer (1984:145–164; 2000:60–72) proposed that seven principles of water allocation operated in the northern Spanish borderlands: Just Title, Prior Use (not to be confused with the prior appropriation of American law), Need, Injury to Third Party, Intent, Legal Right, and Equity and the Common Good.

5. According to D. A. Caponera's discussion of water laws in Muslim countries, the Right of Thirst is "juridically the right to take water to quench one's thirst or to water one's animals" (Caponera 1973:13). Also see Wescoat Jr. (1998:259–169). There is also a Right of Irrigation in Islamic law. Therefore, it seems possible that these ancient principles underlie the acequia water-sharing practices of both sobrante and auxilio. Francesca De Chatel writes that the very term for Islamic law, *Shari`ah*,

is closely related to water. It is included in early Arab dictionaries and originally meant "the place from which one descends to water." Before the advent of Islam in Arabia, the *Shari`ah* was, in fact, a series of rules about water use: the *shuraat al-maa* were the permits that gave rights to drinking water. The term later evolved to include the body of laws and rules given by Allah. Water should be freely available to all, and any Muslim who withholds unneeded water sins against Allah: *"No one can refuse surplus water without sinning against Allah and against man."*

There are two fundamental precepts that guide the rights to water in the Shari`ah: *shafa*, the right of thirst, establishes the universal right for humans to quench their thirst and that of their animals; *shirb*, the right of irrigation, gives all users the right to water their crops. Both rules are interpreted in different ways by the various schools of Islam, and their implementation varies from region to region, from village to village, each community applying the law to suit geographical and social circumstance. [De Chatel 2002:7]

6. Trawick further explicates the six principles underlying the operation of autonomous irrigation communities:

1. Autonomy: The community has and controls its own flow of water.
2. Uniformity: Among water rights: everyone receives water with the same frequency. In technique: everyone irrigates in the same way.
3. Contiguity: Water is distributed to fields in a fixed contiguous order based only on their location along successive canals.
4. Proportionality (equity or fairness): Among rights: no one may use more water than the amount to which the extent of their land entitles them, nor may they legally get it more often than everyone else. Among duties: peoples' contributions to maintenance must be proportional to the amount of irrigated land they have.
5. Regularity: Things are always done in the same way under conditions of scarcity; no exceptions are allowed, and any sudden expansion or irrigation is prohibited.
6. Transparency: Everyone knows the rules and has the ability to confirm, with their own eyes, whether or not those rules are generally being obeyed, to detect and denounce any violations that occur. [Trawick 2001a:367]

7. Other elements of a water right include priority, amount, purpose, and periods and place of use; for irrigation, they include specific tracts of land to which the water right is appurtenant and "other conditions as may be necessary to define the right and its priority." See New Mexico Statute 72-4-19.

8. For Ida M. Luján's account (1999:98–105) of her struggle to earn acceptance and respect as an active parciante on her ditch near the small town of Coyote in Río Arriba County, see "Challenging Tradition, Opening the Headgate." Fabi Romero, a friend of mine who became the first woman mayordomo in San Cristobal in 1996, provided the following account:

I was the first woman to show up to clean ditches in San Cristobal back in 1980. The men just pretended I wasn't there. They seemed embarrassed when I arrived with my gloves and shovel. When Cleofes, who was mayordomo, called the roll for Gabriel Romero [Fabi's father], I answered, "Here." There were side-glances and smirks all around. Cleofes asked me if I wanted to ride around with him, checking on crews and taking water to them. I said I wanted to work with the crew going up through my property and on to the compuerta at the head of the valley. There was muttering among the men when I said that. I don't think they were thrilled to have me, and they did their best to ignore me, but I kept engaging them in conversation and worked my ass off. By the end of the day, they were all quite friendly. The next year, the Peggys and Mary Arellano joined me. After that, it became commonplace for women to be there, and they make up at least 10 percent of the crew. Nobody seems to think it is out of the ordinary anymore. This year [2003] there were about 15 women, including young women I didn't recognize. We all work really hard so nobody will have cause to complain. As for ditch commissions, to the best of my recollection, women have always been on them since I came back in 1979 to take over my parents' property. [E-mail to author, May 8, 2003]

9. David Reichard (1996:28–29) refers to an 1899 water dispute case in which Santo Domingo Pueblo argued for its right to determine its own laws regarding water use rather than conform to the laws of the territory. This implies that the pueblo had its own way of managing irrigation, differing from that of neighboring acequia associations. Yet I have been told that Laguna and Acoma pueblos have adopted the acequia association-mayordomo model for settling water disputes and other forms of internal disputation.

Chapter 2, "Irrigation in Taos"

1. According to Anschuetz (1998:165–167), five accounts by Spanish chroniclers from the late 16th and early 17th centuries describe stream diversion by Pueblo irrigators in the New Mexican territory. These include two from the 1582 Espejo expedition: near Socorro (for the Piro) and near the Acoma and Zuni pueblos. The latter account, recorded by Diego Perez de Luxan, reports "many irrigated corn fields with canals and dams, built as if by Spaniards" (Hammond and Rey 1966:182). Gaspar Castaño de Sosa reported seeing, in 1591, canal irrigation in six villages (Nambé, Tesuque, Pojoaque, Cuyamunque, and possibly Pecos or Jacona and San Ildefonso or San Juan) located in the Tewa and Tano districts north of Santa Fe: "All six of these settlements had canals for irrigation, which would be incredible to anyone who had not seen them with his own eyes. The inhabitants harvest large quantities of corn, beans, and other vegetables" (Hammond and Rey 1966:282).

Another reference to stream irrigation near the confluence of the Río Jemez and another tributary comes from the Chamuscado expedition of 1581 (Hammond and Rey 1966:118). The last dates from 1601, shortly after Oñate's settlement of the colony (Hammond and Rey 1953:626).

2. Tlaxcaltecans may have also transmitted the Matachines dance to the Pueblos, which would explain why some attribute the dance to Montezuma. A suggestive parallel exists between the Matachines dance and ditch cleaning: both involve line formations overseen by an authority figure (mayordomo for the ditch, *abuelo* for the dance) who calls out some of the same commands, such as "Vuelta!" (Turn!) and "Sigue adelante!" (Move forward!).

3. Parsons further describes how the secular Iberian form mixed with aboriginal belief and ritual practice:

> Irrigation by ditch was not unknown to Pueblos before the Conquest, being

practiced at Hawikuh and Acoma and probably elsewhere, but contemporary methods are of Spanish introduction, and so to work on the ditch—cleaning and repair—is naturally in charge of the secular officer, or, at Santo Domingo, on the last day, in charge of the Mexican kachina; but when it comes to opening the ditch, prayer-sticks or feathers are deposited or made by Town chief or shamans, since Water People or Horned Water Serpent control the water's flow, just as they control the water of the Río Grande. [Parsons 1974:1117–1118]

Like others, Parsons observed that the Eastern, or Rio Grande, Pueblos were more dependent on live canal irrigation than the Western Pueblos, where dry farming predominated. As a result, she reports, "the irrigation or ditch-opening ceremonies of the East in charge of clown groups or Town chiefs are not paralleled in the less irrigated or more recently irrigated Western region, nor is the ceremony of general exorcism by the societies cleansing fields, town, and people altogether paralleled" (Parsons 1974:960).

4. Ortiz (1968:117) suggests that before the Tewa started planting wheat, they did not clean their ditches until the vernal equinox. Their Hispano neighbors gradually pressured them to clean the acequias earlier to accommodate the planting date for wheat. He reports that "until recent years Spanish American farmers have all but forced the Tewa to cooperate, by early March, in cleaning and restoring the complex system of irrigation canals they share." Moreover, colonial Catholic rule compelled San Juan Pueblo to reschedule some of its public mass rituals either to precede or to follow the 40 days of Lent. Because the planting and harvesting of wheat took place outside the aboriginal subsistence cycle, the Tewa made these the responsibility of the governor's staff, "an external and independent, but parallel organization [to the indigenous Made People and] the Spanish officials" (Ortiz 1968:174). The pueblo governor enjoys several prerogatives as a result of presiding over the communal aspects of wheat farming: he may receive a portion of each family's wheat harvest for the use of communal machinery; he may rent out a portion of pueblo lands to Hispano farmers; and he may also lease out land to non-Indian stockmen. Ortiz further notes:

> The only other special prerogative the Spanish officials have they share with the *Fiscales* [whose annual duties relate to Catholic ritual activity], and it, too, was introduced by the Spaniards. These two organizations are the only ones exempt from having to work on the irrigation canals while they are in office. Yet the canals are in the governor's over-all charge, and the *Fiscales* have the task of notifying Pueblo residents a month before they are to be cleaned each year. Thus, it seems that the non-aboriginal—and often problematic—traits and activities are placed in the charge of the Spanish-introduced officials, and these officials may avail themselves of whatever advantages may accrue to them because of this fact. [Ortiz 1968:174]

With respect to the process I call acequiazation, Ortiz remarks: "While Harrington (1916:p. 52) and others have noted that the Tewa practiced irrigation before the coming of the Spaniards, they could not have approached in complexity the present system without beasts of burden and metal tools" (Ortiz 1968:117). Also writing along these lines, Frances Leon Quintana concurs that the prehispanic Pueblos had ditches but notes that "the colonists introduced some advanced irrigation techniques such as dams built above the ditch intakes, movable wooden ditch gates, and flumes. They also introduced metal shovels and hoes, as aids in building, cleaning, and diverting ditches" (Quintana 1990:289).

5. Archaeological excavation on Taos Pueblo land has always been prohibited by the tribal council. The single exception took place in 1961, when archaeologists Florence Hawley Ellis and J. J. Brody (1964) were authorized to dig for one day only in the south-side refuse pile in order to establish a stratigraphy for expert testimony in the Taos Blue Lake case. Also see Gordon-McCutchan (1991:77–78).

6. Fowles (2004:451) suggests that stream diversion irrigation at Pot Creek, or T'aitöna, may have developed as part of an experiment in agricultural intensification that continued among Northern Tiwa groups. At least some of those who relocated to Taos from T'aitöna or elsewhere during the late pre-contact centuries could have arrived with the full repertoire of irrigation and water-conservation techniques known to Anasazi farmers. Therefore, cobble mulch and other dry-farm methods may possibly have been complemented by floodwater and some degree of stream diversion. Fowles also challenges the common assumption that Taos district (Pot Creek) was peripheral.

7. David Weber (1996:20 n. 15), citing John Baxter, identifies Santa Gertrudis as La Loma, but Baxter (1990:17–18) gives no real source for this claim. I have never been able to verify it with local historians.

8. Modern parishes, communities, churches, chapels, and moradas (local chapter houses of the Penitente Brotherhood) in the central Taos basin:

> *Nuestra Señora de Guadalupe (Our Lady of Guadalupe Parish)*
>
> Don Fernando (Nuestra Señora de Guadalupe Church)
>
> Taos Pueblo (San Gerónimo Chapel)
>
> Cañon (Nuestra Señora de los Dolores Chapel)
>
> El Prado (Santa Teresa Chapel, formerly Nuestra Señora de los Dolores)
>
> Upper Ranchitos (La Purísima, or Immaculate Conception Chapel)
>
> Lower Ranchitos (San Francisco de Paula, defunct chapel)
>
> La Loma (San Antonio Chapel)

Defunct moradas include Cañón and Lower Ranchitos. Las Cruces, no longer active but still standing and now owned by the Taos Historic Museums (formerly the Kit Carson Museum), is sometimes referred to as Mabel's morada because it is located behind the Mabel Dodge Luhan estate. The San Francisco de Paula (or Pauda) Chapel in Lower Ranchitos is long defunct, and its precise location uncertain.

Another building, formerly a chapel (patron unknown) but now converted to secular use, is located on the main highway in the Placitas area between the Río Pueblo and El Prado.

> *San Francisco de Assisi (Saint Francis Parish)*
> Ranchos (San Francisco Church)
> Talpa (Nuestra Señora de San Juan de los Lagos Chapel and defunct Durán or
> Our Lady of Talpa Chapel)
> Llano Quemado (Nuestra Señora del Carmen Chapel)
> Cordillera (San Isidro Chapel)
> Los Córdovas (San Isidro Chapel)

There are three active moradas and one possible defunct morada in Llano Quemado, according to Harold Ottaway (1975:24). I have been unable to confirm this among elderly individuals in the area.

> *Santísima Trinidad (Holy Trinity Parish)*
> Arroyo Seco (Holy Trinity Church)
> Des Montes
> Valdez (San Antonio Chapel)
> Arroyo Hondo (Nuestra Señora de los Dolores Chapel)
> Las Colonias (Santo Niño de Atocha Chapel)
> San Cristóbal (San Cristóbal Chapel)

There are four extinct moradas: Des Montes, possible patron San Ignacio de Loyola, still standing but now a private residence; Upper Arroyo Hondo, also standing and converted into a private residence; and Lower Arroyo Hondo and Valdez, both falling into ruin. One active morada remains, in Arroyo Seco.

9. Meyer makes the point that "as late as 1793 no measurement of Taos Pueblo land had ever been made...Spain's self-imposed obligation to recognize property rights of Indians extended only to the lands they were using productively at the time of the conquest, and it is impossible to determine if the land subsequently occupied by the town of Taos can be so classified" (Meyer 2000:137).

A major land dispute erupted in 1815 when the governor of Taos Pueblo appealed to the *alcalde mayor* of the ayuntamiento of Don Fernando de Taos to evict Spanish settlers living within the pueblo grant or league meted out in 1793 (Meyer 2000:144). The alcalde passed the potentially explosive case on to the provincial governor, who upheld the Pueblo in principle but did not issue an eviction order. Instead, he ordered the alcalde to work out an equitable and just compromise with the assistance of the Protector of the Indians. Shortly thereafter, a newly appointed alcalde mayor informed the governor that he had remeasured the league as instructed and found that three plazas and a church, all built by vecino labor and involving about 190 families, did indeed encroach on the Pueblo grant. Evidently, these placitas were Don Fernando, Cañon, and Los Estiércoles. No doubt dreading the consequences if these settlements were ejected wholesale, again the governor issued a decree calling for a fair compromise that would minimize injury to both sides. It seems that part of the resulting compromise involved the approval of the Arroyo Hondo land grant in 1815. It was populated by settlers from the town area. That same year, the village of Arroyo Seco was also established. It would soon place new demands on the upper Río Lucero and would lead to endemic conflict over its water and, ultimately, the three-way reparto described in chapter 4.

"Encroachment" by the town of Don Fernando onto Indian land was asserted in the late 19th century after US federal surveyors defined the Pueblo grant, for which a pre-American document was never found (Meyer 2000:137 nn. 279, 280).

10. Despite the fact that Follett (1898:108) probably undercounted the number of ditches in Taos, he concluded that depletion of the Rio Grande above El Paso was caused by increased diversion by new, post-1879 ditches in the San Luís Valley of southern Colorado. Use of water for irrigation in New Mexico, including the Taos Mesa, had not increased substantially since 1880. Finally, Follett (1898:108) concluded that there would be sufficient water to serve one but not two reservoirs above El Paso. According to historian Wells Hutchins (1928:276–277, figure 1), the highest rate of ditch proliferation in New Mexico actually came during the late 19th century, after Americanization. TVAA officials insist that his data do not refer to the Taos Valley; moreover, the US district court has issued orders that confirm pre-1846 priority dates for all community acequias.

11. Under federal subsidy, Pueblo agriculture expanded during the 1930s, followed by a period of steady decline after World War II. In stunning contrast to Follett's count four years earlier, Vlasich reports that 142 acres were farmed at Taos Pueblo in 1900 and 1,338 in 1936 (Vlasich 2005:184, table 5; 1980:25–46). Vlasich indicates that there were 2,015 acres of cropland at the pueblo in 1940 (2005:195, table 7) and 2,369 in 1944, an increase of 17.6 percent (2005:205, table 9).

12. Nonmovers were defined as "people who did not change place of residence over the 5-year period"; intracounty movers "were often young single-parent Hispanic households, a high percentage living in poverty, and not highly educated" (BBER 2000b:35).

Chapter 3, "Dividing the Río Pueblo"

1. Blue Lake is a major feature of Taos Pueblo's sacred geography. It became famous as the result of a 64-year legal battle between Taos Pueblo and the federal government over the ownership and control of the lake and the 64,000 acres of wilderness surrounding it. The Blue Lake case became a milestone in Native American legal history because this sizable tract of aboriginal mountain wilderness was finally restored in 1970 through an act of Congress—and because it succeeded on an argument that linked religious freedom with cultural survival. The cause célèbre of the sacred Blue Lake became synonymous with how Taos Pueblo defined itself to the world and probably to itself. For a tribal-sponsored history of the case,

see Gordon-McCutchan (1991). Also see Bodine (1978). There was local Hispano opposition to, as well as support for, the pueblo's Blue Lake cause. Some Río Pueblo parciantes feared that a pueblo victory would somehow curtail their water; other locals perhaps felt resentment or jealousy.

2. Taos Pueblo is organized into a moiety system, with ceremonial kivas on both the north and south sides. The north side (Winter People) is said to be symbolically associated with hunting, and the south side (Summer People) is symbolically associated with agriculture. It is hard to imagine a more felicitous natural or geological inspiration for a twofold division than the upper banks of the Río Pueblo. Severin Fowles (2004, 2005) has brilliantly reconciled archaeological evidence with Taos oral tradition (culled from Matilda Cox Stevenson's previously unknown field notes) in a novel explanation of Pot Creek Pueblo or T'aitöna prehistory, covering its establishment and abandonment (1320) within about a seventy-year period. Fowles proposes that the moiety was a key structural step taken during this period to accommodate the aggregation of distinct groups who arrived from different places. The dual division was a way of "formalizing the social relationships between a local population and a recently arrived group of immigrants" (Fowles 2005:25). Like other pueblos of the era, T'aitöna was abandoned during a phase of architectural expansion; presumably, some part of the exodus settled at Cornfield Taos. Fowles challenges presumption that the religious activity centered on the great kivas served an integrative function. Instead, he argues that the construction of the great kivas and the emergent hierocratic structure they reflect precipitated the fission and abandonment of T'aitöna.

3. Sources for non-Indian irrigated acreage include the hydrographic survey (New Mexico State Engineer Office 1969, 1995) and the Taos Valley Acequia Association. Their figures far exceed the mere 2,300 acres reported in 1968 by the Bureau of Reclamation (BR) and cited by John Baxter (1990:70)—numbers the TVAA considers erroneous, as confirmed by the state's hydrographic survey. Again citing the BR, Baxter reports that roughly eight hundred acres at Taos Pueblo are irrigated by the Río Pueblo. Historian James Vlasich (2001:371, n. 34), drawing on 1964 data, reports 1,790 irrigated acres at Taos Pueblo. Vlasich also reports an 18 percent (381-acre) loss in irrigated acreage at Taos Pueblo between 1938 and 1964; he provides no figure for the number of acres under irrigation in 1981 (2005:284, table 11). Also see chapter 2, n. 11.

4. This is shown on the Río Pueblo Hydrographic Survey map produced by the Department of Interior Bureau of Indian Affairs in 1989 and revised in 1997.

5. Geoff Bryce and Fred Waltz (personal communication with the author, June 8, 2004), who cited the hydrographic survey (New Mexico State Engineer Office 1969, 1995) as their source.

6. An archaeological and historical survey of Santa Fe's acequia system was completed by historical archaeologist David Snow (1988) in the 1980s. Snow indicates that the Santa Fe acequias were supposedly laid out according to royal ordinances

given to Don Pedro de Peralta in 1609, although little is actually known about their layout and names before 1680 (Snow 1988:5). In any case, they are still much better documented than the Taos ditches.

7. According to Meyer:

> By the time the Taos community received its corporate status the acequias had been carrying water to the fields for years and in the absence of compelling reason there was no need to alter a system that functioned well. Even when the Acequia Madre del Pueblo was extended to run into the town a few years after incorporation it was administered by the parciantes, rather than the town itself. Without question the ayuntamiento of Taos had the power to build and administer a new public acequia and to modify patterns of water allocation but there is no evidence that this power was ever exercised. On the other hand there is ample evidence that the officials of the ayuntamiento exercised their judicial responsibilities when other kinds of water disputes surfaced in the Taos Valley.[Meyer 2000:139]

8. Ralph Meyers (1885–1948) grew up in Colorado and first saw Taos in 1904. He started a curio shop (now owned by his wife's descendants) in 1911 and became well known as a craftsman, photographer, painter, raconteur, and history buff. Rebecca James (1953:27–29) memorialized him in *Allow Me to Present 18 Ladies and Gentlemen.*

9. Another account of ditches in town was provided by my friend Vicente Martínez, a descendant of Padre Antonio José Martínez, owner and (until recently) occupant of the padre's historical home, located west of Taos plaza. I asked Vicente, in his sixties, what he remembered about the acequias in town, and he e-mailed me the following:

> My memories of our little part of the Taos acequia system go back to the '40s when we had a small orchard in the back of our property that needed to be irrigated. I believe that the orchard dated back to the time of Padre Martínez' occupancy of the property. The orchard consisted of a few apple, pear, plum, and berry trees and would have been directly behind my house where the Yaxche School playground is now located.
>
> The ditch, which ran from a slight NE to SW direction, divided the orchard. To irrigate, I used to go up to the compuerta of the Acequia Madre by the Mabel Dodge home to open the water to our ditch. It was great because it took about half a day, or more, to get to our place and I could take my time following it, making sure it wasn't obstructed along the way. From the Acequia Madre, the ditch ran SW through Kit Carson Park, behind the cemetery, and into a little pond (where we would ice skate in the winter) that took forever to fill. It ran west through the park to the main road (Paseo del Pueblo Norte) and crossed over to Armory (Civic Plaza Drive) and ran west along the

south side of the road. There was also another branch from the park that went down Bent Street. Also, near the Acequia Madre compuerta was another ditch that ran NW and came out behind Kachina Lodge and down the west side of Pueblo Road towards your old neighborhood.

Our ditch crossed Placitas Road and ran south along the fence between the street and the old football field and behind the old Parr house, where it went SW towards the Sisters' [the Loretto nuns] convent and irrigated an orchard along the way. I believe that they even diverted it into their little courtyard behind the main convent building. It continued to the front of the convent and ran parallel to a long sidewalk that ran south from the entry to the convent to Don Fernando Street. I seem to remember that the Sisters' stretch was concrete lined. It exited the convent grounds by the main gate on Don Fernando Street, crossed the street and ran SW behind the Romero's territorial home on Don Fernando and Padre Martínez Lane, and towards our orchard.

From there it continued SW towards Manzanares Street and came out somewhere near the old Templeton Laundry (Larry Bell Studio). We quit using the ditch in the early '50s, and sometime after that, my dad removed almost all of the trees. Later, the Town of Taos acquired all of the old water rights in exchange for hookups to the municipal water system. [E-mail to author, March 9, 2004]

Chapter 4, "Dividing the Río Lucero"

1. The Follett Report (1898:88, 160) indicates that 1894 and 1895 were years of average rainfall, whereas 1889 was drier. Follett also estimates that fewer acre-feet of water were used in 1896 than in the two preceding years.

2. This was the land grant that Englishman Arthur Manby, the subject of Taos's most famous murder mystery, swindled and schemed to acquire during the early 20th century. See Waters (1973).

3. Archaeologist Jeffrey Boyer (1991) conducted a test excavation of the Arroyo torreón.

4. The surco was a common unit of liquid measurement, sometimes still used, in apportioning water in community acequias. Its precise size remains a matter of some dispute. Meyer reports that a surco (sometimes rendered *sulco*) came to "slightly over fifty-one gallons per minute, or the amount needed to fill an average trench dug by a simple plow" (Meyer 1984:90). Baxter, citing the Río Lucero case (among others), argues that in New Mexico the surco is a flexible measure whose "size may vary from one community to the next" (Baxter 2000:410–411).

5. For detailed chronicles of the water disputes on the Río Lucero, over the Antonio Martínez land grant, or between Arroyo Seco and Taos Pueblo over the Tenorio Tract, see, for example, Jenkins (1966); Waters (1973); Meyer (1984); Baxter (1990); Meyer and Brescia (1998); and Ebright (2001). Also see note 6, below.

6. The Tenorio Tract is a much-contested area of some 5,696 acres (Ellis n.d.:4–6; Laflin 1941) that lies south of the Arroyo Seco Creek, north and also south or east of the Río Lucero, and north of the Pueblo village. It acquired the name from its sale in 1818 by Miguel Tenorio, acting as agent for the sons of Sebastian Martín and the alleged heirs to the Antonio Martínez grant, to the "sons of the Pueblo." The sale included a corner containing the upper reaches of the river known as la Rinconada {corner} del Río de Lucero (Jenkins 1983:24–52). The Tenorio Tract lies within the overlapping boundaries of both the Antonio Martínez (1716) and Antoine Leroux, or Los Luceros (1742), land grants. Its convoluted legal history derives from claims and counterclaims exerted with respect to both these grants and to Río Lucero water. Strips within it were apparently undergoing allotment to Arroyo Seco settlers as early as 1815—16, and as noted in the text, their encroachment on the water of the Río Lucero had precipitated joint downstream complaints from the pueblo, Don Fernando de Taos, and Los Estiércoles (El Prado).

The New Mexico surveyor general approved the Antoine Leroux grant in 1861 when Taos Pueblo withdrew its initial opposition to the claim because it contained the Tenorio Tract. The pueblo thereupon repurchased the tract, this time from an agent of the Leroux grant heirs. The Antonio Martínez grant was confirmed by the Court of Private Land Claims in 1882 and patented in 1902, the same year Arthur Manby sued to confirm his ambitious claim to a large portion of the grant, including the Tenorio Tract. In 1916, [43]/45 of the entire grant was awarded to Manby and his Taos Valley Land Company (Waters 1973). As a defendant in the case, the pueblo appealed, and in 1918 the New Mexico Supreme Court ruled that the pueblo's Tenorio Tract deed was valid and, moreover, that the Court of Private Land Claim's confirmation of the Antonio Martínez grant was invalid because of the pueblo's ownership of this and another part (the García de la Mora grant) of the previously confirmed Leroux grant. This position was again argued by the United States in 1929.

Hispano "trespassers" were ultimately ejected from parcels on the Tenorio Tract south of the Arroyo Seco Creek as a result of Pueblo Lands Board findings in the 1920s and 1930s. Testimony in the case (*US as Guardian of the Pueblo of Taos {Tenorio Tract} v. Preciliano García et al.*) by both Indian and Hispano witnesses indicated that non-Indians had begun to build houses south of the Arroyo Seco Creek in the late 19th and early 20th centuries and that both Indians and non-Indians had also used Tenorio Tract lands to graze livestock. The pueblo allotted to tribal members parcels that had been occupied and irrigated by Hispanos, and the government installed new ditches and diversion structures for the pueblo's use on the western portion of the tract near Arroyo Seco (Kelly 1994:46–55).

7. See Rivera (1998:69–73) for the text of *Reglas y Regulaciones de la Asequia Madre de Arroyo Seco,* dated 1956. These rules pertain to the self-government and administration of the ditch.

8. This account is based on oral information from Palemon Martínez and Fermín Torres. It differs from what is indicated on the TVAA map, based on the hydro-

graphic survey, which suggests that the Eraclio Martínez ditch is off the La Plaza Lateral and that the latter is off the Acequia Madre del Río Lucero de Arroyo Seco.

9. I define oral historical memory as firsthand information passed by word of mouth from one generation to the next, to a maximum depth of five generations.

10. See Rivera (1998:140–145) for the written text of *Ditch Rules of the El Prado Middle Ditch or Acequia del Medio*, dated 1957.

11. Karavas Tract warranty deed, dated August 8, 1936. The deed lists James Karavas; wife, Noula Karavas; and John Karavas, a single man.

12. By contrast, Tesuque Pueblo, a party to the Aamodt case, sued for this measure of priority calls in May. See "Pueblo wants all water," Doug McClellan, *Albuquerque Journal North*, May 16, 1996, B-1, B-3; also, "Tesuque Pueblo sues to protect its water rights," Karen Peterson, *Santa Fe New Mexican*, May 16, 1996, A-1, A-4.

13. See chapter 1, n. 5. Again, the Right of Thirst is "juridically the right to take water to quench one's thirst or to water one's animals" (Caponera 1973:13). The Right of Irrigation "gives all users the right to irrigate their crops" (De Chatel 2002:7).

14. See Meyer (1984:53–55); Baxter (1997:84–85); and Ebright (2001:3–45).

Chapter 5, "*Respeto and Moral Economy*"

1. For discussions of the honor-shame complex and critiques of the literature, see, for example, J. G. Peristiany, ed. (1966); Julian Pitt-Rivers (1966, 1971); Jane Schneider (1971); David Gilmore, ed. (1987); Joao de Pina-Cabral (1989); Gilmore (1990); Frank Henderson Stewart (1994); and Lyman Johnson and Sonya Lipsett-Rivera, eds. (1998). Ortner (1996) argues persuasively that the emergence of a code of female purity was concurrent with emergence of the state.

2. The Lower Rio Grande Valley variant of this masculine ideal—feo, fuerte, y formal—is noted by folklorist Americo Paredes (1966:121). In this sense, *feo* (ugly) means dangerous if crossed; *fuerte* means physically and psychologically strong; and *formal* means principled, respectful, honorable, reliable, trustworthy, reserved.

3. Brooks's study of the southwest borderlands slave economy argues that indigenous societies brought to the Columbian encounter their own notions of honor and shame:

> Hence any historical view is limited that treats notions of honor in the border-
> lands simply as a type of Mediterranean cultural baggage hauled across the
> Atlantic and deposited on the pristine landscape of El Nuevo Mundo. Honor,
> it has been claimed, served as a distancing value through which Europeans
> defined themselves as superior to natives, who lacked both the quality of and
> capacity for honorable action. In fact, there existed a particular resonance
> between indigenous notions of honor and shame, of male violence and
> exchange imperatives in the region, a resonance persisting well after the
> United States' conquest of the region in 1846. In the Southwest Borderlands,

diverse social traditions of honor and shame, of violence, kinship, and community met, merged, and regenerated in new expressions. Over time, they produced an intricate web of intercultural animosity and affection that lingers
today in the mixed sounds of hand drums and violins, of battle cries and love
songs. [Brooks 2002:9–10]

4. Schneider further elaborates:

> Honor defines the group's social boundaries, contributing to its defense against
> the claims of equivalent competing groups. Honor is also important as a sub-
> stitute for physical violence in the defense of economic interests. The head of a
> family challenges the rest of the world with the idea of his family's honor. His
> "hypersensitive, punctilious posture" (in the words of Caro Baroja 1966) con-
> vinces others to exercise restraint, not so much to avoid physical retaliation as
> to avoid the consequences of continuing rancor. Paradoxically, the idea of
> honor can also serve to legitimate limited aggression, making acts of imposi-
> tion, encroachment, and usurpation morally valid in the eyes of nearly every-
> one except the victim. Especially in bilateral societies, where the exercise of
> collective force and violence is vastly curtailed but family patrimony is
> extremely vulnerable, honor regulates affairs among men. [Schneider 1971:17]

Chapter 6, "Honoring San Isidro"

1. For example, many families in Ranchos, Talpa, and Llano Quemado own lin-
eas in the Cristobal del la Serna land grant.

2. Briggs reports that before 1932 the people of Córdova, in neighboring Rio
Arriba County, observed a vesper, procession, and *velorio* (an all-night prayer watch)
for San Isidro on May 14–15. He recounts a processional format not unlike that in
Los Córdovas before the establishment of the new chapel:

> The wake began after vespers on May 14, the eve of the saint's day. All the
> villagers would gather at the community chapel, where Saint Isidore's image
> was placed on a freshly decorated processional platform…. A procession then
> formed, and the group descended the hillside, crossed the Quemado valley, and
> ascended approximately three miles to the upland dry farms at Las Joyas. The
> journey was punctuated by the rhythm of chanted prayers and of the melodi-
> ous hymn for Saint Isidore.
>
> Upon reaching Las Joyas, the image was taken from the platform and laid
> in a green bower. Córdovans who owned fields at Las Joyas would take turns
> preparing the bower and hosting a wake on the land. The normally early-
> retiring farmers then began an all-night vigil. The darkness around the image
> was broken only by a line of candles. Two or more rezadores sang the many
> stanzas of the hymns, and the people intoned the chorus. This devotional
> concentration was broken only by a communal meal served at midnight.

The end of the wake was signaled when the face of Saint Isidore's image was illuminated by the first direct rays of sunlight. A procession immediately formed around the image, and the saint was carried on the platform at the head of the crowd across all of the Las Joyas fields, down the trail to the beginning of the Quemado valley through each of the valley fields. Upon reaching the plaza the image was returned to its place in the chapel, the populace dispersed. [Briggs 1983:110]

Interestingly enough, Brown described a similar velorio in 1939 for the village of Valdez, formerly San Antonio, in the upper Río Hondo watershed north of Taos:

On the evening of this day [May 15] a procession of the villagers, who are all farmers, carry San Ysidro in state to the farthest farm up the valley. Their host, the owner of this farm, awaits his saintly visitor. In the field near his farm he has prepared a *jacal* or little hut made of willows.

When the procession arrives, San Ysidro is placed within this miniature farm house. The hymn to San Ysidro as well as other alabados interspersed with the praying of the rosary. With all reverence, a good time is had. Gossiping groups take advantage of lulls in the singing and praying. The opportunity for flirtatious interludes is not neglected by younger members of the group.

Near midnight the owner of the farm, who is proud of the honor of having San Ysidro as an overnight guest, summons the group to supper. First, the old folks and the leaders in prayers and singing make their way to the well-laden tables, to partake of the meal amid decorous and dignified conversation. It is a different story when the young folks come to the table. Hilarity and laughter prolong the meal until elder authority asserts itself and the younger ones reluctantly return to the group around the *jacal* or shrine of San Ysidro.

When the rays of the rising sun first show themselves over the mountains on this, San Ysidro's own day, his hymn is sung with renewed vigor. With San Ysidro carried at the front the whole body of people wends its way down the river, following lanes and through fields so that San Ysidro may bless the crops, ensure fertility, and grant a bounteous harvest in the fall.

Slowly the procession follows the winding river, chanting and praying as it goes. Near noon they reach the last farm at the other end of the valley, where the pleased owner awaits them with great quantities of roast mutton, oven-baked bread, pies, and coffee. San Ysidro is temporarily neglected as the crowd scatters to the shade of the cottonwoods to feast on the bounty which has been provided.

On his return to the village San Ysidro is carried through the fields on the opposite bank of the river, so that none should fail to receive the blessings that his passing would bring them. His near approach to the village is heralded by the clear tones of the church bell. It is a tired but happy people who, after ensconcing San Ysidro in his own place in the church, disperse to prepare for the dance that night, confident that their fields would again yield bounteously this year. [Briggs 1978:185–186]

3. I have adopted the honorific title *doña* in referring to Corina Santistevan, out of respect and because she indicated her preference for this form of address from members of my generation. She graciously sponsored my entry into the San Isidro devotional community and acted as my guide and adviser throughout the event, granting me an interview and suggesting others whom I should interview. Her great fondness for my father, even more than my association with the TVAA, was probably the major factor in her decision to help me. She is a retired schoolteacher who worked in California for many years before returning to Taos. Having assisted in Van Dorn Hooker's (1996) history of the St. Francis Church in Ranchos, she is recognized as a knowledgeable local historian. We enjoyed many conversations about Taos history, but our interaction was structured more by the respeto I owed her as my elder than by collegial give and take. This became apparent when she took exception to some part of my interpretation of the folk Catholic sacred landscape, but she would neither explain why nor countenance my attempt to press her about it.

4. Briggs (1988) provides an in-depth linguistic analysis of Nuevomexicano oral performances, including prayers and hymns, with particular focus on *alabados*, the mournful hymns sung during the Lenten season. He asserts that the performance of alabanzas, hymns of praise performed for saints' feast days, is less common today than the performance of alabados (1988:289). This may be true for alabanzas performed from memory rather than read from written texts, such as the ones I reproduce here, which are quite common in the Taos area.

5. A variant of this hymn was recorded by Lorin Brown (1978:156–158) of Córdova in 1939. He identifies it as a "favorite of the people of the rural and sheep-raising sections of New Mexico" (1978:158) and describes a backyard shrine to Santa Inez del Campo where supplicants would burn candles to her in order to find something lost outdoors. Brown records that Santa Inez is "the patron saint of all followers of outdoor pursuits such as sheepherders, cowboys, woodsmen, trappers, and so on. Also, she is the saint whose aid is invoked for the recovery of lost or strayed animals, lost articles of any kind, as well as children who have been lost in the hills or mountains" (Brown 1978:158).

6. The gendering of space is an important dimension of cultural analysis. In Hispano Catholic and, for that matter, Tewa and Tiwa traditions, there are concentric domains of meaning that define spatial-cosmological space and place (see Ortiz 1969). The mountain wilderness seems conventionally accessible only to men in Nuevomexicano tradition; women may enter it escorted by men but not on their own. Doña Maria de la Cabeza manages to pull off excursions into the greater outdoors (beyond village space, perhaps the fields) through prayer. *Parteras* (midwives) would have also enjoyed greater mobility than most women, as is true in Mesoamerica. Of course, premodern, traditional spatial restrictions broke down

in the 20th century, and women in my post–World War II generation grew up free of them. Nonetheless, they still inhere in the ritual-moral or sacred domain. Men, women, and children circumambulate village or community space through the collective act of procession and inscription of the sacred landscape, as shown in chapter 7. It is noteworthy that the plotline of *And Now Miguel* (Krumgold 1953) centers on the young protagonist's eagerness to go into the mountains to herd sheep with his older brothers as a secular rite of passage into manhood. Supplication to make this journey informs Miguel's special prayer during the San Isidro procession, neatly conjoining personal with community aspirations. As a children's book, this story both illustrates and promulgates the production of local subjects. The US State Department film further frames this discourse within that of the nation, then deep in the Cold War (see G. Melendez 2004).

7. Two other variants of this alabanza to San Isidro were recorded by Brown (1978:185–186) and by Briggs (1980:183–184) for the village of Córdova in neighboring Rio Arriba County. Even 40 years after the attenuation of the associated velorio and procession in Córdova, Briggs acknowledges the continuing power of the alabanza to instruct:

> The significance of the hymn and the legend is not exhausted by their use in promoting agricultural success, and they are not exclusively tied to the wake. Forty years after the last Córdovan enactment of the wake, Manuel and Guadalupe [Briggs's informants] used this text (along with many others) to teach me about the saint, Córdova's past, and what it means to be Mexicano. They used it to convey a strong sense of what it means to be a ranchero, a hardworking farmer-rancher. Their words clearly showed that even if Córdovans now work for wages, the values and sentiments expressed by the rancheros of bygone days continue to provide a raison d'etre for their descendants. In other words, each invocation of the hymn and legend articulates the raconteur or vocalist's identification with Mexicano values and with his or her commitment to preserving an important cultural heritage. [Briggs 1983:114]

Chapter 7, "Procession, Water, and Place"

1. Procession and pilgrimage sometimes overlap, for example, when a pilgrimage or some part of it takes processional form. This is true of the annual Good Friday pilgrimage to Chimayó, which departs from various points north and south and arrives at the *santuario* throughout the day. The traditional Good Friday pilgrimage in Tomé, New Mexico, also takes processional form, as does the December 12 Día de Guadalupe pilgrimage up "A Mountain" in Tortugas, New Mexico. Parades and marches are secular, ritual, linear formations that also encode information about the actors' social identities and relationships to place.

2. James Fernandez writes that "by 'architectonic' we may mean the feeling tone a constructed space arouses and the memories it evokes. This arousal and this 'evoca-

tiveness' are the interrelated components of a complex yet somehow coherent experience. It is an experience of past and present, of primary and secondary and emergent qualities, of the present space itself as a physical stimulus coupled with associations, recollections, recallings, memories of the past which arise by means of significant activities that take place in that space or by means of signs that are in some way attached to it" (Fernandez 1992:216).

In Eva and Robert Hunt's discussion of the social organization of irrigation, they identify three types of conceptual models "available to the social anthropologist: local folk, legal/state folk, and scientific" (Hunt and Hunt 1976:392). Whereas the folk model is geared to managing and perpetuating the system, the scientific model aims to explain it. The anthropologist's job, say the Hunts, "is to construct a scientific model which will explain not only the way the irrigation system works, but also the folk models—how they relate to the social reality" (1976:392).

Folk models have "real" and "ideal" components, corresponding to what people say that they (should) do and their actual behavior. Anthropological models incorporate and analyze folk models but might not be recognizable or even agreeable to the people they describe. Trawick's (2001a:366) six principles of irrigation (see chapter 1, n. 6) represent such an anthropological model. Trawick believes that his Andean subjects would agree with his model. He characterizes these principles as "analytic statements, derived from questioning people about local practices and then confirming the information through participant-observation" (2001a:366). His model is relevant because it also describes what takes place on the acequias in northern New Mexico. My study ties the model of irrigation that emerges in Part One to the model of ritual procession described in Part Two. In this chapter, I am proposing an ethnographically revealed, architectonic model that unites the sacred with the irrigated landscape.

3. Color plates 2–5 (maps of Taos basin watersheds and parishes, the St. Francis parish and Río Grande del Rancho watershed, the Nuestra Señora de Guadalupe parish, and the Holy Trinity parish) do not include more ephemeral structures such as calvarios, rock shrines, descansos, and altars.

4. In the canyon above the mouth of the Río Chiquito flows the Río Olla, or Pot Creek. It passes near an ancient pueblo ruin excavated by archaeologists from Southern Methodist University and considered ancestral to both Taos and Picuris Pueblos (also see chapter 2, n. 6; chapter 3, n. 2). Indeed, the entire watershed is evidently strewn with unexcavated pre–Pot Creek Pueblo sites, including one in the Los Córdovas area. Ranchos is reputed to be an old pueblo site, as well as a Genízaro (detribalized and Hispanicized Indian) colonial settlement. Archaeological and historical investigation into these prehispanic and colonial sites is much needed.

5. During the 1940s and 1950s Leandro Durán, whose family owned the chapel, sold the altar screen and bultos to Henry Garnett for display in the Taylor Museum in Colorado Springs, where they now reside. See Wroth (1979:79–87) for a detailed account of the transaction.

6. Verónicas represent the woman said to have wiped sweat from Christ's face with a cloth during the Via Crucis (Way of the Cross); an imprint of his visage was left on the cloth. This act is depicted as the sixth station of the cross.

7. "Peñas Negras" (Black Stones) may refer to the blackish basalt boulders that line the nearby arroyo or to the former use of black lava rocks as grave markers (Gerdes 2006).

8. A close archaeological mapping of the Catholic cultural landscape around Taos is needed. For example, the placement of camposantos in border zones, either between communities or at the periphery of settlement, holds clues to the history of occupation and intercommunity relations in each watershed.

9. The expansion of the old Corpus Christi route to include a mix of new and traditional stations suggests that the 2000 procession in downtown Taos represented a resacralization of increasingly secular, urban space. The 2000 Corpus Christi stations were described in the parish program (June 25) as follows:

> Taos Elementary School: To pray for children, hosted by the Religious Education Committee
>
> Town of Taos civic offices: To pray for civic authorities and social justice, hosted by the Taos Prayer Group
>
> Police station: To pray for peace and justice, hosted by the Taos Guadalupanas
>
> La Fonda Hotel: To pray for travelers, merchants, and career persons, hosted by the Altar Society
>
> Pueblo Alegre Mall: To pray for the unborn and the parents of the aborted child, hosted by the Sacred Heart League
>
> La Loma Chapel: To pray for clergy and for religious and lay ministers, hosted by La Loma mayordomos
>
> Sloping porch (Hattie Trujillo residence): Benediction
>
> Padre Martinez Residence: To pray for ancestors, hosted by the Pastoral Council
>
> Green porch house: To pray for the vocations of married and single life, hosted by the Taos Pueblo Fiscales

A similar act of symbolic reclamation of space threatened by destructive or profane forces was performed in Chimayó in 1999, when the Hermanos Penitentes led a community procession through a town ravaged by the effects of a widely publicized heroin epidemic. The procession started at the Santa Cruz de la Cañada Church and ended at the famed Santuario de Chimayó, stopping to pray in front of five drug houses recently raided by the police (see Glendinning 2005:102–103).

Chapter 8, "Water and the Future of Intercultural Relations"

1. Devon Peña (1998:141–176) argues that traditional Chicano land- and water-management practices in the Río Arriba watershed promoted biodiversity along riparian corridors and created a system of "agroecology," based on local knowledge,

that anticipated the principles of modern conservation biology. His purpose is to refute claims by environmental historians that some agricultural practices by Hispano-Mexicano rancher-farmers (such as overgrazing) have contributed to environmental degradation. He also seeks to "provide a framework to bridge the divide that currently separates environmentalists from Chicano land-grant activists in New Mexico" (1998:171). Although Peña proposes that a place-centered environmental ethic underlies acequia water allocation and management practices, the ethnographic basis for his discussion is less specific than my own, and he refers broadly only to secular practice.

2. Perhaps Telesfor's sentiment points to a difference between acequia-based and indigenous technologies and moral economies: one relies on an irrigated (channelized) landscape and sacralizes a husbanded environment; the other, which at least partly reflects an aboriginal hunting ethos, sacralizes a more "natural" environment, one minimally—or differently—modified by human intervention.

3. This is the large adobe house or hacienda built near the Río Pueblo in Lower Ranchitos by Severino Martínez, the father of Padre Antonio José Martínez, Taos's famous 19th-century priest. In the 1980s the Kit Carson Museum Foundation restored the building and turned it into a museum, now operated by the Taos Historical Museums. See Weber (1996).

4. I am not suggesting that contemporary native Taoseños or Nuevomexicanos are still peasants who might rise up. Nevertheless, the parciante moral economy I describe does resemble patterns anthropologists have observed among peasants in the circum-Mediterranean and Latin America. Nuevomexicanos became postpeasant proletarians and, in some cases, middle-class property owners during the late 19th and early 20th centuries. Kearney argues that the anthropological construct of "peasant" should be jettisoned. Today's ethnographic study must situate these seemingly rural communities within the transnational and global contexts in which their economies are embedded and through which their members move (Kearney 1996:141). The moral economy, like the rural community or village where it arose, belongs to what Raymond Williams (1977) calls "the residual" (see n. 5). The idea of the rural community in modern Western thought and literature is romantic and imbued with nostalgia.

5. Here I draw on Raymond Williams's (1973, 1977) use of these terms and his notion of structures of feeling. Structures of feeling are "meanings and values as they are actively lived and felt" (Williams 1977:132). The residual involves such feelings and, Williams writes,

> by definition has been effectively formed in the past, but it is still active in the cultural process, not only and often not at all as an element of the past, but as an effective element of the present. Thus certain experiences, meanings, and values, which cannot be expressed or substantially verified in terms of the dominant culture, are nevertheless lived and practised on the basis of the

residue—cultural as well as social—of some previous social and cultural institution and formation...the idea of the rural community is predominantly residual, but it is in some limited respects alternative to or oppositional to urban industrial capitalism. [Williams 1977:122]

The emergence of new or refashioned identities that may self-consciously incorporate residual elements is tied, in Williams's view, to the emergence of a new class. Emergent forms may represent novel phases of the dominant culture or be alternative or oppositional to it (1977:123).

6. On the "meaning of water," Strang writes:

The meaning of water as a connective medium of "social being" needs to be reflected in methods of managing resources that are localised, collective, and inclusive, rather than exclusive and alienating. Because social identity is bound up with these connections, some kind of localisation of management would appear to offer a more sustainable way forward than management through distant and centralised institutions. [Strang 2004:251]

Epilogue

1. On the Blue Lake case, see chapter 3, n. 1.

2. It was the introduction of "new water" into the Rio Grande system by the San Juan–Chama Diversion Project that required the quantification of all extant water rights claims and their ranking according to the principle of prior appropriation. This triggered the Rio Grande Pueblo water rights adjudications, including Aamodt and Abeyta. The San Juan–Chama Diversion Project has its origin in the era of big federal dam constructions. Like many other water dramas in the West, it arises from the dividing and damming of the mighty Colorado—a river that does not even flow through the state of New Mexico. In 1948 the Upper Colorado River Basin Compact divided the water of the Colorado River among various western states, including California, Utah, Arizona, and New Mexico. The compact allotted New Mexico roughly 11 percent of Upper Basin water. To secure its entitlement, New Mexico contrived to channel Colorado River water via its tributary, the San Juan River, through mountain tunnels crossing the Continental Divide to flow into the Chama River, a tributary of the Rio Grande. A series of dams and reservoirs was constructed to store and release the water, which amounted to about 110,000 acre-feet per year. The major beneficiaries of this infusion of "new water" included the city of Albuquerque, the Middle Rio Grande Conservancy District, and four proposed irrigation units in northern New Mexico: Llano, Pojoaque, Taos, and Cerro. Virtually all future development in the upper and middle Rio Grande Valley depends upon the acquisition of San Juan–Chama water rights (see Brown and Ingram 1987:58–73; also, for water and dams in the West, see Worster 1985 and Reisner 1986).

Glossary

acequia. A Spanish word of Arabic origin; in New Mexico, an irrigation ditch and also the acequia or community irrigation ditch association that maintains and manages the canals and allocation of water

acequia madre. Lit. "mother ditch"; the main irrigation canal that diverts water from a stream. Smaller ditches, including laterals, divert water off the acequia madre.

alabado. A religious hymn of mourning, typically sung during the Lenten season.

alabanza. A religious hymn of praise sung in honor of a saint

a medias. To farm "a medias" is to sharecrop

anciano. Elder

auxilio. A special dispensation of water granted by the mayordomo upon request in a time of great scarcity and need. Local variant: *arcilio*

bendición. Blessing

bulto. A three-dimensional image or statue of a saint

canoa. A wooden flume, sometimes called a *canova* (lit. canoe), that transports ditch water across an arroyo.

calvario. Lit. Calvary; a tall wooden cross placed near a morada, often on a hillside

capilla. Chapel

campo. Countryside; an unplanted field

camposanto. Cemetery; lit. holy ground

cargo. A duty or obligation

casta. The casta system was a series of stratified ethnic categories applied during the colonial period to the mixed offspring of Spaniards, Indians, and blacks.

ciénega. A marsh or swampy place

chorrito. A small stream of water

communitas. A term applied by anthropoplogist Victor Turner to a sense of community heightened through ritual activity

compadrazgo. Ritual coparenthood

compuerta. A headgate that diverts water from a stream into a mother ditch or from one ditch into another. The vertical drop gate is used to regulate the flow of water.

comisión. The commission or governing body of an acequia association, usually consisting of three elected commissioners, or *comisionados*, who work with the mayordomo to manage ditch business

comisionado. An elected ditch commissioner

costumbre. Custom

coyote. A biethnic Anglo-Hispano or any mix between categories of identity

depósito. Reservoir

derecho de agua. A water right owned by a parciante (irrigator)

desagüe. Drainage ditch

descanso. A small roadside cross that commemorates where someone died in an accident; lit. a rest

despedida. An act of farewell

ejido. Common land

encuentro. Encounter or meeting; in this case, the Good Friday ritual enactment, using statues, of the encounter between the grieving Virgin Mary or Lady of Sorrows and her son, Jesus, during the Via Crucis (Way of the Cross), which culminates in the Crucifixion

entrega(r). In this case, an annual ritual procedure in which the outgoing mayordomos (of the chapel) hand over the saint's statue to the incoming mayordomos; lit. to hand over or surrender (v. *entregar*). Local variant: *entriega*.

función. A religious celebration; lit. function

Hermano(s). Member(s) of the religious lay order known as Los Hermanos de Padre Jesus Nazareno or Los Hermanos Penitentes; lit. brother, or the Brotherhood

la petición del hogar. A prayer to receive a blessing for the home

la limpia. The annual cleaning of an irrigation canal by ditch association members or their surrogates; lit. the cleaning

Las Posadas. A nine-day ritual celebration that reenacts the search by Mary and Joseph for lodging in Bethlehem before the nativity on Christmas Eve

la saca. Another term for the annual ditch cleaning; lit. the taking out (of weeds and refuse from the canal)

lateral. A side ditch off a main canal

limosna. In Los Córdovas, the ritual solicitation of seis (six) reales, or about seventy-five cents, to help pay for a mass; lit. alms or charity

la linea (de arriba, del medio, de abajo). A strip or line of zones (upper, middle, and lower) irrigated by rotation in Arroyo Seco.

luminaria. A ritual bonfire; a series of luminarias light the path of a nocturnal religious procession.

mayordomo de la acequia. The annually elected ditch boss, who allocates water according to custom and works with the commissioners to oversee ditch operations and maintenance

mayordomos de la iglesia (church) or *capilla* (chapel). Usually a married couple who caretakes the local chapel for one year and also serves on a rotational basis in the parish mother church; the couples take responsibility for organizing their chapel saint's day and other celebrations in the Catholic calendar.

morada. A local chapter house belonging to Los Hermanos Penitentes; a kind of chapel containing an altar, religious images, and other artifacts, where the Brothers carry out their ritual activities, such as Lent and Holy Week

multicommunity. A central town surrounded by smaller satellite communities, a characteristic pattern of Spanish colonial settlement in northern New Mexico and also in parts of Spain and Mesoamerica

nicho. A niche where the image of a saint (*santo*) is housed, usually an indentation in an adobe wall or a wood or tin structure.

novena. A nine-day Catholic prayer ceremony

ocote. Pitchy or resinous pine stacked crosswise and ignited to make bonfires or luminarias

ojo. A natural spring; diminutive: *ojito*

oración. Prayer

oratorio. A shrine or private oratory where prayers are offered; may be indoors or outdoors (where it is roofed)

parciante. A water rights owner and irrigator on a ditch; a member of a ditch association

Penitente. A member of Los Hermanos Penitentes; a Good Friday processant

placita. Lit. a little plaza, or settlement

pozo. A hole that is fed or moistened by a spring; diminutive: pozito.

peón. A paid substitute worker sent to help clean the ditch

prima/primo. Cousin

promesa. A promise or vow

psychopompos. A term from the Greek word *psychopompos*, the guide who leads souls to the afterworld or underworld

ranchito. A little ranch

regar. To irrigate

reparto or *repartimiento de agua.* The customary division of water on a river or ditch

respeto. Respect

retablo. A painted, two-dimensional image of a saint

sangría. A small lateral ditch; from *sangriento* (bleeding)

santo. A saint or an image of a saint; lit. holy

sobrante. Excess or surplus irrigation water

surco. A measurement of water used in irrigation, sometimes said to equal the amount of water that passes through the hub of a Mexican cart or wagon wheel

Syrian method. A method of allocating water in proportion to the amount of land under irrigation

tarea. Task; the section of a ditch, marked off by the mayordomo or *rayador* (an individual whose job is to do the marking), one is assigned to clean

temporal. Dry farming, dependent on rainfall

terreno. Land or ground

torreón. A defensive tower constructed of adobe

vecino. Settler, neighbor

vega. Meadow or pasture

viejita/viejito. Diminutive for an older person.

velorio. An all-night prayer watch; a wake

vergüenza. Shame, disgrace

Verónica. A young girl dressed in black during ritual observance of the stations of the cross on Good Friday; named for the woman who soothed Christ's face with a cloth that forever retained his imprint

villa. Town

víspera. Vesper or evening prayer

Yemenite method. A method of allocating water on a rotational or fixed time-release basis

zoquete. Adobe mud plaster

Bibliography

Adams, Eleanor B., and Fray Angelico Chavez, trans. and eds.

1956   The Missions of New Mexico, 1776: A Description by Fray Atanasio Domínguez with Other Contemporary Documents. Albuquerque: University of New Mexico Press.

Adler, Michael A.

1993   *Review of* Greiser and Greiser, Archaeological Analysis of Settlement and Water Use in the Taos Valley. Unpublished MS.

Adler, Michael A., and Herbert W. Dick, eds.

1999   Picuris Pueblo through Time: Eight Centuries of Change in a Northern Rio Grande Pueblo. Dallas: William P. Clements Center for Southwest Studies, Southern Methodist University.

Anschuetz, Kurt F.

1998   Not Waiting for the Rain: Integrated Systems of Water Management by Pre-Columbian Pueblo Farmers in North-Central New Mexico. Ph.D. dissertation, Department of Anthropology, University of Michigan.

2001   Soaking It In: Northern Rio Grande Pueblo Lessons of Water Management and Landscape Ecology. *In* Native Peoples of the Southwest: Negotiating Land, Water, and Ethnicities. Laurie L. Weinstein, ed. Pp. 49–78. Westport, CT: Bergin & Garvey.

Apodaca, Ted, and Lester K. Taylor

1994   Indian Water Rights. Santa Fe: New Mexico Office of the State Engineer.

Apodaca, Ted, and Tammy Zokan

1999   New Mexico Acequia Court Decisions. Santa Fe: New Mexico Office of the State Engineer.

Appadurai, Arjun

1995   The Production of Locality. *In* Counterworks: Managing the Diversity of Knowledge. Richard Fardon, ed. Pp. 205–224. New York: Routledge.

Arbolino, Risa D.

2001   Agricultural Strategies and Labor Organization: An Ethnohistoric Approach to the Study of Prehistoric Farming Systems in the Taos Area of Northern New Mexico. Ph.D. dissertation, Department of Anthropology, Southern Methodist University.

Arnold, Thomas C.

1996   Theory, History, and the Western Waterscape: The Market Culture Thesis. Journal of the Southwest 38(2):215–240.

Baca, Leo, in discussion with the author, July 1995.

Barlow, Maude, and Tony T. Clarke

2002   Blue Gold: The Fight to Stop the Corporate Theft of the World's Water. New York: The New Press.

Baxter, John O.

1990   Spanish Irrigation in Taos Valley. Santa Fe: New Mexico Office of the State Engineer.

1997   Dividing New Mexico's Waters, 1700–1912. Albuquerque: University of New Mexico Press.

2000   Measuring New Mexico's Irrigation Water: How Big Is a Surco? New Mexico Historical Review 75(3):397–413.

Behar, Ruth

1996   The Vulnerable Observer: Anthropology That Breaks Your Heart. Boston: Beacon Press.

Bodine, John J.

1978   Taos Blue Lake Controversy. Journal of Ethnic Studies 6(1):42–48.

1979   Taos Pueblo. *In* The Handbook of Northern American Indians: Southwest, 9. Alfonso Ortiz, ed. Pp. 255–267. Washington, DC: Smithsonian Institution, United States Government Printing Office.

Bohrer, Vorsila L.

1995   The Where, When, and Why of Corn Guardians. *In* Soil, Water, Biology, and Belief in Prehistoric and Traditional Southwestern Agriculture. H. Wolcott Toll, ed. Pp. 361–368. Albuquerque: New Mexico Archaeological Council.

Bond, Benton, in discussion with the author, June 1997.

Boyer, Jeffrey L.

1991   El Torreon de Arroyo Seco: Archaeological Test Excavations at LA A80301, Near Arroyo Seco. Taos County, New Mexico. Unpublished report #90-05B.

1995   Climatic Overview of the Rio Grande Del Rancho Valley: Background for Irrigation. *In* Soil, Water, Biology and Belief in Prehistoric and Traditional Southwestern

Agriculture. H. Wolcott Toll, ed. Pp. 197–208. Albuquerque: New Mexico Archaeological Council.

Brandes, Stanley
1987   Reflections on Honor and Shame in the Mediterranean. Theme issue, "Honor and Shame and the Unity of the Mediterranean," American Anthropological Association 22:121–134.

Brandt, Carol B.
1995   Traditional Agriculture on the Zuni Indian Reservation in the Recent Historic Period. *In* Soil, Water, Biology and Belief in Prehistoric and Traditional Southwestern Agriculture. H. Wolcott Toll, ed. Pp. 291–301. Albuquerque: New Mexico Archaeological Council.

Brandt, Elizabeth
1980   On Secrecy and the Control of Knowledge: Taos Pueblo. *In* Secrecy: A Cross-Cultural Perspective. Stanton K. Tefft, ed. Pp. 123–146. New York: Human Sciences Press.

Briggs, Charles L.
1980   The Woodcarvers of Cordova, New Mexico: Social Dimensions of an Artistic "Revival." Knoxville: University of Tennessee Press.
1981   St. Isidore, Husbandman: Meditation on an Image. El Palacio 87(1).
1983   A Conversation with St. Isidore: The Teachings of the Elders. *In* Hispanic Arts and Ethnohistory in the Southwest: New Papers Inspired by the Work of E. Boyd. Marta Weigle, Claudia Larcombe, and Samuel Larcombe, eds. Pp. 103–116. Santa Fe, NM: Ancient City Press.
1986   Learning How to Ask: A Sociolinguistic Appraisal of the Role of the Interview in Social Science Research. Cambridge and New York: Cambridge University Press.
1988   Competence in Performance: The Creativity of Tradition in Mexicano Verbal Art. Philadelphia: University of Pennsylvania Press.

Brooks, James
2002   Captives & Cousins: Slavery, Kinship, and Community in the Southwest Borderlands. Chapel Hill: University of North Carolina Press.

Brown, Donald N.
1999   Picuris Pueblo in 1890: The Reconstruction of the Picuris Social Structure and Subsistence Activities. *In* Picuris Pueblo through Time: Eight Centuries of Change in a Northern Rio Grande Pueblo. Michael A. Adler and Herbert W. Dick, eds. Pp. 19–37. Dallas, TX: William P. Clements Center for Southwest Studies, Southern Methodist University.

Brown, Lee F., and Helen M. Ingram
1987   Water and Poverty in the Southwest. Tucson: University of Arizona Press.

Brown, Loren W., with Charles L. Briggs and Marta Weigle
1978   Hispano Folklife of New Mexico: The Lorin W. Brown Federal Writers' Project Manuscripts. Albuquerque: University of New Mexico Press.

Bruns, Bryan Randolph, and Ruth S. Meinzen-Dick, eds.
2000   Negotiating Water Rights. New Delhi: Vistaar.

Bureau of Business and Economic Research (BBER)
2000a   Profile of Selected Income and Poverty Characteristics, Taos County, NM, 1990 and 2000 Census. Electronic document, http://www.unm.edu/~bber/census/demoprof/coprofs/taincpov.htm, accessed March 10, 2003.
2000b   A Historical Profile of Taos County Migration at the End of the 20th Century: A Summary and Analysis of Data from the US Census Bureau and Other Sources. Albuquerque: University of New Mexico Press.
2000c   Profiles of General Demographic Characteristics, 2000 and 1990 Census. Electronic document, http://www.unm.edu/~bber/census/demoprof/coprofs/tao.htm, accessed March 10, 2003.

Butzer, Karl W.
1992   The Americas before and after 1492: An Introduction to Current Geographical Research. Annals of the Association of American Geographers 82(3):345–368.

Caponera, Dante A.
1973   Water Laws in Moslem Countries. Part 1, pp. 1–42. Rome: Food and Agriculture Organization of the United Nations.

Carlson, Alvar
1990   The Spanish American Homeland. Baltimore: Johns Hopkins Press.

Caro Baroja, Julio
1965   Honor and Shame: An Historical Account of Several Conflicts. *In* Honor and Shame. J. G. Peristiany, ed. Pp. 79–137. Chicago: University of Chicago Press.

Cash, Marie Romero, and Seigfried Halus
1998   Living Shrines: Home Altars of New Mexico. Santa Fe: Museum of New Mexico Press.

Chambers, Robert
1980   Basic Concepts in the Organization of Irrigation. In Irrigation and Agricultural Development in Asia: Perspectives from the Social Sciences. E. Walter Coward Jr., ed. Pp. 28–50. Ithaca, NY: Cornell University Press.

Chavez, Gabriel, in discussion with the author, May 1996.

Clark, Ira G.
1987   Water in New Mexico: A History of Its Management and Use. Albuquerque: University of New Mexico Press.

Cordell, Linda. S.
1979   Pre-History: Eastern Anasazi. *In* The Handbook of Northern American Indians: Southwest, 9. Alfonso Ortiz, ed. Pp. 141–151. Washington, DC: Smithsonian Institution, United States Government Printing Office.
1989   Northern and Central Rio Grande. *In* Dynamics of Southwest Prehistory.

Linda S. Cordell and George J. Gumerman, eds. Pp. 293–334. Washington, DC: Smithsonian Institution Press.

Coward, E. Walter, Jr.

1979   Principles of Social Organization in an Indigenous Irrigation System. Human Organization 38(1):28–36.

1980a   Irrigation Development: Institutional and Organizational Issues. *In* Irrigation and Agricultural Development in Asia: Perspectives from the Social Sciences. E. Walter Coward Jr., ed. Pp. 15–27. Ithaca, NY: Cornell University Press.

1980b   Management Themes in Community Irrigation Systems. *In* Irrigation and Agricultural Development in Asia: Perspectives from the Social Sciences. E. Walter Coward Jr., ed. Pp. 203–218. Ithaca, NY: Cornell University Press.

Coward, E. Walter, Jr., and Gilbert Levine

1987   Studies of Farmer-Managed Irrigation Systems: Ten Years of Cumulative Knowledge and Changing Research Priorities. *In* Public Intervention in Farmer-Managed Irrigation Systems. E. Walter Coward Jr., ed. Pp. 1–34. DeGana, Sri Lanka: International Management Institute.

Crawford, Stanley G.

1988   Mayordomo: Chronicle of an Acequia in Northern New Mexico. Albuquerque: University of New Mexico Press.

1990   Dancing for Water. Journal of the Southwest 32:265–267.

2003   The River in Winter: New and Selected Essays. Albuquerque: University of New Mexico Press.

Crossland, Charlotte B.

1990   Acequia Rights in Law and Tradition. Journal of the Southwest 32:278–287.

Crown, Patricia L.

1990   The Chronology of the Taos Area Anasazi. *In* Clues to the Past, Papers in Honor of William Sundt. Meliha S. Duran and David T. Kirkpatrick, eds. Pp. 63–74. Archaeological Society of New Mexico Papers, vol. 16. Albuquerque.

Crown, Patricia L., with Janet D. Orcutt and Timothy A. Kohler

1996   Pueblo Cultures in Transition: The Northern Rio Grande. *In* The Prehistoric Pueblo World, AD 1150–1350. Michael A. Adler, ed. Pp. 188–204. Tucson: University of Arizona Press.

Cruz, Ma. Concepción J.

1989   Water as Common Property: The Case of Irrigation Water Rights in the Philippines. *In* Common Property Resources: Ecology and Community-Based Sustainable Development. F. Berkes, ed. Pp. 218–235. London: Belhaven.

de Bruin, Cornelia

2006   Feds guarded about water settlement funding. Taos News, April 13:A1–A12.

De Chatel, Francesca

2002   Drops of Faith: Water in Islam. Electronic document, http://www.islamonline.net, accessed November 28, 2002.

Deutsch, Sarah

1987   No Separate Refuge: Culture, Class, and Gender on an Anglo-Hispanic Frontier in the American Southwest, 1880–1940. New York: Oxford University Press.

Donahue, John M., and Barbara Rose Johnston

1998   Water, Culture, and Power: Local Struggles in a Global Context. Washington, DC: Island Press.

Doolittle, William E.

1992   Agriculture in North America on the Eve of Contact: A Reassessment. Annals of the Association of American Geographers 82(3):386–401.

2000   Cultivated Landscapes of Native North America. Oxford: Oxford University Press.

Dozier, Edward P.

1970   The Pueblo Indians of North America. New York: Holt.

DuMars, Charles T., with Mary O'Leary and Albert E. Utton

1984   Pueblo Indian Water Rights: Struggle for a Precious Resource. Tucson: University of Arizona Press.

Eastman, Clyde

1998   Economics of Small-Scale Irrigated Agriculture in Taos County. Unpublished MS, Department of Agricultural Economics and Agricultural Business, New Mexico State University.

Eastman, Clyde, with Garrey E. Carruthers and James A. Liefer

1971   Evaluation of Attitudes toward Land in North-Central New Mexico. Las Cruces, NM: New Mexico State University, Agricultural Experimental Station.

Eastman, Clyde, and N. A. Meadows

1995   Economic Dimensions of Small-Scale Agriculture. Paper presented at the annual meeting of the Rural Sociological Society, Washington, DC.

Ebright, Malcolm

1985   The Don Fernando de Taos Land Grant: Water Rights on Rio Don Fernando. Unpublished MS.

2001   Sharing the Shortages: Water Litigation and Regulation in Hispanic New Mexico, 1600–1850. New Mexico Historical Review 76(1):3–46.

2005   Whiskey Is for Drinking, Water Is for Fighting: Water Allocation in Territorial New Mexico. Unpublished MS.

Eggan, Fred

1966   The American Indian; Perspectives for the Study of Social Change. The Lewis Henry Morgan Lectures. Chicago: Aldine.

Ellis, Florence H.

1974   Anthropological Data Pertaining to the Taos Land Claim. New York: Garland.

Ellis, Florence H., and J. J. Brody

1964   Stratigraphy and Tribal History at Taos Pueblo. American Antiquity 29(3):316–327.

Ellis, Robert

N.d.   Taos Pueblo. Unpublished MS.

Englebert, Ernest A., and Ann Foley Scheuring, eds.

1984   Water Scarcity: Impacts on Western Agriculture. Berkeley: University of California Press.

Espeland, Wendy N.

1998   The Struggle for Water: Politics, Rationality, and Identity in the American Southwest. Chicago: University of Chicago Press.

Fernandez, James W.

1974   Mission of Metaphor in Expressive Culture. Current Anthropology 12(2):119–146.

1977   Fang Architectonics. Philadelphia: Institute for the Study of Human Issues.

1992   *Review of* Architectonic Inquiry. Semiotica 89(1–3):215–226.

2003   Emergence and Convergence in Some African Sacred Places. *In* The Anthropology of Space and Place: Locating Culture. Setha M. Low and D. Lawrence-Zuñiga, eds. Pp. 187–203. Malden, MA: Blackwell.

Follett, W. W.

1898   Study of the Use of Water for Irrigation on the Rio Grande Del Norte. *In* Senate Document 229, 55th Congress, 2nd Session, Serial Set 3610. Pp. 47–177. Washington, DC: United States Government Printing Office.

Ford, Richard I.

1972   An Ecological Perspective on the Eastern Pueblos. *In* New Perspectives on the Pueblos. Alfonso Ortiz, ed. Pp. 1–17. Albuquerque: University of New Mexico Press.

1977   The Technology of Irrigation in a New Mexico Pueblo. *In* Material Culture: Styles, Organization and Dynamics of Technology. Heather Lecthman and Robert S. Merrill, eds. Pp. 139–154. St. Paul, MN: West Publishing Co.

1987   The New Pueblo Economy: When Cultures Meet, Remembering San Gabriel Del Yunge Oweenge. Pp. 73–91. Santa Fe, NM: Sunstone Press.

Fowles, Severin M.

2004   The Making of Made People: The Prehistoric Evolution of Hierocracy among the Northern Tiwa of New Mexico. Ph.D. dissertation, Department of Anthropology, University of Michigan.

2005   Historical Contingency and the Prehistoric Foundations of Moiety Organization among the Eastern Pueblos. Journal of Anthropological Research 61(1):25–52.

García, Eliseo, in discussion with the author, July 1995.

García, Gus, in discussion with the author, July 1995 and June 1997.

García, Telesfor Eliverio, in discussion with the author, July 1995.

Geertz, Clifford

1959   Form and Variation in Balinese Village Structure. American Anthropologist 61(6):991–1012.

1963   Agricultural Involution. Berkeley: University of California Press.

1973   The Wet and Dry: Tradition Irrigation in Bali and Morocco. Human Ecology
        1(1):23–29.

1980   Organization of Balinease Subak. *In* Irrigation Agricultural Development in Asia. E.
        Walter Coward Jr., ed. Pp. 70–90. Ithaca, NY: Cornell University Press.

Gelles, Paul H.

2000   Water and Power in Highland Peru: The Cultural Politics of Irrigation and
        Development. New Brunswick, NJ: Rutgers University Press.

Gerdes, R. Scott

2006   Making the old, new: Local historian's cemetery restoration efforts come to fruition
        with volunteer help. Taos News, June 1:A11.

Gilmore, David D., ed.

1987   Honor and Shame and the Unity of the Mediterranean. Special publication of the
        American Anthropological Association, no. 2.

1990   On Mediterranean Studies. Current Anthropology 31(4):395–396.

Glendinning, Chellis

2005   Chiva: A Village Takes On the Global Heroin Trade. Gabriola Island, BC: New
        Society Publishers.

Glick, Thomas F.

1970   Irrigation and Society in Medieval Valencia. Cambridge, MA: Belknap Press of
        Harvard University Press.

1972   The Old World Background of the Irrigation System of San Antonio, Texas. El Paso:
        Texas Western Press, University of Texas at El Paso.

Gomez, Joe, in discussion with the author, July 1995.

Gonzales, Lee, in discussion with the author, July 1995.

Gordon-McCutchan, R.C.

1991   The Taos Indians and the Battle for Blue Lake. Santa Fe, NM: Red Crane Books.

Grant, Blanche C.

1983   When Old Trails Were New: The Story of Taos. Glorietta, NM: Rio Grande Press.
[1934]

Gray, John

2003   Open Spaces and Dwelling Places: Being at Home on Hill Farms in the Scottish
        Borders. *In* The Anthropology of Space and Place: Locating Culture. Setha M. Low
        and Denise Lawrence-Zuñiga, eds. Pp. 224–244. Malden, MA: Blackwell Publishers.

Graybill, Andrew

2001   "Strong on the Merits and Powerfully Symbolic": The Return of the Blue Lake to
        Taos Pueblo. New Mexico Historical Review 76:125–160.

Greenleaf, Richard E.

1972   Land and Water in Mexico and New Mexico. New Mexico Historical Review 47:84–112.

Greiser, Sally T., and T. Weber Greiser

1992   Archeological Analysis of Settlement and Water Use in the Taos Valley Prepared for the US Attorney Office in Albuquerque, New Mexico. Unpublished MS.

1995   Prehistoric Irrigation in the Taos Valley. *In* Soil, Water, Biology and Belief in Prehistoric and Traditional Southwestern Agriculture. H. Wolcott Toll, ed. Pp. 221–237. Albuquerque: New Mexico Archaeological Council.

Greiser, Sally T., and James L. Moore

1995   The Case for Prehistoric Irrigation in the Northern Southwest. *In* Soil, Water, Biology, and Belief in Prehistoric and Traditional Southwestern Agriculture. H. Wolcott Toll, ed. Pp. 189–195. Albuquerque: New Mexico Archaeological Council.

Guillet, David

1992   Covering Ground: Communal Water Management and the State in the Peruvian Highlands. Ann Arbor: University of Michigan Press.

Gupta, Akhil

2003   The Song of the Nonaligned World: Transnational Identities and the Reinscription
[1992] of Space in Late Capitalism. *In* The Anthropology of Space and Place: Locating Culture. Setha M. Low and Denise Lawrence-Zuñiga, eds. Pp. 321–336. Malden, MA: Blackwell Publishers.

Gutiérrez, Ramon A.

1982   Report on the Taos Valley Population. Unpublished report.

1984   From Honor to Love: Transformations of the Meaning of Sexuality in Colonial New Mexico. *In* Kinship Ideology and Practice in Latin America. Raymond T. Smith, ed. Pp. 237–263. Chapel Hill: University of North Carolina Press.

1991   When Jesus Came, the Corn Mothers Went Away: Marriage, Sexuality, and Power in New Mexico, 1500–1846. Palo Alto, CA: Stanford University Press.

Hall, G. Emlen

1984   Four Leagues of Pecos: A Legal History of the Pecos Grant, 1800–1933. Albuquerque: University of New Mexico Press.

1987   The Pueblo Grant Labyrinth. *In* Land, Water, and Culture: New Perspectives on Hispanic Land Grants. Susan E. Briggs, Charles L. Van Ness, and John R. Van Ness, eds. Pp. 67–140. Albuquerque: University of New Mexico Press.

2000   Tularosa and the Dismantling of New Mexico Community Ditches. New Mexico Historical Review 75(1):77–106.

2002   High and Dry: The Texas–New Mexico Struggle for the Pecos River. Albuquerque: University of New Mexico Press.

Hammond, George P., and Agapito Rey

1953   Don Juan de Oñate, Colonizer of New Mexico, 1595–1628. Albuquerque: University of New Mexico Press.

1966 The Rediscovery of New Mexico, 1580–1594: The Explorations of Chamuscado, Espejo, Castaño de Sosa, Morlete, and Leyva de Bonilla and Humana. Albuquerque: University of New Mexico Press.

Hardin, Gareth
1968 The Tragedy of the Commons. Science 162:243–248.

Harrington, John Peabody
1916 The Ethnogeography of the Tewa Indians. Annual report of the Bureau of American Ethnology to the Secretary of the Smithsonian Institution, 29. Washington, DC: Government Printing Office.

Hicks, Gregory A., and Devon Peña
2003 Community Acequias in Colorado's Rio Culebra Watershed: A Customary Commons in the Domain of Prior Appropriation. University of Colorado Law Review 74(2):101–200.

Hooker, Van Dorn, and Corina Santistevan
1996 Centuries of Hands: An Architectural History of St. Francis of Assisi Church and Its Missions Ranchos de Taos, New Mexico, and the Historic American Buildings Surveys of St. Francis of Assisi Church and the Chapel of Our Lady of Talpa. Santa Fe, NM: Sunstone Press.

Horgan, Paul
1984 Great River: The Rio Grande in North American History. Austin: Texas Monthly Press.

Hundley, Norris, Jr.
1978 The Dark and Bloody Ground of Indian Water Rights: Confusion Elevated to Principle. The Western Historical Quarterly 9(4):454–482.

Hunt, Robert C.
1988 Size and the Structure of Authority in Canal Irrigation Systems. Journal of Anthropological Research 44(4):335–355.
1989 Appropriate Social Organization? Water User Associations in Bureaucratic Canal Irrigation Systems. Human Organization 48(1):79–90.

Hunt, Robert C., and Eva Hunt
1976 Canal Irrigation and Local Social Organization. Current Anthropology 17(3):389–411.

Hutchins, Wells A.
1928 The Community Acequia: Its Origin and Development. The Southwestern Historical Quarterly 31(3):261–284.

Ilahiane, Hsian
1996 Small-Scale Irrigation in a Multiethnic Oasis Environment: The Case of Zaouit Amelkis Village, Southeast Morocco. Journal of Political Ecology 3:89–106.

Ingram, Helen M.

1990   Water Politics: Continuity and Change. Albuquerque: University of New Mexico Press.

Ingram, Helen M., with Nancy K. Laney and David M. Gillilan

1995   Divided Waters: Bridging the US-Mexico Border. Tucson: University of Arizona Press.

James, Rebecca S.

1953   Allow Me to Present 18 Ladies and Gentlemen and Taos, NM, 1885–1939. Taos, NM: El Crepusculo.

Jeancon, J. A.

1929   Archaeological Investigations in the Taos Valley, New Mexico, during 1920. Smithsonian Miscellaneous Collections 81(12):1–21.

Jenkins, Myra E.

1966   Taos Pueblo and Its Neighbors. New Mexico Historical Review 41(2):85–113.

1978   Acequias in the Taos Area. Unpublished MS.

1983   Development Potential of the Taos Pueblo Area in 1906. Unpublished MS.

Johnson, Lyman, and Sonya Lipsett Rivera, eds.

1988   The Faces of Honor: Sex, Shame, and Violence in Colonial Latin America. Albuquerque: University of New Mexico Press.

Jones, Okah L.

1979   Los Paisanos: Spanish Settlers on the Northern Frontier of New Spain. Norman: University of Oklahoma Press.

Kappel, Wayne

1976   Irrigation's Impact on Society. *In* Irrigation Development and Population Pressure. Theodore E. Downing and McGuire Gibson, eds. Pp. 159–167. Anthropological Papers, vol. 25. Tucson: University of Arizona Press.

Kearney, Michael

1984   World View. Novato, CA: Chandler & Sharp.

1996   Reconceptualizing the Peasantry: Anthropology in Global Perspective. Boulder, CO: Westview Press.

Kelley, William W.

1976   Concepts in the Anthropological Study of Irrigation. American Anthropologist 85(4):880–886.

Kelly, Lawrence C.

1994   Taos Pueblo Land and Water, 1907–1970. Unpublished MS.

Kohler, Timothy A.

1992a   The Prehistory of Sustainability. Population and Environment: A Journal of Interdisciplinary Studies 13(4):237–242.

1992b   Prehistoric Human Impact on the Environment in the Upland North American Southwest. Population and Environment: A Journal of Interdisciplinary Studies 13(4):255–268.

Krumgold, Joseph
1953   And Now Miguel. New York: Crowell.

Laflin, A.
1941   Report on Land Use and Water Rights under Rio Lucero as Affecting the Pueblo of Taos. Unpublished MS.

Lansing, J. Stephen
1987   Balinese "Water Temples" and the Management of Irrigation. American Anthropologist 89(2):326–341.

Leon, Frances L.
1979   Structure of Hispanic-Indian Relations in New Mexico. *In* The Colorado College Studies: The Survival of Spanish American Villages. Paul Kutsche, ed. Pp. 99–106. Colorado Springs, CO: Colorado College.

Levine, Fran
1990   Dividing the Water: The Impact of Water Rights Adjudication on New Mexican Communities. Journal of the Southwest 32:268–277.

Limón, Jose E.
1994   Dancing with the Devil: Society and Cultural Poetics in Mexican-American South Texas. Madison: University of Wisconsin Press.

Lovato, Phil
1974   Las Acequias del Norte. Taos, NM: Kit Carson Memorial Foundation, Inc.

Lowi, Miriam R.
1993   Water and Power: The Politics of a Scarce Resource in the Jordan River Basin. New York: Cambridge University Press.

Luján, Ida M.
1999   Challenging Tradition: Opening the Headgate. *In* Speaking Chicana: Voice, Power, and Identity. D. Letticia Galindo and Maria D. Gonzales, eds. Pp. 98–105. Tucson: University of Arizona Press.

Maass, Arthur, and Raymond L. Anderson, eds.
1986   And the Desert Shall Rejoice: Conflict, Growth, and Justice in Arid Environments. Pp. 11–52, 411–412. Cambridge, MA: MIT Press.

Mabry, Jonathan B., ed.
1996   Canals and Communities: Small-Scale Irrigation Systems. Tucson: University of Arizona Press.

MacCameron, Robert
1997   Environmental Change in Colonial New Mexico. *In* Out of the Woods: Essays in

Environmental History. Char Miller and Hal Rothman, eds. Pp. 79–97. Pittsburgh: University of Pittsburgh Press.

Martínez, Luís, in discussion with the author, July 1995.

Martínez, Palemon, in discussion with the author, July 1995 and June 1997.

Martínez, Robert, in discussion with the author, July 1995.

Martínez Saldaña, Tómas
1998   La Diâspora Tlaxcalteca: Colonizacion Agricola del Norte Mexicano. Tlaxcala, Mexico: Tlaxcallan, Ediciones del Gobierno del Estado de Tlaxcala.

McClellan, Doug
1996   Pueblo wants all water. Albuquerque Journal North, May 16: B1, B3.

McCool, Daniel
1978   Precedent for the Winters Doctrine: Seven Legal Principles. Journal of the Southwest 29(2):164–202.
1987   Command of the Waters: Iron Triangles, Federal Water Development, and Indian Water. Berkeley: University of California Press.

McGuire, Thomas R., with William B. Lord and Mary G. Wallace, eds.
1993   Indian Water in the New West. Tucson: University of Arizona Press.

Melendez, Gabriel
2004   Who Are the Salt of the Earth? Competing Images of Mexican Americans in *Salt of the Earth* and *And Now Miguel*. Unpublished MS, Department of American Studies, University of New Mexico.

Merrill, James L.
1980   Aboriginal Water Rights. Natural Resources Journal 20(1):45–70.

Meyer, Michael C.
1984   Water in the Hispanic Southwest: A Social and Legal History, 1550–1850. Tucson: University of Arizona Press.
2000   New Mexico Hispanic Water Region, 1540–1912, with Special Reference to the Taos Valley. Unpublished MS.

Meyer, Michael C., and M. N. Brescia
1998   The Treaty of Guadalupe Hidalgo as a Living Document: Water and Land Use Issues in Northern New Mexico. New Mexico Historical Review 73(4):321–346.

Miera, Felix, in discussion with the author, July 1995.

Miller, Merton L.
1898   A Preliminary Study of the Pueblo of Taos, New Mexico. Chicago: University of Chicago Press.

Million, René

1962   Variation in Social Responses to the Practice of Irritation Agriculture. *In* Civilization in Arid Lands. R. B. Woodbury, ed. Pp. 56–88. Anthropological Papers, vol. 62. Salt Lake City: University of Utah Press.

Mitchell, William P.

1973   The Hydraulic Hypothesis: A Reappraisal. Current Anthropology 14(5):532–534.

Montoya, Augustín (Atilano), in discussion with the author, February 1996.

Montoya, Ernesto, in discussion with the author, July 1995 and June 1997.

Moore, James L.

1995a   Anasazi Field Systems in the Taos District. *In* Soil, Water, Biology, and Belief in Prehistoric and Traditional Southwestern Agriculture. H. Wolcott Toll, ed. Pp. 13–23. Albuquerque: New Mexico Archaeological Council.

1995b   Prehistoric Irrigation at Pot Creek Pueblo. *In* Soil, Water, Biology, and Belief in Prehistoric and Traditional Southwestern Agriculture. H. Wolcott Toll, ed. Pp. 209–220. Albuquerque: New Mexico Archaeological Council.

Morinis, Alan, ed.

1992   Sacred Journeys: The Anthropology of Pilgrimage. Westport, CT: Greenwood Press.

Mueller, J. E.

1975   Restless River: International Law and the Behavior of the Rio Grande. El Paso: Texas Western Press.

Nabokov, Peter

1970   Tijerina and the Courthouse Raid. Berkeley, CA: Ramparts Press.

Names & Numbers

2003   Taos Telephone Directory. Grand Rapids, MI: Genesis Publisher Services.

Netting, Robert M.

1974   The System Nobody Knows: Village Irrigation in the Swiss Alps. *In* Irrigation's Impact on Society. Theodore E. Downing and McGuire Gibson, eds. Pp. 67–75. Anthropological Papers, vol. 25. Tucson: University of Arizona Press.

New Mexico Office of the State Engineer (OSE)

1969   Rio Pueblo de Taos Hydrographic Survey Report, vol. 2. Santa Fe: New Mexico Office of the State Engineer.

1995   Rio Pueblo de Taos Hydrographic Survey Report, vol. 2. Revised Supplement A. Santa Fe: New Mexico Office of the State Engineer.

2006   Local Negotiating Parties Release Draft Taos Pueblo Water Rights Settlement Agreement. Press release, March 31. www.ose.state.nm.us.

New Mexico Statute

n.d.   Adjudication of Rights. Contents of Decree, 72-4-19. Santa Fe: New Mexico Office of the State Engineer.

Northern New Mexico Legal Services

2000   Acequias and Water Rights, Adjudications in Northern New Mexico. *In* Negotiating Water Rights. Bryan Randolph Bruns and Ruth S. Meinzen-Dick, eds. Pp. 337–350. New Delhi: Vistaar.

Nostrand, Richard L.

1987   The Century of Hispano Expansion. New Mexico Historical Review 62(4):361–386.

1992   The Hispano Homeland. Norman: University of Oklahoma Press.

Ortiz, Alfonso

1968   The Tewa World. Chicago: University of Chicago Press.

1972   New Perspectives on the Pueblos. Albuquerque: University of New Mexico Press.

Ortiz, Orlando, in discussion with the author, July 1995.

Ortner, Sherry B.

1996   The Virgin and the State. *In* Making Gender: The Politics and Erotics of Culture. Pp. 43–58. Boston: Beacon Press.

Ottaway, Harold N.

1975   The Penitente Moradas of the Taos, New Mexico, Area. Ph.D. dissertation, Department of Anthropology, University of Oklahoma.

Pacheco, Elizardo, in discussion with the author, May 1996.

Pacheco, Rudy, in discussion with the author, July 1995.

Paredes, Américo

1966   The Anglo-American in Mexican Folklore. *In* New Voices in American Studies. Ray B. Browne, Donald M. Winkelman, and Allen Hayman, eds. Pp. 113–128. Indianapolis, IN: Purdue University Studies.

Park, Thomas K.

1992   Early Trends toward Class Stratification: Chaos, Common Property, and Flood Recession Agriculture. American Anthropologist 94(1):90–117.

Parsons, Elsie Clews

1970   Taos Pueblo. New York: Johnson Reprint Corp.
[1936]

1974   Pueblo Indian Religion, vols. 1 and 2. Chicago: University of Chicago Press.
[1939]

1991   Mothers and Children at Laguna. *In* Pueblo Mothers and Children: Essays by Elsie Clews Parsons, 1915–1924. Barbara A. Babcock, ed. Pp. 69–75. Santa Fe, NM: Ancient City Press.

Pelcyger, Robert S.

1977   The Winters Doctrine and the Greening of the Reservations. Journal of Contemporary Law 4(1):19–37.

Peña, Devon G.

1998   Chicano Culture, Ecology, Politics: Subversive Kin. Tucson: University of Arizona Press.

Peristiany, J. G., ed.

1966   Honor and Shame: The Values of Mediterranean Society. Chicago: University of Chicago Press.

Peterson, Karen

1996   Tesuque Pueblo sues to protect its water rights. Santa Fe New Mexican, May 16: A16, A-4.

Pielou, E. C.

1998   Fresh Water. Chicago: University of Chicago Press.

Pina-Cabral, João de

1989   The Mediterranean as a Category of Regional Comparison: A Critical View. Current Anthropology 30(3):399–406.

Pisani, Donald J.

1992   To Reclaim a Divided West: Water, Law, and Public Policy, 1848–1902. Albuquerque: University of New Mexico Press.

Pitt-Rivers, Julian A.

1966   Honor and Social Status. *In* Honor and Shame. J. G. Peristiany, ed. Pp. 19–77. Chicago: University of Chicago Press.

1971   The People of the Sierra. Chicago: University of Chicago Press.

Pitt-Rivers, Julian A., and J. G. Peristiany, eds.

1992   Honor and Grace in Anthropology. New York: Cambridge University Press.

Postel, Sandra

1999   Pillar of Sand: Can the Irrigation Miracle Last? New York: W.W. Norton & Co.

Quintana, Bolivar, in discussion with the author, July 1995.

Quintana, Francis, in discussion with the author, July 1995.

Quintana, Frances L.

1990   Land, Water, and the Pueblo-Hispanic Relations in Northern New Mexico. Journal of the Southwest 32(3):288–299.

Ranquist, Harold A.

1976   The Winters Doctrine and How It Grew: Federal Reservation Rights to the Use of Water. Brigham Young University Law Review 1975(3):639–724.

Rappaport, Roy A.

1999   Ritual and Religion in the Making of Humanity. Cambridge and New York: Cambridge University Press.

Reichard, David A.

1996   Water Disputes in Northern New Mexico 1882–1905. Western Legal History 9(1):9–33.

Reisner, Marc

1986   Cadillac Desert: The American West and Its Disappearing Water. New York: Viking.

Rivera, José A.

1998   Acequia Culture: Water, Land, and Community in the Southwest. Albuquerque: University of New Mexico Press.

Rodríguez, Sylvia

1987   Land, Water and Ethnic Identity in Taos. *In* Land, Water, and Culture: New Perspectives on Hispanic Land Grants. Charles L. Briggs and John R. Van Ness, eds. Pp. 313–403. Albuquerque: University of New Mexico Press.

1990   Applied Research on Land and Water in New Mexico: A Critique. Journal of the Southwest 32(3):300–315.

1996   The Matachines Dance: Ritual Symbolism and Interethnic Relations in the Upper Rio Grande Valley. Albuquerque: University of New Mexico Press.

1997   The Taos Fiesta: Invented Tradition and the Infrapolitics of Symbolic Reclamation. Journal of the Southwest 39(1):39–56.

1998   Fiesta Time and Plaza Space: Resistance and Accommodation in a Tourist Town. Journal of American Folklore 111(439):39–56.

2002   Procession and Sacred Landscape in New Mexico. New Mexico Historical Review 77(1):1–26.

2003   Tourism, Difference, and Power in the Borderlands. *In* The Culture of Tourism, The Tourism of Culture. Hal Rothman, ed. Pp. 194–205. Albuquerque: University of New Mexico Press.

Romo, Fernando, in discussion with the author, January 1996.

Rosaldo, Renato

1989   Culture and Truth: The Remaking of Social Analysis. Boston: Beacon Press.

Santistevan, Corina, in discussion with the author, April 1996.

Scarborough, Vernon L.

1988   A Water Storage Adaptation in the American Southwest. Journal of Anthropological Research 44(1):21–40.

1991   Water Management Adaptation in Nonindustrial Complex Societies: An Archaeological Perspective. Archaeological Method and Theory 3:101–154.

2003   Flow of Power: Ancient Water Systems and Landscapes. School of American Research. Santa Fe, NM: SAR Press.

Scarborough, Vernon L., with John W. Schoenfelder and J. Stephen Lansing

1999   Early Statecraft on Bali: The Water Temple Complex and the Decentralization of the Political Economy. Economic Anthropology 20:299–330.

Schimmel, Julie, and Robert R. White

1994   Bert Geer Phillips and the Taos Art Colony. Albuquerque: University of New
        Mexico Press.

Schneider, Jane

1971   Of Vigilance and Virgins: Honor, Shame, Access to Resources in Mediterranean
        Societies. Ethnology 10(1):1–24.

Schneider, Jane, and Peter Schneider

1976   Culture and Political Economy in Western Sicily. New York: Academic Press.

Scott, James C.

1976   The Moral Economy of the Peasant: Rebellion and Subsistence in Southeast Asia.
        New Haven, CT: Yale University Press.

1985   Weapons of the Weak: Everyday Forms of Peasant Resistance. New Haven, CT: Yale
        University Press.

1990   Domination and the Arts of Resistance: Hidden Transcripts. New Haven, CT: Yale
        University Press.

Simmons, Marc

1964   Tlascalans in the Spanish Borderlands. New Mexico Historical Review
        39(2):101–110.

1969   Settlement Patterns and Village Plans in Colonial New Mexico. Journal of the West
        8(1):7–21.

1972   Spanish Irrigation Practices in New Mexico. New Mexico Historical Review
        47(2):135–150.

2001   Spanish Pathways: Readings in the History of Hispanic New Mexico. Albuquerque:
        University of New Mexico Press.

Sklar, Deidre

2001   Dancing with the Virgin: Body and Faith in the Fiesta of Tortugas, New Mexico.
        Berkeley: University of California Press.

Snow, David H.

1979   Rural Hispanic Community Organization in Northern New Mexico: A Historic
        Perspective. *In* The Colorado College Study: The Survival of Spanish-American
        Villages. Paul Kutsche, ed. Pp. 45–52. Colorado Springs, CO: Colorado College.

1988   The Santa Fe Acequia System. Santa Fe, NM: Planning Department, City of Santa
        Fe.

Steele, Thomas J.

1974   Santos and Saints: The Religious Folk Art of Hispanic New Mexico. Santa Fe, NM:
        Ancient City Press.

1998   The Code of Honor in Western Culture. Albuquerque Southwest Hispanic Research
        Institute. Working Paper.

Steward, Julian H., ed.

1955   Irrigation Civilizations: A Comparative Study. Washington, DC: Pan American
        Union.

Stewart, Frank H.
1994   Honor. Chicago: University of Chicago Press.

Strang, Veronica
2004   The Meaning of Water. New York: Berg Publishers.

Taos County Chamber of Commerce
2002   Demographics of Taos: Per Capita, Personal Income, Median Household Income.
        Taos, NM: Taos County Chamber of Commerce.

Tarleton, Thomas, Sr., in discussion with the author, July 1995.

Taylor, William B.
1975   Land and Water Rights in the Viceroyalty of New Spain. New Mexico Historical
        Review 50(3):189–212.

Thompson, E. P.
1964   The Making of the English Working Class. New York: Pantheon Books.

Torres, Donaciano, in discussion with the author, June 1996.

Torres, Ezequiel, in discussion with the author, May 1996.

Torres, Fermín, in discussion with the author, July 1995.

Trawick, Paul B.
2001a   The Moral Economy of Water: Equity and Antiquity in the Andes Commons.
        American Anthropologist 103(2):361–379.
2001b   Successfully Governing the Commons: Principles of Social Organization in an
        Andean Irrigation System. Human Ecology 29(1):1–25.
2003   The Struggle for Water in Peru: Comedy and Tragedy in the Andean Commons.
        Stanford, CA: Stanford University Press.

Trujillo, Feloníz, in discussion with the author, April 1996.

Trujillo, George, in discussion with the author, July 1995.

Trujillo, Stephen, in discussion with the author, July 1995.

Turner, Victor W., and Edith L. Turner
1978   Image and Pilgrimage in Christian Culture: Anthropological Perspectives. New
        York: Columbia University Press.

Tyler, Daniel
1990   The Mythical Pueblo Rights Doctrine: Water Administration in Hispanic New
        Mexico. El Paso: Texas Western Press.
1991   Underground Water in Hispanic New Mexico: A Brief Analysis of Laws, Customs,
        and Disputes. New Mexico Historical Review 66(3):287–301.
1995   The Spanish Colonial Legacy and the Role of Hispanic Custom in Defining New
        Mexico Land and Water Rights. Colonial Latin American Historical Review
        4(2):149–165.

Uphoff, Norman, with M. L. Wickramasinghe and C. M. Wijayaratna
1990   "Optimum" Participation in Irrigation Management: Issues and Evidence from Sri Lanka. Human Organization 49(1):26–40.

Valdez, Facundo
1979   Verguenza. *In* The Colorado College Studies: The Survival of Spanish-American Villages. Paul Kutsche, ed. Pp. 99–106. Colorado Springs, CO: Colorado College.

Valerio, Candido, in discussion with the author, May 1996.

Valerio, Polito, in discussion with the author, May 1996.

Van Ness, John R.
1979   Hispanic Village Organization in Northern New Mexico: Corporate Community Structure in Historical and Comparative Perspective. *In* The Colorado College Studies: The Survival of Spanish-American Villages. Paul Kutsche, ed. Pp. 21–44. Colorado Springs, CO: Colorado College.

Vandermeer, Canute
1971   Water Thievery in a Rice Irrigation System in Taiwan. Annals of the Association of American Geographers 61:156–179.

Vigil, Rafael, in discussion with the author, July 1995.

Vivian, R. Gwinn
1974   Conservation and Diversion Water-Control Systems in the Anasazi Southwest. *In* Irrigation's Impact on Society. Theodore E. Downing and McGuire Gibson, eds. Pp. 95–112. Anthropological Papers, vol. 25. Tucson: University of Arizona Press.

Vlasich, James A.
1980   Transitions in Pueblo Agriculture, 1938–1948. New Mexico Historical Review 55(1):25–46.
2001   Post War Pueblo Indian Culture: Modernization versus Tradition in the Area of Agribusiness. New Mexico Historical Review 76(4):353–381.
2005   Pueblo Indian Agriculture. Albuquerque: University of New Mexico Press.

Ward, Diane Raines
2002   Water Wars: Drought, Flood, Folly, and the Politics of Thirst. New York: Riverhead Books.

Waters, Frank
1973   To Possess the Land: A Biography of Arthur Rochford Manby. Chicago: Sage Books.

Weber, David J.
1992   The Spanish Frontier in North America. New Haven, CT: Yale University Press.
1996   On the Edge of Empire: The Taos Hacienda of Los Martínez. Santa Fe: Museum of New Mexico Press.
1999   What Caused the Pueblo Revolt of 1680? Boston: Bedford/St. Martin's.

Weinstein, Laurie L., ed.

2001 Native Peoples of the Southwest: Negotiating Land, Water, and Ethnicities. Westport, CT: Bergin & Garvey.

Westcoat, James L., Jr.

1998 The "Right of Thirst" for Animals in Islamic Law, a Comparative Approach. *In* Animal Geographies: Place, Politics, and Identity in the Nature-Culture Borderlands. Jennifer R. Wolch and Jody Emel, eds. Pp. 259–279. New York: Verso.

Westphall, Victor

1983 Mercedes Reales: Hispanic Land Grants of the Upper Rio Grande Region. Albuquerque: University of New Mexico Press.

White, Robert R.

1994 Life in Taos, 1898–1911. *In* Bert Geer Phillips and the Taos Art Colony. Julie Schimmel and Robert R. White, eds. Pp. 33–64. Albuquerque: University of New Mexico Press.

Wilkinson, Charles F.

1992 Crossing the Next Meridian: Land, Water, and the Future of the West. Washington, DC: Island Press.

Williams, Raymond

1973 The Country and the City. New York: Oxford University Press.

1977 Marxism and Literature. New York: Oxford University Press.

Wilson, John P.

1988 How the Settlers Farmed: Hispanic Villages and Irrigation Systems in Early Sierra County, 1850–1900. New Mexico Historical Review 63:333–356.

Wilson, Lee

1978 Water Availability and Water Quality in Taos County, NM. Santa Fe, NM: Lee Wilson and Associates, Inc.

Wittfogel, Karl A.

1957 Oriental Despotism; A Comparative Study of Total Power. New Haven, CT: Yale University Press.

Wittfogel, Karl A., and Esther S. Goldfrank

1943 Some Aspects of Pueblo Mythology and Society. Journal of American Folklore 56:17–30.

Woosley, Anne I.

1986 Puebloan Prehistory of the Northern Rio Grande: Settlement, Population, Subsistence. The Kiva 51(3):143–164.

Worster, David

1985 Rivers of Empire: Water, Aridity, and the Growth of the American West. New York: Pantheon Books.

Wozniak, Frank

1997   Irrigation in the Rio Grande Valley, New Mexico: A Study and Annotated Bibliography of the Development of Irrigation Systems. Fort Collins, CO: United States Department of Agriculture.

Wroth, William

1979   The Chapel of Our Lady of Talpa. Colorado Springs, CO: Taylor Museum, Colorado Springs Fine Arts Center.

1983   La Sangre De Cristo: History and Symbolism. *In* Hispanic Arts and Ethnohistory in the Southwest: New Papers Inspired by the Work of E. Boyd. Marta Weigle, Claudia Larcombe, and Samuel Larcombe, eds. Pp. 283–292. Santa Fe, NM: Ancient City Press.

Zumwalt, Rosemary Lévy

1992   Wealth and Rebellion: Elsie Clews Parsons, Anthropologist and Folklorist. Urbana: University of Illinois Press.

Index

Note: Numbers in *italics* indicate figures

Marcus, Josephine & Frank, xxv
María de la Cabeza (wife of San Isidro), 92, 93, 98, 151n6
Martín, Sebastian, 147n6
Martínez, Antonio, 147n6
Martínez, Palemón, 53, 54, 56, 57, 58, 68–69, 147n8
Martínez, Roberto, 47
Martínez, Severino, 155n3
Martínez, Vicente, 110, 145–46n9
Martínez Saldaña, Tómas, 14
Mary. *See* Virgin Mary
mayordomos: and Arroyo Seco's reparto, 57–58; institutional distinctions between kinds of, 83–84; and kinship networks, 87; and religious celebrations, 84, 86, 97; role in acequia practice, 7–8; and water allocation during droughts, 69–71; and water allocation to *parciantes*, 48. *See also parciantes*
Medina, Joe, 83
Medina, María, 83
meetings, and acequia practice, 7
Mexican Americans, nomenclature for, 135n3, 136n2
Mexican American War, 16
Mexico, and history of New Mexico, 16
Meyer, Michael C., 3, 43, 44, 137n4, 142n9, 145n7, 146n4
Meyers, Ralph, 45, 145n8
Miera, Felix, 46–47
Miller, Merton, 23–28, 40, 108
Millicent Rogers Museum (Taos), 43
Montoya, Augustín, 58, 64, 69
Montoya, Ernesto, 63, 67, 69–71
Montoya, J. J., 63–64
moral economy: and *ancianos*, xxiv; and anthropological construct of "peasant," 155n4; and division of water from Río Lucero, 72; and *respeto*, 75–80
Mother's Day, 82–83
multicommunity: and modern Taos, 99; and pre-American settlements in Taos Valley, 21–22
Myers, Lester, 108

New Mexico. *See* specific locations and sub-ject headings
Nostrand, Richard, 16
novenas, and religious celebrations, 76, 84, 86–87, 88–98, 106
Nuestra Señora del Carmen, and feast day procession, 106
Nuestra Señora de Dolores (village), 21
Nuestra Señora de Guadalupe (village/parish), 21, 104, 141n8
Nuestra Señora de San Juan de los Lagos, Chapel of, 105

Old Picuris Pueblo, 17, 18
Oñate, Juan de, 16
oral historical memory, definition of, 148n9
oratorios, and religious rituals, 84, 106
Ortiz, Alfonso, 15, 140–41n4
Ortíz, Orlando, 39, 40, 41
Ortner, Sherry B., 148n1
Ottaway, Harold, 142n8

Pacheco, Elizardo, 53, 54, 55
Pacheco, Mabel & Steve, 84
parciantes: and allocation of water from Río Lucero, 52, 53, 54, 55, 57; and alloca-tion of water from Río Pueblo, 48; and Arroyo Seco's *reparto*, 57–58; and ethno-graphic fieldwork for Taos Valley Acequia Association, xxii–xxiii; and moral economy of water, 76–77. *See also mayordomos*
Paredes, Américo, 148n2
parishes, and watersheds of Taos Basin, 104–107, 141–42n8
Parsons, Elsie Clews, 15, 26, 79, 139–40n3
patriarchy, and role of women in acequia practice, 8–9
Pedlar, Leslie & Skip, 88
Peña, Devon, 154–55n1
Peñas Negras, 106
People of the Sierra (Pitt-Rivers 1971), 77
Phillips, Bert, 27, 108
physiography, of Taos Basin, 19–20
pilgrimages: and observances to Virgin Mary, 82–83; and processions, 102, 152n1
Pitt-Rivers, Julian, 77
place: and gendering of space in cultural

analysis, 151–52n6; narrative and practice in making of, 80; processions and role of water in religious symbolism and practice, 101–13

population, postconquest decline in Indian, 16. *See also* demographics

Pot Creek Pueblo, 17, 18, 19, 153n4

power, of ritual in context of New Mexico, 98–100

prayers, and religious rituals, 88–98

"Preliminary Study of the Pueblo of Taos New Mexico, A" (Miller 1898), 23–28

prior appropriation, doctrine of, 5–6

private/public space, 107

processions: and pilgrimages, 152n1; and roles of water and place in religious symbolism and practice, 101–13. *See also* Corpus Christi procession; San Isidro

public space. *See* private/public space

Pueblo Lands Board, 52–53, 62

Pueblo Revolt of 1680, 14, 16, 20

pueblos: acequia associations and water rights adjudications involving, 9–10; and history of irrigation, 12, 13–16, 139n1, 140n3; and secrecy as cultural norm, xxv, 136n4: Tlaxcaltecans and Matachines dance, 139n2. *See also* Acoma Pueblo; Laguna Pueblo; Old Picuris Pueblo; Pot Creek Pueblo; Santo Domingo Pueblo; Taos Pueblo

Quintana, Frances Leon, 141n4

rain, procession to petition for, 108–109

Ranchitos (town), 29, 35, 46–47, 64, 65

Ranchos (village/parish), 22, 29, 104

Randall, B. G., 44

Rappaport, Roy, 112

real estate, in modern Taos Valley, 30

Reconquest, after Pueblo Revolt of 1680, 14, 16, 20

Reichard, David, 139n9

religion: anthropological theory of, 112; and author's personal experience of rituals, xxiii–xxiv; processions, water, and place in symbolism and practice of,

101–13; ritual participation and connection between acequia practice and, 81–100. *See also* altars; hymns; parishes; rituals; shrines

repartos (customary divisions of water), 48, 57–58

respeto (respect), xxiv, 75–80, 98

Río Chiquito, 19, 105

Río Fernando, 19, 38, 47

Rio Grande, and history of irrigation, 12–13, 156n2

Río Grande del Rancho, 19, 104–105

Río Hondo, 19, 52, 58

Río Lucero: acequia system and allocation of water from, 49–72; Don Fernando land grant and diversion of water from, 38; and irrigation in Ranchitos, 46; and physiography of Taos Basin, 19

Río Pueblo: acequia system and allocation of water from, 35–48; historical difference between Río Lucero watershed and, 50; hydrographic survey map of, 144n4; and physiography of Taos Basin, 19

rituals: power of in context of New Mexico, 98–100; and processions through time, 108–10. *See also oratorios*; pilgrimages; processions; religion

Rivera, José, 137n3

rock shrines, 108

Rodríguez, Justino Olguín, 27

Romero, Fabi, 138–39n8

Romo, Fernando, 53–54, 60–62

Rosenstock, Richard, xv

Sacred Heart Society, 107

St. Francis parish, 105, 106

San Antonio de Padua (saint), 110

San Antonio Society, 107

San Cristóbal (village), 22

sanctity, and religious symbolism of water, 110–12

San Francisco (village/parish), 21, 104

San Francisco de Asís (village/church), 22, 105, 142n8

San Francisco de Paula (village), 21, 22

sangre de Cristo, as place name, 112

Sangre de Cristo Mountains, 19, 112

San Gerónimo (mission/parish), 20

San Isidro (saint), and celebration of feast day, 81–100, 106, 107, 110, 149–50n2, 152n6–7

San Juan Nepomuceno (May 16), 112

Santa Fe (city): and acequia system, 43, 144–45n6; tourism and demography of, 29, 30

Santa Gertrudis (village), 21, 22

Santa Inez, 89, 90

Santísima Trinidad (parish), 104, 142n8

Santistevan, Agapita & Tony, 87

Santistevan, Doña Corina, 6, 84–85, 87, 88, 89, 98–100, 109, 151n3

Santistevan, Juan, 38

Santistevan, Ruben, 85

Santo Domingo Pueblo, 139n9

scarcity, of water in New Mexico context, 79

Schneider, Jane, 79, 149n4

Scott, James, 75–76

Seed, Judge Edward, 51–52

shame. *See* honor-shame complex

sharing, as basic principle of water allocation, 56–57, 72

shrines, 107–108

Simmons, Marc, 14, 15, 17

Simpson, Smith, 38

Singer, Beverly, 79

Sklar, Deidre, 79, 100

Snow, David, 43, 144–45n6

sobrante (surplus) water, 4, 53, 72

space. *See* architectonic spaces; landscape; place; private/public space

Spain: and "acequiazation" of agriculture in Rio Grande Valley, 13–16, 136–37n2; and history of water law in New Mexico, 2, 3. *See also* colonialism and colonial period

statues, and religious celebrations or processions, 83, 84, 86, 107–108

Steele, Father Thomas, 90

Stevenson, Matilda Cox, 26

Strang, Veronica, 156n6

Summer People, of Taos Pueblo, 36, 144n2

Syrian model, of water allocation, 4, 71

Talpa (village), 22

Taos (city): acequia system and ditches in, 41–45; demography and economy of modern, 28–31; history of, 21, 22; and multicommunity, 99

Taos Historical Museum, 43

Taos Pueblo: Blue Lake in sacred geography of, 143–44n1; and Buffalo Pasture wetlands, 64; colonialism and history of, 20–21; description of in 1896, 23–28; establishment of, 18; and fetching of water as traditional duty of children, 78–79; irrigation agreements between non-Indian lands and, 31; and land disputes, 142–43n9, 147n6; moiety system of, 36, 144n2; relationship of with Taos Valley Acequia Association, xxv; Río Lucero acequia system and water allocation, 50, 52, 53, 56, 60, 63, 64, 65, 67–68, 69–71, 72; Río Pueblo acequia system and water allocation, 35–48. *See also* pueblos

Taos Valley: history of acequia system in, 22–23; history of irrigation in, 11–31; multicommunity and pre-American settlements in, 21–22; physiography of, 19–20; pre-Columbian settlement history of, 17–19; as sacred landscape, 103–104

Taos Valley Acequia Association (TVAA), xv, xvii, xxi–xxvi, 36

Tarleton, Thomas, Sr., 41–42, 58–59

Tenorio, Miguel, 52–53, 147n6

Tenorio Tract, 52–53, 54–55, 63, 147n6

Tewa, 15, 140n4, 151n6

thirst. *See* Islamic law

Thompson, E. P., 75

time, and processions as part of Catholic ritual, 108–10

Tiwa, 9, 141n6, 151n6

Torres, Ezequiel, 55–56

Torres, Fermín, 147n8

Torrez, Sylvia, 87

tourism, and modern town of Taos, 27, 28, 29

Trawick, Paul, 5, 76, 138n6, 153n2

Trujillo, Esequiel, 72

Trujillo, Feloníz, 85–86